ABOVE & BEYOND

Also by Casey Sherman:

The Finest Hours (coauthored with Michael J. Tougias)
The Ice Bucket Challenge (coauthored with Dave Wedge)
Boston Strong (coauthored with Dave Wedge)
Animal
Bad Blood
Search for the Strangler
Black Irish
Black Dragon

Also by Michael J. Tougias:

So Close to Home (coauthored with Alison O'Leary)
A Storm Too Soon
Fatal Forecast
Overboard
Rescue of the Bounty (coauthored with Doug Campbell)
Ten Hours Until Dawn
The Finest Hours (coauthored with Casey Sherman)
King Philip's War (coauthored with Eric Schultz)
Until I Have No Country
Quabbin: A History and Explorer's Guide
Derek's Gift (coauthored with Buck Harris)
There's a Porcupine in My Outhouse!
AMC's Best Day Hikes Near Boston (coauthored with Alison O'Leary and John Burke)
The Blizzard of 1978
Inns and Adventures (coauthored with Alison O'Leary)
The Cringe Chronicles (coauthored with Kristin Tougias)

ABOVE &
BEYOND

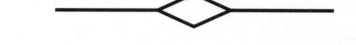

JOHN F. KENNEDY AND AMERICA'S MOST
DANGEROUS COLD WAR SPY MISSION

CASEY SHERMAN & MICHAEL J. TOUGIAS

PUBLICAFFAIRS

New York

PublicAffairs
Hachette Book Group
1290 Avenue of the Americas, New York, NY 10104
www.publicaffairsbooks.com
@Public_Affairs

Printed in the United States of America

First Edition: April 2018

Published by PublicAffairs, an imprint of Perseus Books, LLC, a subsidiary of Hachette Book Group, Inc. The PublicAffairs name and logo is a trademark of the Hachette Book Group.

The Hachette Speakers Bureau provides a wide range of authors for speaking events. To find out more, go to www.hachettespeakersbureau.com or call (866) 376-6591.

The publisher is not responsible for websites (or their content) that are not owned by the publisher.

Print book interior design by Amy Quinn.

Library of Congress Cataloging-in-Publication Data has been applied for.

ISBNs: 978-1-61039-804-6 (hardcover); 978-1-61039-805-3 (ebook)

LSC-C

10 9 8 7 6 5 4 3 2 1

For my mother, Diane Dodd, and for the families of Rudy Anderson and Chuck Maultsby.

—Casey Sherman

For Jerry McIlmoyle and all the pilots who flew over Cuba during the Crisis. And to President John F. Kennedy for his steady hand and thoughtful deliberations.

—Michael Tougias

Contents

Photo insert between pages 184 and 185

CHAPTER ONE

Starbursts

OCTOBER 25, 1962

Captain Jerry McIlmoyle sat in the cramped cockpit of his U-2 spy plane on the runway at McCoy Air Force Base in Orlando, Florida. It was 10 a.m., and the sun was baking the tarmac, causing the thirty-two-year-old pilot to sweat inside his skintight pressure suit and fish-bowl-size helmet. Beads of perspiration ran from his tightly cropped hairline down his forehead and into his bright blue eyes. Another U-2 pilot performed one last equipment check, including inspection of the hose running from the pressure suit to the oxygen supply that ran through the pilot's emergency seat pack. This connection was of particular importance because Jerry would be flying at an altitude no other aircraft could reach—an incredible thirteen miles above Earth. Should something go wrong and the cockpit lose pressure, the flight suit would inflate, providing Jerry's last line of defense against the dangerously thin air of the stratosphere. Without a pressurized cockpit or a functioning pressure suit, Jerry's blood would literally begin to boil, and death would soon follow.

Once the final flight check was completed and the canopy lid sealed, Jerry taxied toward the runway's centerline. The wingspan on the superlight aircraft was so long—103 feet—pogo sticks were needed to keep each wing from nearly scraping the ground. Once at the centerline he engaged the brake and checked that the directional gyro read the same as the runway's compass direction. He then ran the engine up to 80 percent of its maximum RPMs because anything higher would cause the aircraft to start sliding down the runway with its brake locked. Next he checked that all systems were in good operating order and then released the brake, advanced the throttle to 100 percent, and barreled down the runaway, pogo sticks dropping away. When the airspeed indicator passed seventy knots, he began pulling back on the yoke, and the plane became airborne as its speed hit one hundred knots. The rumble of wheels on the runway faded away, and he raised the landing gear. He continued to pull on the yoke and began a forty-five-degree climb.

Airspeed rose to 160 knots. Soon the plane was invisible to the naked eye, its blue coloring the perfect camouflage against the sky. In just thirty minutes the young airman from McCook, Nebraska, had climbed to 72,000 feet, where he could clearly see the curvature of Earth. He had reached his cruising altitude and eased back on the speed, carefully keeping it between 100 and 104 knots. Forty-five minutes later, he had entered the airspace over the island of Cuba.

Now, just east of the capital city of Havana, he maneuvered his plane into position for overflight of his first target. This air force pilot, however, wasn't dropping bombs—in fact his plane carried no weapons at all. Instead, he was after photos of Soviet military installations that included nuclear missiles capable of reaching and destroying cities throughout the United States.

The cockpit was quiet, and Jerry felt calm, even peaceful, despite having entered enemy airspace and knowing Soviet radar was tracking him. This was his third flight over the Communist country in just the last few days, and he focused totally on flying the aircraft, getting the photos, and returning home safely.

Jerry flicked the switch on the cockpit sensor control panel and activated the cameras. Once certain he had photographed target number one, he altered course to the southeast and in approximately forty minutes arrived and filmed his second target. The mission was going as planned, and the clear skies were holding over the 780-mile-long island covered with hills and lush green jungle.

The third and final objective was near the town of Banes, on the northeastern coast of the island. When Jerry arrived, he had been over Cuba for approximately one hour and fifteen minutes. Once over the target he started filming, got the photos he needed, shut the camera off, and started to make his turn for home, thankful for a safe and successful run.

That's when he saw them. Through his tiny rearview mirror, two contrails stretched from Earth all the way toward his aircraft.

He was under fire.

One surface-to-air missile (SAM) had already exploded above and behind him, sending fiery shrapnel in all directions and streaks of white light against the blue sky, a deadly starburst. The second missile exploded a mere second after Jerry first looked into his rearview mirror, this one causing an explosion perhaps 8,000 feet above the plane. The blast sent a burst of adrenaline coursing through the pilot's body, even though he could not hear or feel the impact. His muscles clenched, and his entire body felt as if it were shrinking. This was a natural, physiological survival response. But Jerry knew it was fruitless as he had no place to hide.

Was a third missile streaking up beneath him—out of sight?

He craned his neck around as best he could in the cumbersome helmet and flight suit but did not see a third contrail. Then he made an instant decision. He banked the plane and, during the turn, flicked the cameras on—he wanted to get the contrails and starbursts on film. Despite the near miss of the missiles and the adrenaline, Jerry felt calm. Seeing the explosions meant to kill him but not hearing or feeling a thing was a surreal experience—like watching the movie of your life from the front row. But this was all too real.

He had his pictures. Now it was time to get the hell out of there.

He turned the aircraft once again for home and took a deep breath, relieved to be looking north toward a horizon where ocean met sky. Less than two minutes had passed since he noticed the contrails.

On the flight home he replayed those intense moments again and again in his mind, still trying to come to grips with what had just happened.

Just a second or two more over his last target and he probably would have been blown out of the sky. It was the initial turn toward home that had saved his life. The Russians had likely aimed the SAMs at a location ahead of the U-2 in the direction it was then flying, but Jerry had changed course in the nick of time. Just one piece of shrapnel hitting the U-2 in the engine could have blown it to pieces. And even if the shrapnel missed the engine, a hit to just about any other area would have crippled the fragile plane, sending it tumbling thirteen miles down before it smacked into the Cuban earth.

Jerry wondered why the red light intended to warn him that a missile was locked onto his aircraft had not come on. The device that activated it had adequately warned him more than once during the flight, by displaying a yellow light in the cockpit, that the Soviets were painting him with radar. But the light never changed to red to indicate an incoming missile. He tried to put himself in the enemy's position. Maybe the Soviets had turned off their guidance systems to deprive him of a warning? They could've gambled that they could hit him without it. Either way, it was a miracle he was alive.

He reflected appreciatively on his years of arduous training, which had helped him stay calm and given him the presence of mind to get the contrails on film. Jerry had been in the air force since 1951, long enough to know that without the pictures, some might doubt him, and he thought it imperative that the decision-makers, as well as his fellow pilots, understand the increased risk. He knew how important these black-and-white images would be, as his experience marked the first time during this growing Cuban crisis that any American airman had been fired upon.

A sense of peace washed over Jerry as he saw the green landmass of Florida far in the distance. Despite the close call with the SAMs, his relief at cheating death blended with a feeling of serenity, a sensation he almost always experienced when flying the U-2. The silence made him feel like the only man alive, and when cruising and not taking photos, he could be alone with his thoughts and felt closer to God. There was a radio in the cockpit, but that could only be used in code, and only to alert friendly military aircraft of his entry and exit from Cuban airspace. At times Jerry felt more astronaut than pilot, sealed off from the earth below. Many pilots who entered the U-2 program washed out not just because of the myriad dangers and challenges associated with flying in the stratosphere but also because of the isolation they felt, particularly on long missions. These spy planes flew alone, never in squadrons, and secrecy was paramount.

Upon his landing at McCoy, members of the Physiological Support Team helped Jerry out of the cockpit and removed his helmet, welcoming him home. They then escorted him into an air-conditioned van for the drive to the building where he would do his usual post-flight intelligence debriefing. He wanted to make sure that he had every detail right. Jerry stepped out of the van into a blast of hot air generated by the burning Florida sun. He began to sweat again. He entered the building and then an office where several men from the American intelligence community awaited him. Shown a chair, he sat down but could not get comfortable. Jerry knew he was about to give his superiors information they did not want to hear. But he also realized that he simply had to come out and say it. He stared at the men in the room, took a deep breath, and spoke.

"I was shot at over Cuba."

The intelligence men stared hard at Jerry and then looked at each other, as if having a telepathic conversation.

"Are you sure?" one of the men asked, furrowing his brow.

"Yes, sir, I took pictures of the missiles' contrails," Jerry replied with confidence. "They stretched from the ground all the way behind and above my aircraft." He went on to explain in detail how he maneuvered the plane to secure pictures, the location from which the missiles had been fired, and the approximate distance of the starbursts from his plane. The intelligence officers scribbled away on notepads, recording each detail. After an hour of questioning, the officers excused McIlmoyle and thanked him for his time. Jerry returned to his quarters, while the debriefing notes went immediately to the Pentagon.

Back at the barracks where the pilots lived, Jerry felt obliged to give his fellow U-2 drivers, as they were called, fair warning. He repeated the details of how he had eluded two SAMs and got photos.

Some of the pilots took him at his word; others peppered him with questions. One of McIlmoyle's flying mates did not appear overly concerned by the details of his near-death experience in the skies over Cuba. Major Rudy Anderson asked no questions as the answers might allow fear and hesitation to enter his mind. Any realization that the enemy had fired missiles—thereby turning surveillance missions into combat missions in a defenseless aircraft—might lead Anderson to perform his duties with extra caution instead of based on his instinct and training. Anderson could not let that happen. He was ready to push himself to the limit and separate himself from the pack. Rudy Anderson was determined to fly more missions over Cuba than the other ten members of his squadron during the increasingly volatile showdown between the United States and the Soviet Union.

THE NEXT MORNING, as Jerry walked out of the Psychological Support Center, about to head across the tarmac, he heard a booming voice behind him.

"I'd like to have a word with you."

Jerry turned. He did not know the man, but he knew what his heavily decorated uniform represented. He was a three-star general and had flown down from Washington, DC, that very morning for one purpose: to deliver a stern message to Jerry, which he did without preamble.

"There was nothing on your film," said the general. "Therefore you were not shot at."

Stunned, Jerry began to protest. "But I got those pictures."

The general was unmoved. "You were *not* shot at, so we are going to destroy your intelligence report. Is that okay with you?"

For a moment, McIlmoyle forgot he was speaking to a three-star general. His temper rose. He knew what he had seen. He knew what he had experienced.

"No, it's not okay," Jerry replied firmly, "because I know I was fired on."

The general shot the captain a piercing look. He had not flown from the nation's capital for argument or debate. "Well that's what we are going to do, because we don't think you were."

Jerry shook his head in frustration. "Do whatever you want, but I know what happened."

The general stood stock-still, then slowly, subtly shook his head no, all the while staring into Jerry's eyes.

The message was delivered.

McIlmoyle was outraged, but he was no fool. The general was so many ranks above him, further argument would be fruitless and downright dangerous for his military career. Jerry held his tongue and walked away, not sure why this general was so adamant that he had not been shot at. But it hardly mattered: a general had flown all the way to Florida to tell him in person. That was all he needed to know.

NOT UNTIL MANY years later, when Jerry himself was a brigadier general working in Washington, was he able to confirm what he had known all along: the Soviets had in fact launched two SAMs at his U-2. At this time Jerry was in charge of the nuclear codes, serving under newly elected president Ronald Reagan. He had just briefed the president, and some CIA people were also at the meeting. When the discussion adjourned, one of the CIA men said to Jerry, "If there's anything we can do for you, just ask."

Jerry asked. He explained about the incident over Cuba many years earlier and inquired if the CIA men could locate the photo analysts who examined the film he had taken on that October day in 1962.

It took a few phone calls, but the CIA found the analyst who had studied the photos Jerry took decades before. The analyst called Jerry and after introducing himself, said, "Sir, you were most definitely fired on with two SAMs."

CHAPTER TWO

Born to Fly

THREE HUNDRED THIRTY-SIX miles. That was the distance separating two young boys who were born to fly. Rudolf Anderson Jr. grew up in the foothills of the Blue Ridge Mountains in Greenville, South Carolina. Born on September 15, 1927, in nearby Spartanburg, he was raised in a small, well-kept home at 6 Tomassece Avenue. He shared the 1920s three-bedroom bungalow with his parents, older sister, Elizabeth, and their cousin Peggy, who came to live with them when her parents died.

The land that Rudy Anderson, his family, and his fellow towns-people called home had once been off-limits to white people. Members of the Cherokee tribe, whose ancestors migrated to the area from the Great Lakes region in ancient times, had once used it as their hunting ground and forbidden colonists to enter on penalty of death.

The Native Americans lost control over this sacred land thanks to a conniving colonist named Richard Pearis, a man they had grown to trust. The Irish-born Pearis had spent decades trading with the Cherokee Nation and led a band of Indian warriors in the battle to reclaim Fort Duquesne in modern-day Pittsburgh, Pennsylvania, on behalf of British forces during the French–Indian War. In 1770, Pearis and a trading partner presented letters from Cherokee tribe leaders declaring their willingness to cede to the colony of Virginia. The letters had been forged. When the plot was finally uncovered, however, Pearis had already begun transferring 10,000 acres over to white settlers.

Loyalties were divided during the Revolutionary War, but the community stood united during the Civil War, when the town became a major supplier of arms, food, and clothing for the Confederacy. The commitment to service and country passed from generation to generation. The town served as a training center for army recruits during World War I and became home to the Greenville Army Base at the beginning of World War II. The US Army's Third Air Base began medium bomber training there in the early 1940s with its twin-engine B-25 Mitchell aircraft.

Young Rudy Anderson found the sound and fury emanating from these planes as they took off and landed in Greenville intoxicating. Fixated on air travel since he could walk, as a young boy Anderson studied the navigational paths of honeybees and learned that the flying insects used the sun as a reference point for both navigation and communication. He was always eager to share this knowledge with his classmates at Augusta Circle Elementary School. When not in school, he busied himself building wooden model airplanes in his bedroom. A photograph taken during one of those long, hot summers typical of Greenville shows a shirtless young Anderson crouching in the backyard of his home, holding a model airplane nearly the length of his small body. A look of determination and pride blankets his face as he shows off his wooden aircraft.

The boy also found inspiration across the street from his home in a neighbor who piloted prop planes at the nearby airstrip. Long backyard discussions about flying soon led to short plane rides high above Greenville's sprawling tobacco and cotton fields. For Anderson, no sensation matched it. He and the pilot were masters of the sky, and he was hooked immediately. Anderson learned about all types of aircraft and eventually logged his own hours in the cockpit. He was the all-American boy in every sense.

He joined Boy Scout Troop 19 at Camp Old Indian, where he took long hikes and learned basic and advanced scout craft, eventually earning an Eagle Scout badge. His scoutmaster called Anderson "a good scout who took bravery to the limits." His father, Rudy Sr., who owned one of the largest nurseries in town and specialized in cross-breeding hybrid roses, fostered the boy's love of nature.

In his free time, Anderson played softball for the Buncombe Street Methodist Church softball team. He was an athlete, a scholar, and a prized catch for the young ladies of Greenville. The towheaded boy, who had proudly displayed his model airplane in that earlier photograph, grew rapidly into a strapping young man with light brown hair and soft eyes.

"He was so handsome," Annelle Powell recalled years later. "Or maybe he wasn't. We just loved him so. We thought he was."[1] Rudy Anderson was graced with a powerful yet polite personality to match his broad shoulders and movie star looks. But his love life took a backseat to his academic career and dream of flying. The quote "Good humor is the calm blue sky of the soul" accompanies a photo of Anderson in his 1944 high school yearbook.

He believed that his destiny lay not on the ground but in the heavens. Upon graduation, Anderson enrolled at Clemson University and continued his training as a respected major in the university's Reserve Officers' Training Corps (ROTC) program, the first of its kind at Clemson. Leadership came naturally to the Eagle Scout. He also made friends easily, thanks to his giving nature.

"I went to ROTC summer camp with Rudy in Mississippi in 1948," fellow cadet Richard Sublette recalled years later. "Rudy was the only one of my friends who had a car during that time."[2]

Sublette says Anderson would stand guard in the camp parking lot at night, allowing his buddies, also supposed to be on watch, to sit in his car and run down the battery playing the radio.

That same year, Anderson was nearly killed in an accident—not drilling on the parade ground but while chasing a pigeon in his dormitory. The wayward bird had slipped in through a window on the third floor. Anderson and others had tried to shoo it away, but the creature would not budge. He took a running start at the bird and chased it down the hallway. When the pigeon made it to the window, Rudy could not stop his momentum and followed the bird into the night sky. He landed hard on an iron and concrete gangplank above the front entrance of the dormitory. Anderson suffered a broken pelvis, sprained wrist, and deep gash on his forehead. He was conscious when he arrived at the university hospital, where Dr. Lee Milford, the college physician who treated him, said his surviving the fall was a miracle.[3]

When it became clear that Anderson would recover fully, some began to poke fun at the bizarre circumstances surrounding the accident.

A letter soon arrived at the office of Clemson's president on a postcard postmarked in Greenville:

> Gentlemen: I read in the paper that one of your distinguished senior students fell out of a third story window while chasing a pigeon down the hall. It did not state whether he caught the pigeon or not. This has me worried because I have often wondered whether a Clemson man is capable of catching a pigeon or not. Yours truly, A Cute Pigeon.[4]

After graduating from college in 1948, Anderson spent nearly three years working in the textile industry as a cost accountant for Dunean Mill, a cotton manufacturer in Greenville. The mill employed hundreds of people, and its owners labored to foster a sense of community among the workers. There were hot dog suppers, Halloween carnivals, fishing club banquets, and annual Fourth of July pig chases.

It was the perfect place to work and raise a family. But Rudy Anderson felt grounded. He wanted more. He was born to fly.

On November 6, 1951, he took the oath of enlistment in the US Air Force: "I, Rudolf Anderson, do solemnly swear that I will support and defend the Constitution of the United States of America against all enemies foreign and domestic," he pledged. "That I bear true faith and allegiance to the same; And that I will obey the orders of the President of the United States and the orders of the officers appointed over me, according to regulations and the Uniform Code of Military Justice, so help me God."

CHARLES "CHUCK" MAULTSBY, a year older than Rudy Anderson, was also from Greenville—the other one, a few hundred miles away in North Carolina. Like Anderson, Maultsby was born with flying in his blood, though he had a vastly different childhood.

Chuck Maultsby was the fourth of five children born to Isaac Wayne Maultsby and his wife, Cecelia Lash Maultsby. During the first years of his life, his father was rarely at home. Wayne Maultsby, a shoemaker by trade, traveled around the South by motorcycle, looking for work and returning home for just a couple of days each month to spend time with his wife and children.

The family later settled in Greensboro, living in a two-bedroom wood-frame house with no plumbing. They were poor, but Cecelia hid the hardship from her children as best she could. Cecelia's sister Inez often donated food and clothing, while Maultsby's grandmother covered the electric bill when the small house went dark. Cecelia paid this generosity forward by welcoming down-on-their-luck travelers into their home for warmth and something to eat. It was the height of the Great Depression, and despite their financial woes, Cecelia's home was a beacon of light for transients, who had marked the location with chalk so that others could benefit from the woman's goodwill.

For young Maultsby, the visitors provided welcome entertainment as they shared stories about their travels far and wide. The pivotal moment of Maultsby's childhood occurred when a mail plane flew dangerously low over the house. The loud noise frightened the boy and his four sisters. Cecelia explained that there was nothing to fear, and Maultsby soon found himself feeling excited each time the craft buzzed past their tiny home.

Cecelia encouraged her son's interest in planes and read to him stories about Charles Lindbergh and daring pilots from World War I. The boy soon paid his first visit to a local airstrip and took a sightseeing flight aboard a Ford trimotor, a big metal plane with two engines on the wings and one on the nose. The flight lasted just a few minutes, but the memories stayed with Maultsby for a lifetime. He savored the smells of gasoline and hydraulic fluid. His stomach tightened during takeoff, his eyes widening as the aircraft climbed into the blue sky above. The boy felt as if he could reach out and touch the clouds. He peered down at the farmland and houses below. They got smaller and smaller as the trimotor soared. He returned to Earth a short time later, exhilarated.

As Maultsby grew more attached to the airfield in Greensboro, his family was uprooted again. Isaac Maultsby moved Cecelia and the children to Danville, Virginia, to open a shoe-repair shop. Financial prospects for the family appeared bright for the first time that the boy could remember. They had rented a sprawling two-story home in a decent neighborhood, and the children had enrolled in school. But these days of happiness and prosperity were short-lived.

A sudden visit from Maultsby's grandmother was a welcome surprise until the children overheard a quiet conversation among her, Isaac, and Cecelia.

Cecelia's mother had been startled to see a massive, grapefruit-sized growth on her daughter's neck. It had metastasized over time, and yet Isaac had neglected to get his wife proper medical attention. The conversation between Maultsby's father and grandmother turned heated until they had agreed on a plan of action. The next day, Cecelia was gone, taken to the hospital for an emergency operation. The young boy never saw his mother again.

Cecelia Maultsby died on the operating table. Chuck Maultsby was just eight years old. Upon learning of his mother's death, he hid in a dark shed, away from his father, and sobbed over his loss. Isaac Maultsby forbade his children to cry, which he considered a sign of weakness.

Maultsby and his four sisters were now alone with their father, who showed little compassion for his children. To teach his son how to swim, Isaac simply threw the boy off a bridge into a river below.

"It seemed like an eternity until my body hit the water," Maultsby recalled years later in his memoir. "I felt myself sinking deeper into the inky black water finally hitting bottom. I instinctively began thrashing my arms and legs which brought me to the surface."[5]

The current swept the boy up onto the riverbank, where he laid facedown, coughing and sputtering river water. His father had not moved from his spot on the bridge. The boy could hear him laughing.

Isaac sent his daughters off to a boarding school for girls, while he and Chuck moved out of their rented home and into the back of his shoe-repair shop. The boy slept on a cot and bathed at the local YMCA. He also endured repeated beatings by his father. Fortunately for Chuck, the responsibilities of parenthood were too much for Isaac, who eventually sent his son to live with Cecelia's sister Inez and her husband, Louis, in Norfolk, Virginia. Isaac never said good-bye and did not reappear in his son's life for another eight years.

Aunt Inez filled a deep void in Chuck Maultsby's life. She nurtured the boy much as his mother had done. He now had structure and freedom from fear that a simple mistake would lead to a thrashing. He began to explore the city of Norfolk on his bicycle, eventually discovering a small airstrip fifteen minutes away from his new home.

The exhilaration he had experienced back in Greensboro returned. Maultsby hung around the airport, studying planes and getting to know the pilots. He watched while engines were overhauled and wings recovered. Occasionally, he offered to wax and polish planes in exchange for a ride in the heavens. Pilots admired his pluck and unquenchable thirst for knowledge.

Later, while attending Holy Trinity High School in Norfolk, he learned about a private airport that offered flying lessons for eight dollars a session. The place, Glenrock Airport, consisted of a grass runway, a tiny operations shack, and two small hangars. It had received some recent notoriety with a visit from famed pilot Douglas "Wrong Way" Corrigan. Corrigan had become a folk hero of sorts when in 1938 he "accidentally" flew to Ireland during what was supposed to be a transcontinental flight. Corrigan flew his plane, a nine-year-old, specially constructed Curtiss Robin nicknamed *Sunshine*, from Long Beach, California, to Brooklyn, New York. Supposed to return to Long Beach, he instead headed in the opposite direction, landing safely at Baldonnel Aerodome in Dublin. Corrigan told aviation officials that, disoriented by heavy cloud cover and low-light conditions, he had flown the wrong way. Reporters gobbled up the story. But pilots close to Corrigan knew how skilled he was in the cockpit and suspected him of pulling a publicity stunt. It worked. Young Chuck Maultsby had read the tale but could not have known then how an event in his own future would one day draw comparisons to Corrigan's flying feat.

At first blush, Maultsby was not impressed by the conditions of Glenrock Airport. "I inspected the hangars and I thought they were a disgrace," he recalled. "There were motor and airplane pieces scattered everywhere on the dirt floor of the hangars amongst the trash and oily rags. It made me wonder about the airworthiness of the planes."[6]

He learned that he would need eight hours, at seven and a half dollars per hour, to obtain a student permit to fly solo. Sixty dollars was far too much to ask of his aunt Inez and uncle Louis, so he took several jobs after school as a drugstore delivery boy, theater usher, and soda jerk to pay for the lessons.

Maultsby jumped on his bicycle each Saturday and pedaled twenty-eight miles round-trip to the airfield for training. His first lesson was a basic orientation flight. His instructor took him through the preflight checks and drilled him on every detail. Maultsby recited the instructions back to the pilot verbatim several times before they took off in the J-3 Piper Cub, a monoplane with a single rectangular wing.

The plane was the Model T of aviation. The Cub was lightweight and affordable and easy to mass-produce. On his first flight, the young pilot was allowed to fly straight and make a few simple turns. His calm demeanor in the cockpit impressed the instructor. Soon Maultsby was learning to taxi, take off, approach, and land.

His confidence grew with each lesson, and he was allowed to fly solo on his sixteenth birthday. He savored the experience, as he would not fly again for another three years. The United States was now a fully committed Allied power in World War II, and all J-3 Piper Cubs were being turned over to the Civil Air Patrol. Glenrock Airport was shuttered, and a teenaged Maultsby had to look for other opportunities to support the growing war effort.

CHAPTER THREE

11 Alive

AUGUST 2, 1943

Twenty-six-year-old US Navy lieutenant Jack Kennedy motored his patrol torpedo (PT) boat through the darkness off Vanga Point, just northwest of Kolombangara, a circular island in the Blackett Strait of the Solomon Island chain.

It was just after midnight, and the sky was black. With no moon and no stars, the darkness was total.[1] Kennedy and his crew were navigating the waters virtually blindfolded and alone. The men had become separated from a fifteen-boat formation sometime before midnight while trying to avoid a Japanese searchlight. Kennedy's mission was simple—to engage, damage, and turn back Japanese destroyers serving as supply ships to reinforce Emperor Hirohito's troops. The convoy they were waiting for consisted of four Japanese warships in total: the *Amagiri*, *Arashi*, *Hagikaze*, and *Shigure*. The destroyers belonged to Japan's 8th Fleet, which also included five heavy cruisers and two light cruisers. The *Tokyo Express*, as it was called, had to make its resupply missions at night due to Allied air superiority in the South Pacific.

The destroyers were not due to sail through the area for another hour or so. American code breakers had unlocked the Imperial Navy's schedule and predicted an arrival time of about 1 a.m.

Another patrol torpedo boat, PT-159, had engaged the enemy a short time before and several miles away, but Kennedy knew nothing of this. The boat's captain, Lieutenant Henry "Hank" Brantingham of Fayetteville, Arkansas, had mistaken four blips on the radar screen for Japanese barges when in fact they represented four enemy destroyers carrying heavy guns and more than 1,000 troops. The approaching warships were also sailing under the invisible protection of several armed Japanese floatplanes flown by pilots eager to strafe any and all Allied intruders. Believing that he had the advantage over what he had presumed were ill-equipped barges, Brantingham aligned his boat with nearby PT-157, and together they forged an attack. The American sailors soon realized their mistake as the destroyers immediately opened fire on the small patrol boats. PT-157 launched four torpedoes, but none made contact with the enemy. Outgunned and outnumbered, the patrol torpedo boats moved out of firing position and zigzagged their way for more than ten miles before they found themselves out of danger.

To complicate matters even more, Commander Thomas Warfield, the man in charge of the PT formation, had ordered PT-159, the only boat with radar, back to base. Without radar coverage and separated from the nearest American boat by at least 1,000 yards, Kennedy took a defensive posture and laid down a smoke screen with the boat's stern-mounted generators while waiting for the *Tokyo Express* to enter the area en route to a Japanese military base on the island of Kolombangara.

The Japanese destroyers had now successfully breached four American picket lines, raining lightning down upon the patrol boats while evading a myriad of torpedoes launched in their direction. Thus far, not one of twenty-four torpedoes fired at the Japanese had hit its mark. The Japanese convoy arrived at the island outpost at approximately 12:30 a.m. and unloaded troops and supplies. The destroyers set sail again nearly two hours later. By this time, Kennedy's boat was patrolling the waters north of the island along with two other lost boats: PT-162 and PT-169.

A heavy mist lay over the water. Kennedy guided PT-109 quietly along, utilizing only one of the patrol boat's three 1,500-horsepower engines. Four crewmembers were off duty and had fallen asleep on deck, while the remaining six were on high alert at their stations at the gun turrets both forward and aft, next to the machine gun on the port side and on the forward deck next to the big 37 mm gun.

Ensign Barney Ross saw it first—the dark outline of a massive vessel headed directly toward them from about 1,000 yards away. Before Ross could utter a word, crewmate Harold Marney, a normally quiet nineteen-year-old sailor from Springfield, Massachusetts, shouted a warning from his position by the forward gun turret.

"Ship at two o'clock!"[2]

Lieutenant Kennedy believed it to be another PT boat fumbling around in the darkness. As the vessel drew closer, he noticed the huge phosphorescent wake of a massive ship. The destroyer *Amagiri* was bearing down on them at a speed of thirty-four knots with no signs of shifting course. Kennedy jerked the wheel in an attempt to fire off a torpedo. He ordered his men to prepare to launch a torpedo while Ensign Ross worked feverishly to stuff a shell into the 37 mm antitank gun. But *Amagiri* was closing in fast—too fast for the crewmembers to avoid collision.

The men of PT-109 braced for impact.

This is how it feels to be killed, Kennedy thought.

Amagiri looked like a giant orca as it nearly swallowed PT-109 whole. The destroyer plowed into the small vessel just feet away from Kennedy's position in the cockpit, tossing the young lieutenant violently against the steel bulkhead. The destroyer continued to eat away at the boat, tearing off a huge chunk of the starboard stern. PT-109 began to sink.

Harold Marney was thrown from the vessel and disappeared below the waterline. Fellow crewmember Andrew Jackson Kirksey, a twenty-five-year-old torpedo man from Reynolds, Georgia, also fell out of the boat and into the black, cold water along with twisted metal from the broken vessel's aft section. Seven more men were picked up and tossed into the ocean like toy soldiers.

Darkness then turned to daylight as a tower of fire and smoke fed on gallons of gasoline that had leaked from the boat.

Kennedy, though knocked off his feet and onto his back, remained inside the wreckage of PT-109. Another sailor, Patrick "Pappy" Mc-Mahon, a motor machinist's mate from Wyanet, Illinois, found himself trapped in the engine room as torrents of water and flames flooded the small space. McMahon pulled his knees up close to his chest and waited to die. Seconds later, *Amagiri*'s propellers, working like a giant vacuum inhaling everything in their path, sucked him out of the engine room. McMahon should have been cut to ribbons but some-how managed to evade the massive blades as the turbulent ocean spit him back out moments later. When he breached the surface, McMa-hon found himself surrounded by a ring of fire, five hundred yards away from Kennedy and the sinking PT-109. Flames licked his body, burning his arms and chest, as he attempted to swim to safety.

Kennedy struggled to his feet and called out to his men.

"Who's aboard?" he shouted.

Edman Mauer, a young quartermaster from St. Louis, called back, as did radioman John Maguire. Like Kennedy, Mauer had been knocked to the deck. He suffered a deep bruise to his right shoulder but was otherwise okay. Maguire had been standing close to Kennedy at the time of impact but, instead of getting knocked down, was tossed out of the cockpit and into the ocean, where he was at the mercy of the destroyer's rear gunners, who were firing at will.

Maguire swam back to the patrol boat and climbed onto the sink-ing hull. The boat's gas tank was still partially filled, and knowing that it could explode at any moment, Kennedy ordered the two sailors to abandon ship. The men jumped into the sea, where they joined eight other survivors treading water amid the flames and debris from PT-109. Two sailors, Marney and Kirksey, never reemerged after getting thrown into the ocean. Their bodies were never found.

Of the survivors, the man in the worst shape appeared to be Pappy McMahon. He had sustained second- and third-degree burns on his torso, chest, and face.

Kennedy swam over to McMahon and assessed his injuries.

"How are you, Mac?"[3]

McMahon was barely conscious. He mumbled a response and in-dicated that he could not move his arms or legs. At age thirty-seven, Pappy was the oldest member of the crew and a full decade older than Kennedy, his commander. Exempt from military service because of his age, McMahon had enlisted in the navy anyway. Now here he was somewhere in the Pacific Ocean, drawing what could be his last breaths while ingesting seawater and gasoline fumes. There was no way that the man could make it back to the broken vessel on his own, so Kennedy lifted McMahon onto his back and clenched the strap of Pappy's life jacket in his teeth. The young lieutenant pushed back through the black, choppy water, towing McMahon toward the wreck of PT-109. The predawn winds howled, and the strong current served as a formidable barrier to the rescue. Yet Kennedy kept fighting against the waves and the pain screaming through his head, shoulders, and legs and especially his lower back. The journey took an hour to complete. Several others also scrambled back to the wreckage.

Another survivor, Gerry Zinser, was attempting to swim in the direction of the bow's hull when his entire body was overcome by pain.

"Please, God, don't let me pass out! Bring the boat!"

The boat was splintered and not operational. No other help was on the way.

Zinser, a machinist's mate first-class and career navy man from Belleville, Illinois, had been standing near the engine hatch at the time of the collision. He was immediately hurled into the air and into the water. Zinser had been knocked totally unconscious, but his life jacket kept him afloat. He woke up about ten to fifteen minutes later. Surrounded by small fires, he was burned on the arm and chest.

Three other crewmen, including radioman John Maguire, tried to pull Zinser through the water, but they too struggled against the stiff current. The men needed help. Kennedy, a strong swimmer, swam the breaststroke toward the sound of Zinser's quivering voice. His body scorched, the Illinois native was ready to give up. When Kennedy finally reached him, he grabbed Zinser's shoulder and began shaking him.

"I will not allow you to die!" Kennedy shouted.[4]

The lieutenant helped escort Zinser back to PT-109. Soon other men emerged from the smoky water, some by their own will and others through the strength and power of their comrades who had refused to let them die.

It had now been three hours since the Japanese destroyer rammed PT-109. *Amagiri* was long gone. The bow was all that remained of the eighty-foot-long torpedo patrol boat. The stern section, where the engine room was located, had sunk soon after impact. Two crewmembers were still missing. Kennedy and others called out for Marney and Kirksey but heard nothing. The young commander soon came to grips with the painful reality that he had lost two men under his watch.

The eleven exhausted survivors of PT-109 waited for help, but unaware that a Japanese destroyer had rammed the vessel, the other patrol torpedo boat commanders were not coordinating a rescue attempt.

Kennedy had a flare gun, but firing it while adrift in hostile waters was too dangerous. He feared that the signal might alert the enemy and trigger a second attack. The battered and burned crewmembers grabbed hold of the broken vessel and found brief moments of sleep as darkness turned to dawn.

The next morning, Kennedy asked his men if they were willing to fight if the Japanese discovered their position, which was now three miles southeast of Kolombangara Island, then occupied by 10,000 Japanese soldiers. "Fight with what?" a crewmember asked. The men were low on arms—they had only a submachine gun, a few knives, and six pistols among them. The men said they would engage the enemy if the fight was fair. But if the Japanese sent out an overwhelming force to dispatch the remaining crewmembers of PT-109, the best option was surrender.

"We're no good to anybody dead," quartermaster Edman Mauer said.[5]

Fighting became less of an option as the morning wore on. The sea continued to swallow what remained of the vessel. Soon all eleven men were struggling to hang on to only fifteen feet of wood and metal sticking out of the ocean. By early afternoon, only one foot of the boat remained above water. It was time for Kennedy and his crew to abandon ship.

The commander scanned the horizon, looking for land not crawling with enemy troops. Soon, he spotted a tiny island that appeared deserted. The decision was made. They would swim for it. Kennedy drew the crew's attention to a large piece of wood from the wreckage floating in the water.

"I'll take McMahon with me," he said. "The rest of you can swim together on this plank."[6]

McMahon knew that he would be dead weight in the water and that Kennedy's only chance to reach the island was to swim alone.

"You go on with the other men," McMahon told Kennedy. "Don't worry about me."

The young commander would hear none of it.

"You're coming, Pappy," he said. "Only the good die young."

Just as he had done hours before, Kennedy bit on the leather strap attached to McMahon's life vest and started to swim. Their safe haven stood 3.4 miles in the distance. Kennedy swam the breaststroke for

fifteen minutes straight before taking a brief rest. He continued to
swim in intervals with McMahon on his back. The other men made
the journey kicking their legs behind a flotation device jerry-rigged
from a pair of two-by-eight wooden planks. It took four long hours
for the men to reach their destination, Kasolo Island.

As arduous as the marathon swim was, the most difficult moments
for Kennedy occurred when he reached shallow water. He cut his
legs and arms badly on jagged coral as he struggled toward the beach.
Once he reached land, Kennedy vomited violently—coughing up the
seawater he had swallowed during the four-hour swim. Both he and
McMahon then crawled toward a nearby tree line for cover. Amazingly, Kennedy had reached the island before the other PT-109 survivors swimming with the assistance of the flotation device.

Now reunited, the survivors hid themselves in the thick bushes
and flora of the island, away from the angry eyes of the enemy. The
only food on the island was coconuts, but when the men ate them,
they all got sick.

Kennedy took stock of the welfare of his crew. Beaten by the enemy and tortured by the ocean, they were now starving and losing
hope. The young commander pondered whether any of them would
survive this ordeal—especially Pappy McMahon.

"McMahon's burns, which covered his face, body and arms, fes-
tered, grew hard, and cracked in the salt water, and his skin peeled
off," Kennedy later wrote.

Hope of rescue was dim. In this hostile location, there was a
greater chance that the men would be mowed down by Japanese soldiers or left to rot and die on the island. If Kennedy wanted help, he
would have to go find it. He remembered that for the past several
nights, PT boats had made their runs through a nearby channel. Kennedy believed that in order to save his men, he would have to put his
own life on the line and swim by himself into Ferguson Passage in
the hope of alerting a passing boat to their desperate situation and the
position of his men. Despite pleas from his crew not to go—that it was
a suicide mission—Kennedy grabbed a lantern and waded back into
the cold, dark water. His men watched him go, believing they would
never see him alive again.

Kennedy swam for about a half mile before reaching a patch of
land called Leorava Island. After a brief rest, he swam for another two

miles before reaching the Ferguson Passage. The night sky was the color of charcoal, as it had been on the previous evening. Kennedy had a .38 pistol tied to a lanyard around his neck and a battle lantern. He planned to fire three warning shots into the sky and then flash his lantern in hopes that his fellow PT boatmen would spot him. The young lieutenant waited, treading water, for several minutes as the stiff current pummeled his body. With no American vessel in sight, he decided to turn around and swim back to his men on Kasolo Island. Allowing the current to do most of the work this time, Kennedy floated and swam for several more hours in the never-ending sea. Just before dawn, he washed up on a coral reef jutting out from Leorava Island. He could hardly believe that the current had taken him back to the same spot where he had rested briefly the night before. He fought his way to the sand and fell into a deep sleep.

Later that morning, as the hot sun began to bake his rough skin and open wounds, Kennedy awoke and dragged himself back to the water. About a half mile now separated him from his crew. The young commander had been in the ocean on and off for the past thirty hours and had reached a point beyond fatigue. He had put his body and mind through an ordeal that would have broken most men. The survivors waiting back on Kasolo were now trying to cope with the thought that their leader was dead—that he had succumbed to the dangerous ocean. At around noontime, the stranded sailors saw a figure emerge from the gentle waves rolling up to the shore of the island. It was Lieutenant Kennedy. The young PT skipper fell to the sand and slipped into unconsciousness. His fellow survivors carried him into the thick green cover of the island, where he slept for several hours.

That evening, Ensign Barney Ross, the first to spot the Japanese destroyer on that ill-fated night, attempted the same swim Kennedy had and achieved the same result. The survivors had to come up with a new plan.

Morale was getting low as hunger gripped the crew. The young commander did his best to keep everyone's spirits up, while privately he voiced anger to two of his senior men about the navy's apparent decision to leave them all for dead. Kennedy was also growing more concerned for the survival of Pappy McMahon. If not treated soon, the sailor's burns would become infected, and he would surely die.

Ferguson Passage remained their salvation. Just beyond the body of water was Rendova Island, which served as the US Navy's major base for patrol torpedo boats. Getting closer to Ferguson Passage was their only chance of rescue. There was another island, bigger than Kasolo, on the horizon. It was a short distance from Ferguson Passage, but there was no telling whether Japanese troops had occupied it or not. Kennedy looked out at the faraway island of Olasana and decided that he must put the lives of his men at great risk in order to save them.

Once again, Kennedy hoisted the injured McMahon onto his back and returned to the water. The others followed on the makeshift raft. After another grueling swim, they arrived at Olasana Island, which was much bigger than the previous atoll. Kennedy and crew discussed whether to search the island for any sign of the enemy but decided it was a bad idea.

"Why go looking for trouble?" one survivor asked.[7]

The men agreed to remain in place near the beach and on constant watch. There were no Japanese soldiers on Olasana Island. There was no food or freshwater either. To make matters worse, that night six PT boats passed through the area but the weather was too bad and the seas too rough to attempt a swim in their direction. As the sun rose on Thursday, August 5, some survivors took to prayer, while others were convinced they would die stranded on the island. To cheer each other up, they took to repeating Kennedy's phrase: "Only the good die young."

The young lieutenant felt his strength returning and asked Barney Ross, the strongest swimmer among the crew, to accompany him on an hour-long swim to nearby Nauru Island, a four-hundred-yard-wide atoll thirty-eight miles north of Rendova Island. They made it to the island with relative ease and soon after found a box of rations left behind by the Japanese. The men, who had not eaten for days, devoured a few small bags of crackers and candy, washed down with potable rainwater collected in a fifty-gallon catchment drum. With their thirst and hunger abated, Kennedy and Ross continued to explore the small island and discovered an old wooden canoe. Kennedy paddled the one-man canoe into Ferguson Passage that night but, finding no PT boats in sight, returned to Nauru, loaded the canoe with the drum of drinking water, and ferried it back to his men on Olasana Island.

Kennedy paddled overnight, hoping that his men would greet the water drum as a welcome surprise. But the survivors had a surprise of their own to share with their young skipper.

"We're saved! Two locals have found us!" they cheered.[8]

The survivors introduced Kennedy to two native scouts who had stumbled on the island in search of food. The native peoples of the Solomon Islands hated their Japanese occupiers and had proven strong supporters of the Allied cause. They were organized and inspired by Allied spies known as "coastwatchers," brave men who lived behind enemy lines reporting on Japanese troop movements and building coalitions among the tribes. The native scouts agreed to take Kennedy back through Ferguson Passage in their canoe. They placed him in the bottom of the vessel and covered him with coconut leaves. Kennedy told the scouts to take him back to Nauru Island to rendezvous with Barney Ross, but Ross had decided to swim back to Olasana Island on his own. The scouts found Ross midway between the two small islands and pulled him aboard the canoe.

Once back on Nauru, Kennedy reexamined his options. He concluded that the tribesmen offered them the best chance for survival. The native islanders, Biuku Gasa and Eroni Kumana, were young like Kennedy and had been schooled by Seventh Day Adventist missionaries. Still, they did not speak much English. Kennedy filled in the communications gaps with pidgin: words, gestures, and body language that the tribesmen understood. He needed Gasa and Kumana to deliver a message to the PT base at Rendova but had nothing to write with or on. Gasa looked up at a coconut tree and came up with a clever solution. He ordered Kumana to climb the tall tree and retrieve a hanging fruit.

"We natives have lots of 'papers,'" Gasa explained to Kennedy. "You can write a message inside this husk of coconut."[9]

Kennedy thought the idea was ingenious. Using his knife, he dug into the sturdy husk and carved out this message:

NAURO ISL
NATIVE KNOWS POS'IT
HE CAN PILOT
11 ALIVE
NEED SMALL BOAT
KENNEDY

The scouts took the husk, along with another note to serve as backup written by fellow survivor Lenny Thom, a native of Sandusky, Ohio, and Kennedy's executive officer, and headed out to sea. Kennedy now had two new concerns. There was a good chance the tribesmen would not make it all the way to Rendova as they were traveling in shark-infested waters made more treacherous by steady Japanese patrols. They could easily be killed or captured. If the coconut and emergency message fell into enemy hands, the eleven men left from PT-109 would surely be doomed.

Gasa and Kumana paddled seven miles east of Nauru to the island of Wana Wana, where they rendezvoused with a senior scout who worked directly under Lieutenant Reginald Evans, a coastwatcher from Sydney, Australia. Coincidently, Evans had witnessed the Japanese attack on PT-109 from his bamboo hut hidden high atop a mountain on the island of Kolombangara. Evans conferred with the scouts at a secret jungle location on the island of Gomu. The coastwatcher was shocked to hear that eleven men had survived the fiery collision with the Japanese destroyer *Amagiri*. Evans would need to mount a rescue mission, but it would take some time to plan and execute. In the meantime, he sent the scouts back to Nauru with supplies for the starving survivors. He also sent this note to Kennedy:

To Senior Officer, Naru Is. Friday 11 p.m.

Have just learnt of your presence on Naru Is. & also that two natives have taken news to Rendova. I strongly advise you return immediately to here in this canoe & by the time you arrive here I will be in Radio communication with authorities at Rendova & we can finalise plans to collect balance of party. Will warn aviation of your crossing Ferguson Passage.

A. R. Evans Lt RANVR

On the morning of August 7, five days into the PT crew's ordeal, a long canoe holding seven scouts and filled with supplies arrived on the shores of Nauru Island. Kennedy and Ross climbed in and guided the scouts to Olasana Island, where their nine comrades awaited them. The scouts handed out potatoes, yams, roast beef hash, and fish, which the starving survivors heated on a small cooking stove. While the men filled their empty bellies, an exhausted Kennedy got back into the canoe and headed for another nearby island to meet with Reginald "Reg" Evans.

When the coastwatcher first encountered the young lieutenant, he saw immediately that Kennedy had been through hell.

"He looked like a very tired, a very haggard and a very, very, sunburned young man," Evans recalled several years later.[10]

The Aussie offered Kennedy a cup of tea and advised him to travel to the safe haven of Rendova Island while PT boats were dispatched to rescue the remaining survivors. But these were Kennedy's men, and the suggestion that he would not see this rescue to the very end was unthinkable. Instead, the skipper joined the rescue party aboard PT-157 and returned to Olasana Island in the predawn hours of August 8, 1943. The survivors of PT-109 were all asleep in the bushes when help finally arrived. Kennedy called out to his men as, one by one, they stumbled slowly out of the jungle toward salvation.

For the next two hours, the survivors, including a badly burned Pappy McMahon, were carefully loaded onto the rescue boat. As they motored out to sea, Kennedy was escorted to a bunk belowdecks. Fatigued and overwhelmed by the emotions of the moment, he collapsed on the bunk and wept for the men he had saved and the two sailors he could not—Harold Marney and Andrew Jackson Kirksey.

CHAPTER FOUR

The Pacifist

RUDY ANDERSON ABHORRED war but loved his country and loved to fly. In fact, he was driven to become the best pilot in the world, and his enlistment in the US Air Force (USAF) gave him the opportunity to test his skills in the military's most sophisticated aircraft against other top pilots, friend and foe.

In June 1950, the nascent Cold War reached its first point of crisis. An estimated 75,000 troops from the Soviet-backed Democratic People's Republic of Korea marched south across the Thirty-Eighth Parallel into the Republic of Korea. A month later, the United States, under the auspices of a United Nations police action, took up arms to defend South Korea.

Both Rudy Anderson and Chuck Maultsby would soon enter the fray, but with different objectives in mind. While Maultsby hungered for the opportunity to fight the enemy in the skies over Korea, Anderson decided he could better serve the cause flying reconnaissance missions to protect and alert North Atlantic Treaty Organization (NATO) troops. He had no thirst for dogfighting.

Anderson was assigned to the 15th Tactical Reconnaissance Squadron based at Kimpo, Korea. His mission was to obtain photographic evidence of enemy troop movements and supply lines. The 15th Squadron, originally part of the Army Air Service, had provided key aerial reconnaissance for the D-day landings in June 1944. Its pilots prided themselves on serving as eyes in the sky for American military operations, a feeling handed down from the World War II airmen to the next generation serving in Korea. Rudy was trained on the elusive F-86 Sabre, the US Air Force's premier jet fighter at the time. Developed after World War II as America's first swept-wing fighter, the F-86 Sabre cut down on aerodynamic drag at superhigh speeds. It was fast and lethal: armed with six .50-caliber machine guns, three on each side of the pilot, it could reach speeds of 690 mph at sea level. It also offered the perfect solution for recon squadrons hampered by the Chinese-supplied MiG-15s that dominated the skies above the Thirty-Eighth Parallel. The 15th Squadron was tasked with identifying prisoner of war camps in a region known as MiG Alley, where the Yalu River spills into the Yellow Sea—a mission fraught with risk. The squadron had already lost twelve men since the beginning of the conflict, and the American reconnaissance planes—the RF-80 and RB-26—were slow and made for easy targets for enemy fighters. Finally, someone came up with the idea to modify the faster F-86 Sabre for reconnaissance missions. Cameras fitted on each side of the fuselage replaced the guns. The modified jets, renamed RF-86s, flew into the hostile area in mixed formation with F-86 fighters for protection, captured evidence of POW camps, and returned safely to base at Kimpo, "Home of the MiG Killers."

Robert Ross flew with Rudy Anderson in Korea. A native of Pittsburgh, Pennsylvania, Ross joined the 15th Tactical Reconnaissance Squadron in early March 1954, as it was moving from Korea to Komaki, Japan. He had trained with Rudy at Moody Air Force Base and was quick to admit that Anderson's piloting and leadership skills were a cut above the rest.

"Everything impressed you about Rudy," Ross recalled. "He was physically strong and vertically erect. You never saw him slouching. Most important was the way he handled the men. He wasn't prone to shouting or beating his chest. Rudy led in the best way—quietly and by example."[1]

Anderson was Ross's first flying partner in Korea. They were assigned to fly to three different points across the Sea of Japan before returning to Komaki.

"I was flying wing on Rudy's left, and I was reasonably close," Ross remembered. "He was always watching me and charting my progress."

Ross's plane then leveled off at 13,000 feet instead of 23,000 feet—a dangerously low altitude that exposed his aircraft and Anderson's to enemy fighters. But Rudy did not panic. He called out to Ross on the mic.

"Hey, Bob, we won't make it in this altitude. Please readjust," he said calmly.

Ross quickly realized his mistake and made the proper adjustments so both could return to base safely.

"We finished the mission as requested," Ross said. "Rudy could've hammered me for making a mistake like that, but he didn't. I thought he was the perfect flight leader."

"Alone, unarmed, and unafraid." This was the battle cry for all USAF reconnaissance pilots in Korea. But when it came to the most sensitive and dangerous missions, it was best to fly not solo but in pairs. Anderson and fellow pilot Robert J. Depew were teamed up for four daring, "off the books" missions. These top-secret flights took the pilots where they were not supposed to be. During pre-dawn hours, Anderson and Depew climbed into the cockpits of their RF-86s, rolled down the runway, and watched the small base at Komaki disappear behind them. From there, they crossed the Sea of Japan and landed briefly at K-8, the air base at Kunsan, South Korea, where they loaded their cameras and refueled their drop tanks. There they received details for the next leg of their mission. Briefed on their targets, they headed back into the sky. Both pilots understood they were making an unauthorized flight out of North Korea and into China. If something went wrong, they would be on their own, with only one another to count on for their survival. Flying at approximately 54,000 feet, Anderson and Depew traveled across the Yellow Sea and over Dairen, China, home to Soviet-occupied Port Arthur. The pilots flew in tight formation, only five hundred to eight hundred feet apart. They had visuals on each other to look for contrails. If Anderson could see Depew's contrails, that meant they could also be seen from the ground. The top-secret mission would be top-secret no more, and they would have to abort immediately. Fortunately for the pilots, they managed to meet their targets, take their photos, and return safely to friendly soil.

ALTHOUGH A RECONNAISSANCE pilot was utterly defenseless and susceptible to enemy attack at any time, the job suited Anderson's personality perfectly as he was a closet pacifist who had confided to family members that he could not justify killing anyone—even in combat.

Upon his return home from the war, he was sent for additional training at Moody Air Force Base near Valdosta, Georgia. The base was first used during World War II to train single-engine pilots to fly twin-engine combat aircraft. Moody had also served as an internment camp for German POWs. The base itself was massive, the largest Anderson had ever seen, with eight long runways and more than 160 buildings of various sizes and shapes spread out over 9,000 acres. The base was a temporary home for over 4,000 airmen all eager to prove their worth. Flight instructors schooled Anderson and his fellow pilots on navigational instruments of the F-80 Shooting Star, the USAF's first turbojet-powered combat aircraft. They also received extensive training on aerial photography. Airmen like Anderson then photographed assigned targets, such as ports and the occasional communications line, at differing altitudes. A thorough understanding of geography was a key element in recon training. The airmen pored over maps and studied photographs to identify every river, hilltop, and valley deemed important to their mission. By all accounts, Anderson excelled both in the classroom and in the air. He also made the most of his brief time spent off base.

When he could break away from the classroom and the cockpit, he and a few air force buddies drove to Valdosta, nine miles south of Moody Air Force Base. Valdosta was a state college town lined with two-story brick buildings and storefronts that carried bold signs promoting anything from billiards to broomsticks. The town was also slowly emerging from the racial strife that plagued the South in the early to mid-twentieth century. In 1918, murderous white mobs lynched thirteen African Americans, including a young pregnant woman, in retaliation for the shooting of a white planter by a black farmhand. Twenty-five years later, the community celebrated a young Georgia high school student named Martin Luther King Jr. by voting him second place in a local scholastic oratory contest.

Anderson drove to Valdosta to pick up a friend who was taking courses at the state college there. It was here that he met a young coed named Jane Corbett. With flowing red hair, sparkling blue eyes, and a porcelain complexion that earned her the nickname "Doll," Jane was the ideal catch for the fraternity boys on campus. In high school, a friend had pressured her to enter a beauty contest simply because she did not want to enter it alone. Jane reluctantly entered and won. She always said that it was the single most embarrassing moment of her life because she never sought attention and had always downplayed her good looks.

"On a good day, I won't scare people off, or their pets," she often said.

Jane was born and raised in neighboring Pearson, Georgia. Her parents, Francis and Lilla Mae Corbett, owned a small business in the heart of town, where they sold ice along with sausage and ham cooked in a smokehouse in the back of the store. But the family-run business barely turned a profit, and the Corbetts, like most folks in southern Georgia, survived week to week on meager earnings.

Jane was the typical middle child. She never received the same attention from her parents as her older sister, Frances, or younger brother, William, whom the family called "Boy." Instead, Jane forged her own path, finding passion in education, art, and athletics. She skipped two grades in high school despite constant scolding for her reluctance to take notes in class.

"Taking notes is unnecessary if you pay attention," she told her teachers.[2]

Jane loved to paint with oils and acrylics and was a pivotal player on her high school basketball team, which won a state title. She also demonstrated a real talent for horseback riding. Trained in the English style, using the reins for direction and speed, Jane raced across local fields and hills, experiencing a sense of freedom similar to the exhilaration Rudy felt soaring high above the Georgia countryside.

But their first encounter was anything but graceful. A heavy rain had begun to fall as Rudy waited for his friend under the portico of West Hall at Valdosta State College. At the same time, Jane was wrapping up a sorority chapter meeting and left the building with her head down and the hood of her coat shielding her from the squall. She barreled into Rudy, nearly toppling them both over. Jane was always convinced that the collision was no accident and that destiny had intervened. Both were smitten from then on.

Rudy and Jane were drawn together by their spirit of adventure and love of laughter. Jane's beauty drew comparisons to screen siren Rita Hayworth, and although she attracted many admirers, some would-be suitors found her sharp wit intimidating. Jane was quick on her feet and fiercely independent. Rudy Anderson was the only young man with both the confidence and the keen sense of humor to impress her. They looked like the perfect couple—youthful and beautiful, as they strolled down Valdosta's quaint Main Street during those brief moments when Rudy was on leave. Their closest friends described them as soul mates.

"I knew immediately that he was the one," Jane would later tell their children.

But her parents had serious reservations about the air force pilot. Rudy was seven years older than Jane, had already graduated college, and had been to war. Jane Corbett was young and had never traveled far from home. When Rudy met Jane's mother and father, he was polite but determined.

"I intend to marry your daughter as soon as she graduates from college, and I would like your permission to do so," he told Jane's father, Francis Corbett.[3]

The Corbetts saw both meaning and love in Rudy's words and soon began to treat him like a second son. Jane joked that her parents only kept her around so Rudy would visit them.

Rudy's parents also had initial misgivings about the union because Jane was so much younger than their son. She was twenty-one to his twenty-eight. They also knew nothing about her.

"I've met the only girl for me, and I'm going to marry her," he told them.[4]

They later became smitten with Jane as well. She graduated from college in 1955. The two wed the following November and moved to Spokane, Washington, where Rudy was assigned to Fairchild Air Force Base.

CHAPTER FIVE

The Warrior

CHUCK MAULTSBY HAD no questions of conscience when it came to combat. He saw himself as a patriot willing to kill or be killed for his country. In 1943, he entered his senior year at Holy Trinity High School in Norfolk, Virginia. He had not flown for one full year and was eager to get back in the air and into the fight against Germany and Japan. Maultsby paid frequent visits to Norfolk Municipal Airport, which served as a transition school for Army Air Corps pilots assigned to operational units in Europe. He wanted to trade places with them in the worst way, but he was still a year away from his eighteenth birthday. The Army Air Corps did, however, have a preaviation cadet program open to high school students as long as they could pass a physical and mental aptitude test. Both examinations were of great concern to him.

Maultsby considered himself an average student at best, and he was a puny teenager. At 130 pounds and just over five feet tall, he fell short of the program's standards by five pounds and a half inch of height. He ate six pounds of bananas on his way to Langley Hospital for his weigh-in. As he stepped onto the scale, he was relieved to see that his banana binge had worked. He now weighed 136 pounds. The examiner measured his height next. Maultsby closed his eyes and prayed. The examiner brought the horizontal bar down until it rested on his head. The man paused.

"Stand up straight," he barked.[1]

The examiner then shoved his thumb into Chuck's spine, the force nearly lifting him off his feet. For a split second, Maultsby measured five-foot-six. The aspiring pilot passed his exams and was ordered to report for duty at Fort George G. Meade in July 1944. He would be the first member of his family to enter the military since his uncle Patsy had served during World War I—an ominous reminder for his aunt Inez, who seldom talked about her brother's wartime experiences. Maultsby managed to form a narrative from bits and pieces of conversation that suggested his uncle Patsy had been gassed in battle and then spent time in a German prisoner of war camp. Patsy made it back home but was never the same. He lived for just a short while longer—killed by a fall as he stepped out of a bathtub.

Chuck forced the image of his uncle Patsy to the back of his mind as he was shipped from Fort Meade to Keesler Field in Biloxi, Mississippi, where he spent the next eight weeks undergoing basic training in the searing heat of the southern sun. He spent countless hours learning how to shoot a rifle, listening to lectures, and participating in psychomotor tests. Aptitude for these tests would determine whether cadets would move on to bombardier, navigator, or pilot training next. Maultsby scored high marks and qualified for all—but chose pilot training, as flying was his first and only love.

Designated an "on-the-line trainee," he was transferred to Greenville Army Air Base in Mississippi, where he began training on Stearman PT-17 and North American AT-6 Texan biplanes. He spent a year at the training center and was eventually commissioned as a second lieutenant. He had recorded hundreds of hours in the cockpit and was eager to join the fight against the German Luftwaffe or the Imperial Japanese Navy Air Service. Maultsby thought he was about to get his chance when the barracks lights flickered on in the middle of the night, and the pilots were ordered to gather their belongings and ship out. They went by train to Montgomery, Alabama, but were diverted along the journey to Tyndall Field in Panama City, Florida. As a fighter pilot, Chuck Maultsby was ready and able, but the military refused to send him into the fray. World War II was winding down, and aerial combat operations were almost over. With Hitler's war machine decimated, the Allies were assured victory in Europe. The Empire of Japan would soon surrender as well, following the atomic bomb drops on Hiroshima and Nagasaki. War heroes were coming home in droves, while Maultsby and his fellow pilots performed menial duties on base, such as flight line maintenance and mess hall cleanup.

Discharged in November 1945, Chuck Maultsby was in no hurry to get out of uniform. He told his family that he planned to enroll at the Virginia Military Institute in Lexington. The challenge was coming up with the tuition. The Army Air Corps had given him some money, but he spent most of the small sum on new clothes. His aunt Inez had given all his clothes to the Salvation Army, not that they would fit him anymore anyway. Maultsby had undergone a major growth spurt while in the army and now stood five feet, seven inches. He had also gained ten pounds of muscle. He realized that if he wanted his basic financial needs met, he would have to go to the man who had turned his back on him time after time—his father.

By now, Chuck's father, Isaac, was a successful businessman with a string of shoe-repair shops. Inez also confirmed that Isaac had just returned from a long vacation in Europe and was flush with cash.

The mere thought of asking his father for money sickened him, but he swallowed his pride. Isaac's answer was predictable, made not for love of his son but as a way to grow his own small business. He told Chuck that he would not spare a cent for the young man's education but would instead bankroll Chuck's very own shoe-repair shop.

Resentment of his father's failure to seek proper medical care for his mother and subsequent brutal treatment and abandonment of him and his siblings had sent Chuck down a different path. Emulating his father in any way, in business or otherwise, was not an option. He declined Isaac's offer and walked out of his life.

Maultsby put a pin in his dream of college and took a job as a mail carrier, which gave him a little money to continue his pilot training back at Glenrock Airport, which had reopened after the war. Several months later, he became eligible for the GI Bill and applied for enrollment at the Northrop Aeronautical Institute in Hawthorne, California. A few weeks later, he received his acceptance letter in the mail and made his way to the West Coast. The schoolwork was difficult and the environment very businesslike. Maultsby shared an apartment in nearby Manhattan Beach with four other students—veterans like him and serious-minded men. When he wanted to blow off a little steam, he took a bus to Hollywood and played tourist. He once saw Clark

Gable washing his car and Howard Hughes testing his *Spruce Goose* in Long Beach Harbor. Maultsby was not the type to be starstruck and only found himself at a loss for words once, when he stopped into a small Manhattan Beach diner called the White Stop Café. He took a seat at the counter and watched as a young waitress with brown hair tied up in a ponytail emerged from the kitchen with a pencil and paper in hand.

"She was the cutest thing God ever made," Maultsby recalled. "She had large, beautiful soft hazel eyes and the longest lashes I'd ever seen."[2]

The pretty waitress took his order and disappeared into the kitchen. Drawn to her immediately, he inquired of the café owner, "Who's the little tootie that just waited on me?"

He later discovered that the "tootie" was the café owner's daughter. Jeanne was still in high school but acted more mature than the bobbysoxers dressed in poodle skirts, with their socks rolled at the ankle. She usually wore slacks, a turtleneck, and just a hint of lipstick. Neither had a car so they courted by trolley, bus, or a borrowed car on occasion. They fell hard for each other and soon began to talk of marriage.

With the blessing of Jeanne's parents, the couple wed in March 1949, after Chuck had successfully completed his education and training at Northrop. A month later, Jeanne announced she was pregnant. Chuck found work as a draftsman and took other odd jobs while he awaited approval of his application to join the US Air Force.

He was ordered to report for duty in March 1950, just a month after the birth of their first child, Charles Wayne Maultsby II. Jeanne tended to her newborn while Charles Sr. sweated out basic training at Perrin Air Force Base in Sherman, Texas. He ran, lifted weights, and drilled with other recruits, while also learning Morse code, aircraft recognition, flight planning, and meteorology. To keep their minds sharp, these future combat pilots had to commit trivial data to memory, like how many jelly beans it would take to fill the water tower on base or how many rivets there were in the port wing of an AT-6.

Mealtimes were Pygmalion-like exercises to improve posture. Pilots were ordered to sit on the first six inches of their chairs, ramrod straight, with their eyes focused directly ahead. They could not look down at their plates but instead had to raise their forks in a straight vertical line and lift them horizontally to their mouths. Seldom did a morsel of food remain on the fork long enough to eat. Nearly half of the cadets washed out of the program.

Chuck survived basic training and graduated to fighter school at Williams Air Force Base in Mesa, Arizona, where Jeanne and Chuckie, as the baby was called, joined him. The couple settled in nicely and made friends easily with other cadets on base, including a young hot shot and future Mercury Seven astronaut named Virgil "Gus" Grissom. Like Maultsby, Grissom had served in the Army Air Force during World War II but not seen combat.

General Henry Russell Spicer served as commanding officer at the base. Spicer, a living legend, had been flying for the US military since 1933. The Colorado Springs native was a rigid man with a mustache as thick as a hairbrush and a piercing gaze under a heavy brow. He had earned a reputation for quick decision-making while stationed in Hawaii as a second lieutenant in the 6th Pursuit Squadron in the late 1930s. When the United States entered World War II after the December 1941 bombing of Pearl Harbor, Spicer shipped out to England to lead the 66th Fighter Wing, tasked with escorting heavy bombers, such as the B-17 Flying Fortress, on raids over occupied Europe. Spicer led fourteen missions and downed three German aircraft before he was shot down over the English Channel in early March 1944. He managed to bail out of his P-51 Mustang but spent two days adrift in the bone-chilling waters off France before making it ashore at German-occupied Cherbourg. A group of German soldiers then spotted him as he lay on the beach, too injured to walk and suffering from frostbite to his hands and feet.

Spicer surrendered without struggle but refused to talk under heavy interrogation. He was sent to a prisoner of war camp at Barth, Germany, where he spent months recuperating. Spicer walked the perimeter of the camp routinely while rubbing his legs to regain the circulation he had lost to the frigid waters of the English Channel. Despite his frailty, Spicer, then a colonel, challenged his captors at every opportunity. Installed as senior officer at North No. 2 Compound at Stalag Luft 1, he grew increasingly angry about the Germans' heavy-handed treatment of his men, many of whom spent weeks in the cooler for minor transgressions such as failing to salute a German soldier of lower rank.

Spicer had also grown frustrated with friendly relationships he observed between the prisoners and their captors. On November 1, 1944, he gathered his men in front of his barracks and addressed the group in a stern voice loud enough for the German guards to hear. He ran down a list of grievances and reminded the Allied POWs that they were still at war with Germany.

"They are still our enemies and are doing everything they can to win this war," Spicer shouted. "Don't let them fool you around this camp as they are dirty, lying sneaks and can't be trusted."[3]

He then told the men that if they all had to stay in the camp for fifteen years to see all the Germans killed, it would be worth it. Spicer's passionate speech drew loud cheers among the camp's 1,800 POWs but outraged his captors. Spicer was immediately hauled off and placed in solitary confinement awaiting court-martial by a German tribunal. The Germans sentenced him to death by firing squad following six months in isolation. The extended prison sentence turned out to be a lifesaver for the American airman. The day before he was scheduled to face the firing squad, Soviet troops liberated Stalag Luft 1.

General Spicer carried this strength and tenacity with him during his command at Williams Air Force Base. For Chuck Maultsby, Gus Grissom, and the other cadets, fighter pilot school was much different from basic flying school. There were no more cafeteria exercises or trivial facts to commit to memory. Instead, General Spicer and other flight instructors who had stared down the enemy in the skies during World War II schooled the young pilots on every facet of air war.

The cadets learned loops, rolls, and other aerobatic maneuvers to evade an enemy. They trained extensively in the F–80 Shooting Star, practicing start and emergency procedures and how to rise and lower gear flaps. The F–80 was a sophisticated fighter jet but easy for pilots to operate on takeoff. Cadets would simply "kick the tires and light the fire," as the phrase went on the base. The real challenge came in the air as pilots tried to get accustomed to the thrust and speed of the Shooting Star. Chuck put in nearly sixty-five hours of flight time before graduating in May 1951. At the ceremony, General Spicer wished the cadets Godspeed and a safe return from Korea. He then pinned a pair of wings on Maultsby's uniform while Jeanne had the honor of pinning a gold bar on her husband's right shoulder.

Next was Fighter Gunnery School at Nellis Air Force Base near Las Vegas, Nevada. This would be the final stop to prepare the cadets for combat as 90 percent of all pilots graduating from the program would head overseas to the escalating conflict in Korea. Nellis was one of the largest and busiest air bases in the United States, with a takeoff or landing occurring every twenty seconds. Named after local fighter pilot William Harrell Nellis, who flew seventy combat missions during World War II before he was shot down and killed during the Battle of the Bulge, the air base had earned the nickname "Home of the Fighter Pilot" because it pitted the best against the best. These elite cadets tested themselves and one another each day for eight weeks from sunup to sundown. Maultsby and his fellow combat pilots learned the deadly arts of dive-bombing, skip-bombing, high- and low-angle strafing, tactical firing on convoys, and air-to-air combat at altitudes of 12,000 and 20,000 feet. The pilots chased after one another in the skies over the Nevada desert in a fiercely competitive environment.

"Anytime you were airborne, you were subject to being pursued by another aircraft," Maultsby wrote years later. "If you didn't see him [an aggressor] and he got your tail number, you owed him a beer when you landed."[4]

He flew eighty sorties in less than thirty days. He spent more time in the air than he did on the ground. He and the other cadets were as combat ready as they could possibly be. The training was over. It was now time for the real thing.

Maultsby was ordered to Japan in August 1951. Jeanne and Chuckie, now eighteen months old, drove to Los Angeles International Airport to see him off. Chuck and Jeanne did not say goodbye—it sounded too final. Instead, they hugged tightly and kissed silently before he boarded the plane. Wife and child remained on the tarmac as the large aircraft taxied down the runway. Maultsby gazed out the window and watched as his entire world receded in his view. At that moment, he wondered if he would ever return home to them.

He was assigned to the 26th Fighter Interceptor Squadron at Naha Air Base in Okinawa. The squadron was ordered to protect the island from the threat of Chinese combat aircraft. The base was small, and the men were housed in Quonset huts. During World War II, the Japanese had used the base to launch kamikaze attacks against American ships. One former kamikaze pilot, who never had the chance to complete his mission, now worked as a bartender at the officers' club.

As Maultsby awaited his first combat mission, he kept his reflexes sharp through air-to-ground gunnery training at an auxiliary field nearby. As he returned from one practice mission, he began to experience engine trouble on final approach. He pushed the throttle full forward, but the F-80's power was limited, and the jet's engine refused to accelerate. As he reached the ground, the right wing dipped and scraped the runway, sending the fighter jet end over end, with the pilot trapped at the controls. The violent thrusts rattled him, and his head slammed against the console. The plane turned over several times before coming to a dead stop. Dazed, but still conscious, Maultsby worked desperately to free himself from the cockpit, fearing the plane might explode. He pulled himself out of the wreck and crawled to the top of a nearby ravine. Looking back, he was shocked to see that the nose, wings, and tail were completely destroyed. A crash vehicle was dispatched to the scene, and as the driver got out and surveyed the crash, he called to Maultsby, who was now standing a few yards away.

"Where's the pilot?" the driver asked.

"I am the pilot."

"No, I mean the pilot who was in that thing!"[5]

Inspecting the twisted wreckage, the emergency driver was flabbergasted that anyone could have walked away from the crash. Maultsby's squadron mates could hardly believe it either. They looked at him as if he were a ghost. The story of his miraculous survival grew and was later immortalized at the crash site, which was renamed Maultsby's Canyon.

He was growing more anxious to enter the fight in Korea as he realized that he was still one hundred combat missions away from reuniting with Jeanne and Chuckie back in the United States. Up to that point, the only enemy he had faced was Mother Nature. Soon after he survived the training crash, a massive typhoon hit Okinawa and nearly destroyed their small base. Hurricane-force winds ripped his Quonset hut from its foundation and blew it away. He and others waited out the typhoon in the concrete officers' club. When the weather finally abated, he returned to his quarters to find nothing left.

Maultsby was soon dispatched to Korea and assigned to the 35th Squadron of the 8th Fighter-Bomber Group at K-13 near the city of Suwon. The base, attacked and lost to the North Koreans twice since 1950, had returned to American control. It was now used to stage patrols along the Yalu River and the deadly MiG Alley.

Maultsby entered the fray immediately. He undertook missions to destroy roads, canals, and enemy trains. He bombarded enemy troops with rockets and napalm. He was ordered into the air sixteen times and successfully completed each task in textbook fashion.

Maultsby was then briefed on his next mission—a major attack on a convoy of tanks, armored vehicles, troop transports, and supply trucks outside Kunu-ri, North Korea, just eighty kilometers from the Chinese border. The area was of critical importance to the enemy, and Chuck knew it would be heavily defended. On the day of the mission, he climbed into the cockpit of an F-80 Shooting Star and waited for his turn to lift off. The squadron took off in pairs, with a 1,000-pound bomb tucked beneath each wing.

As he taxied down the runway, Maultsby discovered that a circuit breaker had become dislodged, which meant that he would have to apply extra force on the stick during the bombing run and the return to base. Such a long flight would be torture on his arms, and he briefly considered turning back for repairs. But the mission could not wait, so he continued soaring into the sky and into formation with the other American bombers.

Despite intelligence estimates, the pilots truly had no idea what they were about to face in Kunu-ri. The enemy had set a trap for the squadron by bringing in dozens of heavy guns to launch a counterattack against the bombers.

Chuck Maultsby knew he was in trouble the moment he reached the target. Antiaircraft fire blanketed the skies.

"Great clouds of oily, black smoke erupted everywhere in the sky," he recalled.[6]

Realizing there was no way to penetrate this deadly shield with glide bombing, the squadron leader ordered his men to begin dive-bombing maneuvers instead. Maultsby pushed his plane into a deep dive toward a line of railcars below. The next moment, the F-80 shook violently as a shell slammed into its side, then exploded just feet behind the cockpit, tearing off the left side of the plane. The wind-screen shattered, sending jagged pieces into his face as hot, sharp metal shards from the exploded shell pounded the back of his seat. Flames poured into what remained of the cockpit, and the instrument panel melted before his eyes. Maultsby's left arm was now on fire. Immediately, he stuck his arm out of the plane, allowing the wind to snuff the flames.

The shell explosion destroyed the control system, and he could no longer manage the large F-80. The only instrument still working was the bomb-release lever. He squeezed it hard with his right hand and released the heavy payload of bombs toward the target. As a result, the plane became much lighter and pitched up instantly. Maultsby felt his muscles tighten and contract with the pressure of the g-forces. His head fell between his knees. He strained to look up but could not lift his head. Stuck in this position with the F-80 now spiraling out of control, he grabbed hold of the ejection handles and with all his remaining strength pulled them back, activating an explosive charge. The pilot's seat shot up like a rocket from the distressed F-80, narrowly missing the plane's canopy, which would have severed both his legs. The thunder of the airstream pounded Maultsby's eardrums as he kicked wildly, attempting to break free of his seat. The pilot chute opened, and he was now floating in the cold Korean air, surrounded by three squadrons of American jet fighters and streams of lightning shooting up from enemy antiaircraft guns on the ground. A volley of gunfire struck the chute, and he could hear bullets zip by his head. He closed his eyes and prayed. *If death should come, let it come quickly.*

As he fell, the snowy earth rose up quickly to meet him. The trajectory of the parachute was pushing him dead center onto his own target. Much to his surprise, he landed softly in the thick snow without harm. The pale color of his parachute made for the ideal camouflage against the glistening whiteness. Still, Chuck was in the center of the aerial target and had to find cover immediately, or a bomb dropped by his own squadron would kill him. He struggled out of his harness and spotted a hill several yards in the distance.

Get behind the hill and away from the firing, he thought to himself. *Disappear from sight and run for it while the Chinese are focusing all their attention on the sky.*[7]

He sprinted toward the hill and then felt the ground give away under his boots. Two 1,000-pound bombs exploded less than a football field away, transforming the landscape into Satan's version of a Salvador Dali painting. It was all surreal. The ground vibrated and rippled. Trees erupted into torches. The sky bled.

Maultsby fell to the ground as if trapped by gravity. Each time he got up to run a few more steps, the force of another bomb knocked him back down into the snow. This macabre dance caught the attention of a group of Chinese soldiers, who started chasing after him with rifles ready. The enemy closed the distance easily and surrounded the downed pilot. He raised his shaking arms in surrender. Just as when Williams Air Force Base commander Henry Spicer reached shore in Cherbourg, France, during World War II, his protégé Chuck Maultsby was now helpless and in the hands of the enemy.

Jeanne Maultsby had not heard from her husband for at least two weeks and was sick with worry. Chuck had always been dutiful in his letter writing. He never withheld the danger of his job from her and, not wanting her to hear about the accident from some other source, like a newspaper reporter, had even mailed her photos of the F-80 crash he had walked away from during the training exercise in Japan. Jeanne grew more concerned when awoken by her toddler's screams in the middle of the night. Little Chuckie was covered in sweat and calling for his father over and over again. She comforted him until he fell back to sleep. The outburst was totally out of character for the normally happy little boy. Jeanne saw his unusual behavior as a premonition that something terrible had happened to her husband.

The next day, her hunch was confirmed when a strange woman arrived on her doorstep and asked if she could come inside. She was holding a telegram. Jeanne showed her to the couch and both sat down. There was a moment of awkward silence as the stranger fumbled with the telegram. Finally she opened it and informed Jeanne that Chuck had been lost during a mission on January 5, 1951, and was now declared missing in action.

Maultsby, held in isolation for several weeks, was not sure whether he would ever see a friendly face again or even survive at all. He was taken up the Ch'ongch'on River to the coal city of Anju, North Korea, and interrogated along with another American pilot. The two prisoners were held together in what Maultsby later described as a small prison cave dug into the side of a hill.

"The cave was not quite high enough for a man to stand or lie with his feet outstretched," he recalled. "We slept and lived in filthy straw, passed our body waste almost like animals and endured all the discomfort and sometimes the horror of living in a stinking hole in the ground infested with all manner of insect life and rodents."[8]

In keeping with the fighting spirit of his former commander and mentor General Spicer, Maultsby too discovered ways to challenge his captors. He and his fellow American captive attempted to dig and claw their way out of their cave until their fingers bled. And then they dug some more. But the fortification of their crude prison cell was surprisingly strong, and fed only one bowl of rice and a few drops of water each day, they were growing weaker. But worse than the malnourishment were the physical beatings. While the prison guards pounded his broken body, Chuck Maultsby dug his own hole, deep within his mind, and locked himself away from the excruciating pain.

"You must have resilience, belief in yourself, in your country," he later wrote. "If you believe, you can stand anything."[9]

Weeks stretched into months and eventually years. Maultsby suffered a seemingly endless wave of beatings, followed by hour after hour in the interrogation room, and yet he refused to provide his captors with a morsel of information. He dug in deeper when they threatened him with death. Chuck Maultsby was a warrior, trained to kill and ready to give his life for his cause. He just hoped that his wife and only son would one day understand.

Maultsby had no knowledge that cease-fire talks had been ongoing since 1951 and had nearly fallen apart several times over the issue of POWs. The North Koreans and Chinese demanded that all prisoners of war be turned over to their respective countries, but representatives of the UN forces argued for allowing prisoners to choose where they wanted to spend the rest of their lives. Finally the two sides struck a deal in late July 1953. The armistice agreement called a cease-fire and established a new border between North and South Korea along the Thirty-Eighth Parallel. The repatriation of prisoners, called Operation Big Switch, began a month later. Chuck Maultsby was one of 3,597 American POWs to be returned home.

CHAPTER SIX

The Angel

As the Cold War dragged into its second decade, CIA director Allen Dulles was hard at work on a new program: comprehensive overhead reconnaissance. With the help of the US Air Force, Dulles was creating an aerial spying system he believed was essential to preventing a nuclear showdown with Russia. One of his most essential partners was famed reconnaissance pilot and MIT-educated scientist Colonel Richard Leghorn of Winchester, Massachusetts. Leghorn had flown nearly one hundred secret missions over Hitler's so-called Fortress Europe during World War II and provided aerial reconnaissance of the epic and bloody fight for control of the beaches of Normandy, France, on June 6, 1944: D-day. Leghorn made three daring passes over the area in an unarmed aircraft. "In the face of intense fire from some of the strongest anti-aircraft installments in Western Europe, Richard Leghorn photographed bridges, rail junctions, airfields and other targets."[1]

The camera in Leghorn's plane and those in other reconnaissance aircraft had no gyrostabilizing mechanisms and could not withstand shock. This affected the quality of the photographs. Still, analysts later determined that at least 80 percent of useful military intelligence during the war came from aerial reconnaissance photos.

After leading the Army Air Force's 67th Reconnaissance Group during World War II, Leghorn returned to the United States and went back to work at Eastman Kodak. He had seen firsthand the devastation of warfare and continued to stress the need for what he termed "pre-D-day reconnaissance" against America's future foes.[2] In 1946, during temporary duty for the US Army Air Force, he witnessed Operation Crossroads, the first atomic weapons detonation since the bombings of Japan. Leghorn photographed nuclear explosions at Bikini Atoll in the Marshall Islands from the air. The US military had lined up ninety-five target ships, including captured Japanese and German warships and submarines, in Bikini Lagoon and detonated two twenty-three-kiloton nuclear bombs above and below the surface. Leghorn flew at a distance just beyond the mushroom cloud of the underwater detonation and captured photos of a radioactive wall of water some 6,000 feet high that vaporized the armada of seized warships. Leghorn could not imagine the destruction of an American city from a Soviet bomb of equal power. He would do everything in his power to prevent such an apocalypse. In his mind, reconnaissance was the key.

Until then, the US military had relied on aerial photographs of Russian military buildup taken by the German Luftwaffe during World War II. In the early 1950s, when NATO pilots flying converted Boeing RB-47s tried to penetrate Soviet airspace, they were immediately shot down by Russia's feared MiG-15s and later the MiG-17s, which could fly at heights of 45,000 feet. Leghorn's idea was to build an aircraft that could soar above 65,000 feet and keep safely out of the crosshairs of Soviet fighters. He also pushed for peripheral long-range photography, satellites, free balloons, and vertical takeoff and landing vehicles that would be of exceptional use to clandestine intelligence collectors.

Recalled to duty during the Korean War, Colonel Leghorn had planned the secret missions over denied territories performed by Rudy Anderson and other reconnaissance pilots.

Leghorn pushed his new plan on the Pentagon, where he initially met with resistance from those who wanted the aircraft designed not only for reconnaissance but for battle. He finally convinced the military brass that a spy plane weighed down by heavy airframes and armor plating could never reach the heights necessary to avoid radar and antiaircraft fire.

When the initiative was brought to Dulles, he was initially reluctant to allocate agency resources for such a project. But Edwin H. Land, cofounder of Polaroid and head of a presidential task force called

Project 3, Technological Capabilities Panel, urged him on. In a letter sent to the CIA director on November 5, 1954, Land advised Dulles that aerial photography was "the kind of action that is right for the contemporary version of the CIA; a modern and scientific way for an Agency that is always supposed to be looking, to do its looking."[3]

The objectives for the new program as Land defined them were to provide adequate locations of newly discovered Russian targets, an appraisal through test range photos of Soviet guided missile development, and improved estimates of the Soviet Union's ability to produce and deliver nuclear weapons.

The Project 3 presidential panel wanted the program operational within twenty months. Edwin Land informed Dulles that a quick turnaround was needed because the Russians were making advancements of their own to develop radars, interceptors, and guided missile defense systems that could reach the 70,000-foot region.

The race was on.

Now convinced of the project's importance, Dulles looked to the one man he had complete faith in to lead the effort, his special assistant Richard Bissell. Dulles was a Princeton graduate, and like him, Bissell was the product of privilege as his father had served as president of Hartford Fire Insurance, the second-largest insurance agency in the country. Wealth, stature, and a keen intelligence helped pave the way for the younger Bissell's entry to Groton, Yale University, and the London School of Economics. He scored high marks wherever he went, but no traditional text could measure Bissell's level of determination to get the job done. For that, one would have to travel to Pinnacle Rock, a six-hundred-foot cliff located just outside Hartford. There Bissell, at twenty-one years old, had fallen off a seventy-foot ledge and nearly died. After a brief case of amnesia and months of intense physical therapy, he returned to the site alone, successfully made the climb, and conquered his fear. Espionage was also in his blood. An ancestor, Daniel Bissell, had served as a spy in George Washington's Continental Army during the Revolutionary War.

Bespectacled, pale, and painfully shy, Bissell did not project outward confidence but had a quick mind and a keen attention to detail. He was also no stranger to big and demanding projects. In the late 1940s, Bissell had served as one of the key architects of the Marshall Plan to rebuild much of Western Europe following World War II.[4]

Dulles called Bissell into his large mahogany-lined office, where they discussed a packet of top-secret documents that laid out the need to build a high-altitude reconnaissance aircraft. Bissell had been studying the dossier since Thanksgiving. The CIA director then ordered him to attend a meeting with air force officials the following day at the Pentagon, where they discussed how to pay for the program. For their part, the air force would divert Pratt & Whitney J57 engines currently being produced for B-52 bombers and F-100s to the top-secret project. When Bissell asked who would pay for the airframes to be built by engineers at American defense contractor Lockheed Martin, the senior airmen made it clear that the CIA would have to come up with the money.

Dick Bissell would have to dig deep into the agency's Contingency Reserve Fund, set up to support covert actions, to kick-start the project. It was given the code name AQUATONE.

With a blank check for $35 million from the Contingency Reserve Fund approved by President Dwight Eisenhower, Bissell began building his large project staff consisting of over five hundred CIA and air force personnel and eventually set up shop on the fifth floor of the Matomic Building at 1717 H Street NW in Washington, DC. The first task was to negotiate a contract for the airframes with Lockheed Martin. The contractor offered to deliver twenty airframes and a two-seat training model for $26 million. Bissell rejected the offer as it would leave him very little to pay for cameras and life-support gear. The parties eventually agreed on a fixed price of $22.5 million and signed a formal contract in March 1955. Lockheed Martin pledged to deliver the very first model in just five months. Engineers were confident they could meet the deadline because the airframes were relatively easy to build. Lockheed had recently created a prototype for a new lightweight fighter called the XF-104. The design called for a single engine, thin wings, and a sleek design. The company would replicate this model for America's new spy plane.

Lockheed's top engineer, Clarence "Kelly" Johnson, assembled a crew of his best engineers, draftsmen, and mechanics and went to work on the project at the company's Advanced Development facility, better known as Skunk Works, in Burbank, California. The top-secret facility took its nickname from the run-down distillery featured in the *Lil' Abner* comic strip. There, Kelly Johnson and his small army worked around the clock with near-full autonomy. So secret was the project that Bissell sent the first check for $1.256 million not to Skunk Works but directly to Johnson's home.

Dick Bissell was confident that Johnson would put the money to good use. At forty-five-years old, Johnson was already a legend in his field. The son of Swedish immigrants, he grew up on the Upper Peninsula of Michigan in a small town called Ishpeming.

In rugged, rural Ishpeming, men found work in the iron ore mines while their boys challenged one another on the local ball fields. Many of the children were especially cruel to Johnson and teased him mercilessly about his first name, Clarence. The young tormentors called him "Clara" and then "Kelly" after the popular song "Has Anybody Here Seen Kelly?" The nickname stuck. His family was among the poorest in town. Johnson's mother took in laundry to put food on the table, while he delivered the wash to neighborhood customers in his wagon or, during the winter months, in his sled. As a young boy, he feared a lifetime of poverty and anonymity and dreamed about returning triumphantly to his hometown, "not on the back streets, but on the best streets."[5]

Driven to succeed, Johnson discovered a passion for aircraft design as a teenager. He excelled academically and was granted a full scholarship to the University of Michigan, where he studied aeronautical engineering. After earning his master's degree, he was hired as a tool designer at Lockheed. Johnson was both brash and bookish. With a wide face and a narrow set of eyes, he looked like he was always squinting or searching for an answer. He pored over calculus and engineering textbooks in his spare time. Johnson's brain was always working, and he rose quickly in the company. In 1938, he joined a team of Lockheed executives on a trip to England, where they were trying to sell the British on a new militarized version of the Model 14 Super Electra, Lockheed's civilian and cargo carrier. The British Air Ministry was not initially sold on the idea, so Johnson spent the next seventy-two hours improving on the design, ultimately winning the contract and an order for 250 airplanes—at the time the largest order ever placed with an American manufacturer.

Five years later, in 1944, while Lockheed engineers worked six days a week, in multiple shifts, to produce twenty-eight airplanes each day for the war effort, Johnson took on the task of designing a fighter plane to match superior jet fighters being produced in Germany. He set up a secret shop under a circus tent and over the next 150 days perfected the design for the P-80 Shooting Star. With that, Skunk Works was born.

Now, a full decade later, Johnson and his team faced a new challenge. The Skunk Works staff drew up plans for the U-2. Normally, a reconnaissance plane's designation would fit with its mission. But instead of incorporating an *R* for "reconnaissance," the air force chose a different letter for its secret spy plane, *U*, for "utility." Only two other utility planes existed at the time: U-1 and U-3. Both the army and navy used the U-1 Otter to deliver cargo to makeshift airfields in remote places such as Antarctica. The U-3, dubbed the "Blue Canoe," was the military version of a Cessna 310 transport used by the air force to shuttle light cargo and administrative personnel. The brains at Skunk Works nicknamed their new U-2 spy plane "Angel" because it was to fly to the heavens.

Johnson drafted a twenty-three-page report outlining both the obstacles and the solutions in designing the U-2. First, he had to account for weight and fuel capacity. The aircraft needed a large fuel supply for long, intercontinental flights, but it had to be lightweight in order to achieve altitudes of more than 70,000 feet. He confronted this challenge by attaching the tail assembly to the main body of the airframe with only three tension bolts. Another way to build a lighter aircraft was to construct the U-2 with two separate wing panels attached to the fuselage sides. This way, engineers could place the camera ahead of the engine and behind the pilot, improving the plane's center of gravity.

Fragility was also a major issue. Johnson and his team needed to protect the pilots from gusts of wind, which could destroy the plane at altitudes below 35,000 feet. They devised a "gust control" mechanism similar to that found on a sailplane. The engineers set the horizontal stabilizers and ailerons on the trailing edge of each wing in a position that allowed the U-2 to remain slightly nose up, which would protect the plane from wind gusts. Flight at elevations above 50,000 feet was also fraught with peril. This altitude level was known as "the chimney." If a pilot flew too slowly, the U-2 would stall and fall into a tailspin. If a U-2 pilot flew too fast, the aircraft could break apart in midair.

Another problem arose over the likelihood that the plane's fuel would boil and burn off at ultrahigh altitudes. Shell Oil was contracted to develop a new low-vapor-pressure kerosene fuel to hold in specially designed tanks.

But how would the seven-ton spy plane land? The landing gear is normally one of an aircraft's heaviest mechanisms. Johnson and his team designed a new structure with a hydraulic shock absorber called an "oleostrut," with two lightweight wheels in the front and a pair of small mounted wheels under the tail. The landing gear resembled a bicycle and weighed just over two hundred pounds. The plane was also equipped with detachable pogo sticks to keep it level during takeoff.

As design of the airframe neared completion in Southern California, project manager Dick Bissell looked to Colonel Richard Leghorn and other experts for development of the new spy plane's high-powered cameras. Among the leaders in this field was James G. Baker, a Kentucky-born astronomer with a PhD from Harvard, and Richard Perkin, cofounder of the optical design company Perkin-Elmer in Norwalk, Connecticut.

During World War II, the pair collaborated on the design of a forty-eight-inch focal-length scanning camera, which was mounted on a modified B-36 bomber. The experimental camera was then tested at 34,000 feet over a golf course in Fort Worth, Texas. It could identify and distinguish two golf balls on a putting green. The camera had the accuracy needed for the job but weighed more than a ton and therefore could not be used in the U-2.

The new spy plane had a payload limit of only 450 pounds. Baker and Perkin decided to modify an aerial framing camera called the K-38, already in use by the air force, to make it more compact. The system they came up with had three twenty-four-inch K-38 cameras designed to shoot vertically, left, and right. Called the A-2 camera system, it also employed sophisticated lenses and increased the sharpness of each photograph. Baker worked to grind the objective lenses until they could resolve sixty lines per millimeter—a vast improvement over existing lenses. The optics team would continue to improve on the design over time until the camera system was light and accurate enough to fit into Kelly Johnson's U-2 airframe.

Once the camera was sharp enough, the weight just right, and the logistics problems solved, the Angel would fly so high as to be all but invisible.

CHAPTER SEVEN

The Dragon Lady

IN EARLY SPRING 1955, Dick Bissell, Kelly Johnson, and Colonel Osmund Ritland, the air force's senior officer on the U-2 project, took a small Beechcraft airplane over the vast open spaces of Nevada, searching for the ideal place to test their new spy plane. As they flew close to the northeast corner of the Atomic Energy Commission's proving ground, they recognized an old airstrip next to a large salt flat at a place called Groom Lake. It was a desolate landscape, but for security purposes, the location was an absolute dream. Bald Mountain, with an elevation of 9,549 feet, to the north and the Papoose Mountain range to the south overshadowed the flat plain. As there wasn't a living soul for miles in all directions, the CIA could test the aircraft in total secrecy. Bissell convinced the Atomic Energy Commission to acquire the parched, dusty rectangular piece of land—known only by its map designation, Area 51—for the project's use.

For the next several months, workers labored building a 6,000-foot paved runway, secured the perimeter with fencing, and rolled in a few dozen trailers to serve as temporary housing for engineers, test pilots, and support staff, which included CIA officers doubling as security guards. With no roads or nearby towns, the secret base still looked bleak. Anyone working on the U-2 training facility had to be flown onto the base and back out again. The training would be dangerous, but the immediate threat to these top-secret workers was rattlesnakes. The CIA issued employees heavy-duty work boots to stomp on any rattlers that entered their quarters. As a joke, Kelly Johnson began calling the site "Paradise Ranch." The name stuck and was later shortened to "the Ranch."

Debate persisted over which department or military branch would oversee the U-2 project. By now, the US Navy had also become keenly interested in the spy plane. US Air Force chief of staff Nathan Twining wanted the Strategic Air Command (SAC), located at Offutt Air Force Base near Omaha, Nebraska, to run the program. But CIA director Allen Dulles didn't trust SAC head General Curtis LeMay, the youngest four-star general since Ulysses S. Grant, and fought the idea vigorously. The dispute went all the way to the White House where President Dwight Eisenhower would make the final decision. After much contemplation, the president sided with the CIA.

"I want this whole thing to be a civilian operation," Eisenhower wrote. "If uniformed personnel of the armed services of the United States fly over Russia, it is an act of war—legally—and I don't want any part of it."[1]

In April 1955, Bissell signed a contract with the air force and the navy to assume primary oversight of all security for the overhead reconnaissance project. Now the CIA not only had control of the mission but would have to take full responsibility should something go wrong.

Under the auspices of the CIA, the program began to take on the unique characteristics of the agency. To veil the U-2 program in secrecy, the experimental aircraft were referred to not as planes but as "articles." The brave men manning them were called "drivers," not pilots. The idea was to give the enemy no written or verbal indication of the true nature of the U-2 program.

Still, the CIA needed the air force's experience and expertise, so Director Dulles and air force chief of staff Twining came up with a compromise, code-named OILSTONE, whereby the air force would take responsibility for pilot selection and training, mission development, and operational support, while the agency handled cameras, film processing, and operational security.[2] The air force, however, would keep the project at arm's length. All technical personnel (photography, technology, and maintenance) would be specially trained civilians. In a top-secret document outlining the organizational concept for Operation Oilstone, the air force stressed the imperative that

"OILSTONE appear to friendly governments as a project of the CIA rather than of the Air Force."

The first U-2 spy plane, called Article 341, was disassembled and transported in a huge C-124 cargo plane to Groom Lake on July 25, 1955. Kelly Johnson had delivered the plane in eight months, not five as agreed on in the initial contract. Dick Bissell and his partners in the air force were thrilled with the result. It took six full days for engineers to reassemble the U-2's wings and tail in preparation for its very first flight.

The man at the controls for the U-2's maiden flight was Tony LeVier, Lockheed's top test pilot. An adrenaline junkie with a cool demeanor and lightning-fast reflexes, LeVier was a champion air racer known for his acrobatic style and speed. Kelly Johnson had used him to test the Shooting Star, and LeVier responded by pushing the aircraft to the ungodly speed of 565 mph. Engineer and pilot made for a good team.

"I like LeVier to fly my aircraft first because he always brings back the answers," Johnson once told reporters.[3]

But the partnership had nearly killed the gutsy pilot during a previous test flight, when the plane's turbine crumbled in midair and cut the tail off. LeVier bailed out at the last second and suffered a hard fall. Although his parachute had deployed correctly, he landed badly, breaking his back. After his recuperation, the fearless airman returned to the skies with zero trepidation.

In 1954, he gained legendary status testing the XF-104 Starfighter—a single-engine aircraft designed by Kelly Johnson to reach supersonic speeds—for the air force. LeVier got a feel for the new plane with high-speed taxiing tests at Edwards Air Force Base in February of that year before going full throttle a month later, in a twenty-minute flight over the high desert of Southern California. LeVier pushed the Starfighter over the 1,000-mile-per-hour threshold, becoming the first pilot to achieve such a feat. Awed reporters called the aircraft "a missile with a man in it."

Now that man was at Groom Lake and about to test another of Johnson's space-age designs. During LeVier's first taxi trial of the new U-2, he took the aircraft to fifty knots. He then pushed the speed to seventy knots in a second trial and suddenly found himself airborne—a surprise as LeVier had had no intention of flying that day. The pilot immediately started back toward the ground, but the dry lake bed had no markings by which to judge distance or altitude. LeVier was landing virtually blind. The U-2 made contact with the ground and bounced twice before he regained control. On the second landing, the spy plane skidded about one hundred yards before coming to a stop.

The brakes caught fire, and Bissell and Johnson doused the flames with an extinguisher as LeVier climbed out of the cockpit. Later, when debriefed by Johnson about the U-2's performance, the pilot said the brakes performed poorly and also noted that the absence of markings on the runway made it nearly impossible to determine just how high the aircraft was off the ground. Other than damaged brakes and a few blown tires, however, the U-2 was in decent shape. Engineers focused on the brakes problem, while the ground crew put down proper distance markers on and near the runway—all in preparation for the spy plane's first planned flight on August 4, 1955, with LeVier once again at the controls.

The pilot climbed back into the tiny cockpit of the U-2 and took off, reaching an altitude of 8,000 feet before leveling off. LeVier tested the control systems, flaps, and overall stability before attempting his first landing approach. Johnson had instructed LeVier to make initial contact with the forward landing gear and then let the aircraft settle on its back wheel. When he attempted this maneuver, the plane skidded and bounced back into the air. LeVier tried the landing technique several more times with the same result. Finally, he decided to land the plane with its rear wheel making contact first. That technique worked perfectly.

The pilot tested the U-2 nineteen more times while exploring its maximum speed of Mach 0.85 and stress limit of 2.5 gs. He also pushed the plane higher than any other aircraft had soared in sustained flight—52,000 feet. On September 8, 1955, LeVier climbed to 65,600 feet in the U-2, the secret aircraft's initial design altitude.

Dick Bissell had confidence in the performance and durability of the U-2. Now he had to find and train men willing to fly it over enemy territory. President Eisenhower opposed using US military personnel to man the aircraft. He preferred "non-American" pilots to give the United States cover in case a U-2 crashed or was shot down over the Soviet Union or China. Discreet feelers went out to skilled pilots around the world to gauge their interest in the covert

project. The CIA offered high pay for qualified candidates. Air force
lieutenant colonel Leo P. Geary was in charge of training the foreign
pilots selected. A Boston native with a degree in chemistry from Tufts
University and a knack for languages, Geary had flown B-24 bombers during World War II. The first pilots trained for the mission came
from Taiwan. Colonel Geary brought them to the United States for
preliminary training at Luke Air Force Base near Phoenix, Arizona.
The training session was a disaster as only a handful of recruits graduated from the program. The pilots could barely speak English and
simply were not as skilled as American airmen. Those who failed the
program were released from duty under strict orders never to reveal
what they had learned and seen.

Once again, Bissell faced a serious problem. How could the CIA
use American pilots on unlawful missions while maintaining deniability for the White House? The agency would have to employ the
deadly tactics perfected by the Nazis in World War II. Bissell consulted
with Dr. Alexander Batlin in the Technical Services Division of the
agency's Directorate of Plans. Bissell feared that a U-2 pilot captured
in hostile territory might give up operational secrets under torture.
According to Dr. Batlin, liquid potassium cyanide was the only solution. He reminded Bissell that Nazi war criminal Hermann Goering
committed suicide by ingesting cyanide on the eve of his execution
for war crimes in 1946. Goering bit down on a thin glass capsule filled
with poison and was dead within fifteen seconds, taking with him any
remaining secrets of Adolf Hitler's fallen empire. Bissell knew that he
could not order a pilot to commit suicide for his country. Still, if a
captured airman had the option of a quick death over slow and painful
torture, the odds were fair that he would bite the capsule and keep
his secrets. Bissell went ahead and ordered the capsules, called L-pills,
which would be offered to each pilot before his mission.

Of course, the pilots were not briefed about this possibility during
training. Foreknowledge of such a choice would no doubt have dis-
suaded many from participating in the program. These men were
not kamikaze pilots, after all. They were highly skilled airmen who,
despite the inherent danger of flying, had every intention of surviving their missions. Another potential drawback for some was the re-
quirement that they resign their air force rank and seniority and fly
the spy plane as civilians employed by the CIA. The agency tried to

compensate for this by paying the U-2 pilots four times what they earned in the air force and promising them future reinstatement when they had completed their overflight missions for the CIA.

Only six pilots made the cut to fly in the first wave of the U-2 spy program. The attrition rate was high among candidates because the mental and physical exams conducted by the CIA were more rigorous than those of the air force. Colonel Richard Leghorn assisted in vetting candidates for the program. He knew better than anyone what it felt like to fly over enemy territory "unafraid, unarmed, and alone."

Once Leghorn and others successfully screened candidates for the top-secret program, they handed pilots the flight manual for the Shooting Star and ordered them to memorize it. The training would use that plane to simulate the U-2's floating tendencies during takeoff.

The original group of six flew from Burbank to Groom Lake to begin their training in January 1956. Since Area 51 did not officially exist, the pilots got post office boxes in North Hollywood, California, for their mail. The had all flown with the strategic Air Command and were tasked with learning to fly the U-2 to become trainers on the aircraft and teach the next wave of pilots for future missions behind the Iron Curtain.

The spy planes had only one seat, so the pilots took their direction from the ground by radio. The "drivers" were fighter pilots by training, and their aggressive nature made for a difficult transition to flying the defenseless U-2, a fragile aircraft with long, narrow wings that operated more like a glider than an interceptor or bomber. Speed was also an issue as the U-2 would break apart if pushed beyond Mach 0.8, or 453 mph. The aircraft was less "angel" than "dragon lady," as far as the pilots were concerned. No matter how experienced, a pilot never knew what to expect when he entered the cockpit. Like the Dragon Lady of comic book lore, the U-2 was both mysterious and beyond control.

CHAPTER EIGHT

Ready and Eager to Go

AFTER DOZENS OF test flights, the first class of U-2 pilots had sufficiently "checked out" the new aircraft for efficiency and performance. The spy plane had a range of 2,950 miles, meaning that it could cross continents, and its altitude ceiling of 72,000 feet was beyond the reach of Soviet radar. It was now time to put these strange birds to the test.

Dick Bissell began searching for operational bases in Europe. Great Britain was the first logical choice as the United States' closest ally, and the U-2 squadron could fly out of Lakenheath Royal Air Force (RAF) Base in Suffolk, England, also home to the Strategic Air Command's 307th Bombardment Wing. The CIA sent four spy planes to England in late April 1956.

British prime minister Anthony Eden had initially approved the idea but got spooked when Soviet premier Nikita Khrushchev paid his first official visit to the United Kingdom that same month. Khrushchev was riding a positive wave of international support after denouncing the purges and crimes of his predecessor, Joseph Stalin, earlier in the year. Khrushchev and his top deputy, Nikolai Bulganin, had traveled to England aboard the Soviet cruiser *Ordzhonikidze*. The diplomatic mission turned haywire when Lionel Crabbe, a frogman employed by the British spymasters at MI-6, tried to inspect the vessel's propeller in Portsmouth Harbor. The incident sparked a formal protest from the Soviets and caused major commotion in the halls of Parliament. The diver was never seen alive again. Two fishermen discovered Crabbe's remains—minus his head and both hands—more than a year later.

The prime minister became leery of further weakening his country's relations with Russia. Bissell promised Eden that only one U-2 would be based at Lakenheath. He lied. The CIA flew four spy planes out of England, including one U-2 that later penetrated the British radar network. Believing an enemy aircraft was flying over its soil, the RAF scrambled fighter planes to intercept the aerial invader. The American pilot was forced to identify himself or be shot out of the sky. Overflights from Britain were immediately suspended.

President Dwight Eisenhower was also concerned that the top-secret program could heat up the Cold War. He believed that the United States would lose the moral high ground it had attained over the Soviet Union after World War II if the U-2 program were compromised and exposed. But the fear that the Soviet Union had surpassed the United States in long-range bomber and missile technology also weighed heavily on the commander in chief. The blustery Khrushchev predicted the Soviet Union was close to achieving air superiority in the spring of 1956.

"I am quite sure that we shall have very soon a guided missile with a hydrogen bomb warhead which could hit any point in the world," Khrushchev boasted.[1]

These sobering words from the Russian leader proved the deciding factor in Eisenhower's decision to approve reconnaissance flights over the Soviet Union.

Bissell then moved the four U-2s from Lakenheath RAF Base to an American airfield in Wiesbaden, West Germany—without notifying West German officials.

U-2 pilot Carl Overstreet flew the first operational mission of America's new spy plane on June 20, 1956. A native of Bedford County, Virginia, Overstreet had been flying since he was sixteen years old. Like Rudy Anderson and Chuck Maultsby, he piloted jets for the air force in Korea before the CIA recruited him to fly over Soviet satellite countries. Overstreet's mission was to fly over Poland and East Germany, which he did undetected by enemy radar. The CIA flew two more missions over Eastern Europe in early July with equal stealth and success. Initial reports satisfied Eisenhower, and Bissell told him that his pilots were "ready and eager to go in beyond the [Soviet] satellites."[2]

On July 4, 1956, the U-2 program celebrated America's Independence Day with its first overflight of the Soviet Union itself. The pilot at the controls was Hervey Stockman of Princeton, New Jersey. With a youthful smile and tousled hair, Stockman, or "Studdie," as his friends called him, had attended Princeton University before joining the Army Air Corps in World War II, flying P-51 Mustangs out of England. Now he was back in Europe and about to fly the most important mission of his life.

In the cockpit of a U-2 equipped with an A-2 camera, Stockman took off into dark skies from Wiesbaden just before 6 a.m. During the mission, he soared over Poland and Belorussia before turning north to Leningrad. He took photos of the city's naval shipyards, where the Soviets had concentrated their growing submarine program, and made an inventory of Russia's new Bison long-range heavy bombers, which were fueled up and ready to engage. Stockman was not sure whether Soviet radar had painted the U-2, but he managed to return to Wiesbaden safely despite heavy wind damage to the plane's fuel tank.

According to his family, the ruptured fuel tank caused gas to spill out all over the runway, causing concern that the plane would blow up. But Stockman refused to leave the cockpit until he had finished his flight log. "I had just flown the length of the Soviet Union," he said. "I wasn't concerned about a leaky gas tank."[3]

The next day, Stockman's squadron mate Carmine Vito continued the search for the Soviets' dreaded Bison Bomber on a flight that took him more than two hundred kilometers past Moscow. Vito captured photographs of the airframe plant where the Bisons were built and the bomber arsenal where they were tested, as well as a missile plant and a rocket-engine plant.

Dick Bissell soon learned that Soviet radar had discovered the first two flights over the Soviet Union and that the Russians had tried to intercept the spy planes but been unsuccessful because the radar could not track them consistently. The CIA also learned that the Soviets' radar coverage was most vulnerable around their most vital military installations.

Film from the initial flights was flown back to the United States for developing, and the quality of the photographs was considered acceptable despite occasional cloud cover. Most alarming, however, were miniscule images of Soviet MiGs in pursuit of the U-2s—proof that the Soviets had tracked the spy planes long enough to launch their warplanes and also that the MiGs were no match for the U-2s at ultrahigh altitude.

The Russians responded immediately with a protest letter hand-delivered to the US embassy in Moscow. The Soviets expressed outrage that American twin-engine medium-range bombers had made overflights across their country. They made no mention of an odd-looking glider-type aircraft. No Russian pilot got a clear enough visual on the U-2, so the project remained secret for the time being.

Still, the note disturbed President Eisenhower enough to suspend the flights. His main concern was that the American people would lose confidence in his administration if the program—hence, violation of international law—were exposed.

Bissell continued to stress the need for such flights, but his arguments had hit the White House wall.

THROUGHOUT HIS ADMINISTRATION, President Eisenhower worked tirelessly to strengthen relations with the Soviet Union, even though many in- and outside the United States government were working against him. The so-called Communist threat had become a cottage industry for politicians, civic leaders, and businessmen who preyed upon the collective fear that Red Army tanks would one day roll down Pennsylvania Avenue. To ease Cold War tensions, Eisenhower and Khrushchev agreed to an exchange of visits to further the cause of peace. The trips to Washington, DC, and Moscow, planned for the fall of 1959, would mark the first time leaders of both the United States and the Soviet Union paid an official visit to the other's country.

Premier Khrushchev's twelve-day tour of America included a private summit with the president and a formal tea with members of the Foreign Relations Committee. Several senators refused the invitation on the grounds that they would not entertain conversation of any kind with a man they considered America's archenemy and a clear and present danger to the United States. One lawmaker who did not consider turning down such an opportunity was Jack Kennedy, the junior US senator from Massachusetts, then building the foundation for a run at the White House in 1960.

Kennedy arrived late at the heavily guarded, soundproof ceremonial chamber of the Foreign Relations Committee for his audience with Khrushchev on September 16, 1959.

The Russian premier had only been on US soil for two days, but his crooked smile had already begun to fade; it didn't brighten at the sight of the young American politician who had strolled in late yet seemed completely unruffled and unhurried. As a junior committee member, Kennedy was relegated to the sidelines for the ninety-minute meeting, at which discussion ranged from American overseas bases to Russian subversion and the space race. Khrushchev's words were important, but equally important to Kennedy were his mannerisms. The young senator kept a watchful eye on the Soviet leader and wrote, "Tea—vodka—if we drank all the time, we could not launch rockets to the moon."

He then jotted down his thoughts on Khrushchev's appearance. "Tan suit—French cuffs—short, stocky, two red ribbons, two stars."[4]

After the meeting, Kennedy was introduced to Khrushchev, who remarked that he looked too young to be a senator.

"I've heard a lot about you," Khrushchev said. "People say you have a great future ahead of you in politics."

The Russian had no idea at the time how their lives would become intertwined. And to gain better perspective about Kennedy's possible future in politics, Nikita Khrushchev would have been well served to examine the man's past.

AFTER SURVIVING THE ramming of his patrol torpedo boat in August 1943, Jack Kennedy was declared a hero for the lengths to which he went to save the lives of his crewmen in the Solomon Islands. The *New York Times* headline read, "Kennedy's Son Is Hero in Pacific as Destroyer Splits His PT Boat." Not to be outdone, editors at the *Herald Tribune* called Kennedy's actions a "blazing new saga in PT boat annals."

Jack Kennedy was uncomfortable with the attention foisted on him by the media in a story no doubt foisted on them by his father, Joseph Kennedy Sr., a multimillionaire banker, film mogul, and former US ambassador to Great Britain. Countless servicemen performed heroic and courageous acts on a daily basis during the height of the war, and each deserved his own banner headline. When asked much later about his gallantry, Jack Kennedy responded sheepishly that he did not feel like much of a hero because the Japanese had cut his PT boat in half, killing two of his crew. In a letter to his parents after the incident, Kennedy reflected on the loss of those men and the futility of war.

It certainly brought home how real the war is—and when I read the papers from home—how superficial is most of the talking and thinking about it. When I read that we will fight Japs for years if necessary and will sacrifice hundreds of thousands if we must—I always like to check from where he's talking—it's seldom out here [in the war zone]. People get so used to talking about billions of dollars and millions of soldiers that thousands dead sounds like drops in a bucket. But if those thousands want to live as much as the ten I saw—they should measure their words with great care.[5]

Kennedy would experience the heavy toll of war once again the following year when his older brother, Joe, a twenty-nine-year-old US Navy lieutenant, died while piloting a B-24 Liberator packed with 20,000 pounds of explosives. The aircraft exploded in midair over the English Channel with Kennedy and others on board.

The loss devastated the Kennedy clan, particularly Joe Sr., who had been grooming his eldest son for a career in politics and pursuit of the presidency. Now that torch would pass to Jack.

The younger Kennedy was undoubtedly up to the task intellectually. He had the right background—the best private schools and a degree from Harvard. But could he handle the physical rigors of a long, grueling campaign?

Jack had been dealing with lower-back problems since his football-playing days in prep school and had long slept with a plywood board under his mattress for support. The collision in the South Pacific, followed by days of grueling swims, had nearly crippled him. Life as a politician only compounded the problem. Years of travel in planes, trains, and automobiles, crisscrossing the country on the campaign trail, would increasingly endanger Kennedy's health, already jeopardized by Addison's disease, a withering of the adrenal glands, which produce adrenaline and other hormones. Kennedy had collapsed twice, once during a parade while campaigning for a congressional seat in Boston in 1946 and again a year later during a congressional visit to Great Britain. The second scare landed him in a London hospital, where his chronic condition was officially diagnosed. A London doctor told Kennedy confidante Pamela Churchill, Winston Churchill's daughter, "That American friend of yours, he hasn't got a year to live."[6]

This refrain was familiar to Joseph Kennedy and his wife, Rose, who had worried about Jack's physical welfare since his birth in 1917. In his youth, he had always been suffering or recovering from one malady or another. Be it a bout with scarlet fever at the age of three or severe abdominal issues that caused drastic weight loss during his boarding school days at the posh Choate Academy, Jack Kennedy's health had always been a grave concern for his parents and medical professionals.

By the time he entered the US Senate in 1954, the pain in his lower back had become intolerable—he needed crutches just to climb a flight of stairs. X-rays revealed that his fourth lumbar vertebra had narrowed, causing the bones supporting his spinal column to collapse. Later X-rays showed that his fifth lumbar vertebra had fully collapsed. Doctors warned Kennedy that he could lose the ability to walk and suggested an operation to strengthen his lower back through fusions of the spine and sacroiliac. The surgery would be risky under normal circumstances, but the Addison's disease made it truly life threatening. Because the steroids used to control that condition weakened his immune system, there was a strong risk of deadly infection. Believing surgery his only option, Kennedy was willing to take the gamble.

"Even if the risks are fifty-fifty," he explained to his father, "I'd rather be dead than spend the rest of my life hobbling on crutches and paralyzed by pain."[7]

Kennedy entered the New York Hospital for Special Surgery on October 10, 1954, but did not receive the operation until eleven days later. Surgeons had to postpone the procedure three times to ensure an extended metabolic workup prior to, during, and after surgery. During the operation, which lasted three hours, a metal plate was inserted to stabilize Kennedy's lower spine. While everything went as planned on the operating table, doctors knew the biggest threat to Kennedy's life would lay in his recovery. Almost immediately after the procedure the young senator suffered a urinary tract infection that sent him into a coma. Joe Sr. sent for the family priest, Father John Cavanaugh, who arrived at the hospital a short time later to administer Last Rites.

But Jack eventually regained consciousness, and his condition slowly improved. This Lazarus-like recovery was a testament to the young politician's uncanny will. But unlike the PT-109 incident, this story could not be shared with the press corps as it could cause irreparable harm to the junior senator from Massachusetts, who, unbeknownst to many, aspired to the executive office.

Spinal-fusion surgery did little to alleviate the pain in Kennedy's back. Over the next three years, he would be hospitalized nine more times for a total of forty-five days. He could no longer bend over or grab an object out of his immediate reach. Yet, during this time, he campaigned vigorously for the 1956 vice presidential nomination as running mate to Democratic nominee Adlai Stevenson, former governor of Illinois, who had decided that delegates at the Democratic National Convention would choose his running mate. The delegates selected Tennessee senator Estes Kefauver. Stevenson's decision outraged Kennedy, but it turned out to be a blessing for him as Dwight D. Eisenhower and Richard M. Nixon steamrolled the Democratic ticket in the general election. Spared the stain of defeat, Kennedy slowly began to mount his own campaign to succeed Eisenhower in the Oval Office.

CHAPTER NINE

From Thunderbird to UFO

WHEN CHUCK MAULTSBY stepped off the plane from Korea and back into the lives of his wife and child, he fought desperately in his darkest hours to swallow the horror, pain, and indignity he had suffered for two-and-a-half years as a prisoner of war at the hands of the Red Chinese.

His body healed, but his psyche remained scarred. Still, he had survived, and that was all that mattered now. Jeanne needed a husband, Chuckie needed a father, and his country needed a fighter pilot. He'd missed nearly 1,000 nights in his wife's warm embrace, two of his son's birthday parties, and countless hours bonding with his squadron mates at a job they all believed was the greatest in the world.

Shortly after his return home, Maultsby was assigned to the 3594th Squadron of the 3595 Flying Training Wing operating out of Nellis Air Force Base. Nellis was crawling with combat vets, many of whom had completed one hundred missions in Korea. At least six squadron mates had been prisoners of war like him.

Despite his efforts to focus not on the past but on his future as a pilot, his squadron mates often lured Maultsby into conversations about his time as a POW. His fellow airmen could hardly believe what he had endured in the prison cave in Anju. Many considered him a hero. He answered their questions plainly, without embellishment. Maultsby figured that his insight might be useful if they ever ended up captured behind enemy lines. One pilot did not ask questions: the squadron's flight leader, who had recorded several enemy kills during his combat tours in Korea. Tired of all the attention paid to Maultsby, he pulled him aside and lashed out.

"You know, Maultsby, it doesn't take any skill to become a POW," the flight leader barked.[1]

But it was not a test of skill that drew pilots to Maultsby; it was a test of will. As a POW, he had mentally outwitted his captors and physically outlasted them. The flight leader did not understand that— at least not then. Eventually he would learn the value of Maultsby's toughness during his own six years as a prisoner of war in Vietnam.

Chuck Maultsby had no time for such petty jealousies, though. He had nearly three lost years to make up. He focused on quiet mornings with his family and important events such as Thanksgiving and Christmas. As a young boy, he had always yearned for a Lionel train set for Christmas, but his father never granted that wish. Determined that his son would never want for anything, he bought the finest train set in the store window and spent hours setting it up around the tree to make Chuckie's Christmas morning as magical as those he dreamed of as a child.

Chuck and Jeanne welcomed another son, Shawn, in late 1954, shortly before he was promoted to captain and flight commander of the 3525th Squadron. He then headed to squadron officers' school in Montgomery, Alabama, with his growing family in tow. Soon after, he got to train on the F-100 Super Sabre while also competing with the Nellis Air Force Base gunnery team, the Lone Tigers, against the best squadrons from around the world.

Every two years, squadrons sent their top guns to Nellis to go head-to-head in what was dubbed "fighter pilot Olympics." Maultsby's team took the top prize—the William Tell Trophy—and its members got the opportunity to audition for the Thunderbirds, the air force's elite demonstration squadron. Maultsby had been itching for an overseas assignment to Germany, but the chance to fly for the Thunderbirds was too good to pass up. On the morning of his tryout, he flew with Major Robby Robinson, leader of the squadron. It was a flight unlike any other he had experienced. Major Robinson took him through the paces of formation aerobatics, rolling left to right until they were upside down, pulling into a loop, and performing barrel rolls while pulling five gs. They landed after twenty minutes, and as he climbed out of the cockpit, Maultsby found himself soaked in sweat with his right arm dragging. Major Robinson said nothing about his performance in the tryout flight, and Chuck figured he had not made the team.

The next day, he was ordered to T-bird Ops, where Robinson and other members of the elite team met him with smiles and congratulatory slaps on the back. Maultsby was now one of them. He took position as the right wingman on the Thunderbirds' diamond formation and traveled with the team, performing aerobatic stunts before large crowds around the world. When not flying, Maultsby spent his time visiting sick children in hospitals, making public appearances, and conducting media interviews. This former prisoner of war was now a goodwill ambassador for the US Air Force.

To keep sharp, the Thunderbirds had to practice at least once a day, and even though not on combat duty, all pilots were to report anything unusual in the skies. During one practice flight, Maultsby spotted what looked like a glider flying at an incredible altitude about 15,000 feet above his plane. The mysterious craft appeared to be headed toward the gunnery ranges at Nellis Air Force Base. Maultsby followed until it broke off in the opposite direction from Nellis. He had never seen an aircraft like it before. When he landed, Maultsby rushed over to Base Ops and reported the strange sighting.

U-2 training missions coincided with an increase in UFO sightings in the Nevada desert. During daylight flights, the plane's silver airframe sometimes caught and reflected sunlight, rendering it briefly visible to people on the ground. Commercial airliners flew at around 15,000 feet, and military planes rarely climbed above 40,000 feet. Most people could not imagine that an aircraft could reach 60,000 feet or higher. Terrified citizens wrote letters to their town and state representatives, who forwarded them to a unit at Wright-Patterson Air Force Base in Dayton, Ohio, tasked with investigating these unexplained phenomena. By comparing UFO sightings with U-2 flight logs, the investigators accounted for most of the reports. The program's secrecy, however, prevented the air force from sharing this information with the public, and therefore the hysteria surrounding UFOs in the 1950s continued to grow.

Hours after Maultsby filed his report and returned home to Jeanne and the kids, he received a knock on the door from a man in civilian clothes. He identified himself as a CIA employee and showed Maultsby his badge.

"Captain Maultsby, you didn't see anything today."

Maultsby started to walk him through his report, describing the strange UFO he had seen during his practice run, but the man quickly cut him off. "Captain Maultsby, you didn't see a thing to-day." Then turning to leave, he repeated, "You understand, you didn't see a thing!"[2] Whatever he'd seen was clearly secret—and clearly man-made.

SOON AFTER, ANOTHER man approached Maultsby to ask if he would like to join a volunteer program that paid up to $30,000 a year. He found the offer enticing as he and Jeanne had been scraping by on a meager captain's salary for years. When he asked what the mission en-tailed, the man simply told him he would be reassigned to a weather station in the middle of the desert. At that moment, Maultsby knew he would soon be manning the controls of that mysterious UFO.

After accepting the lucrative but secret assignment, he was sent to the Lovelace Foundation for Medical Education and Research in Albuquerque, New Mexico, for rigorous physical and psychologi-cal tests that the Mercury 7 space program would later use to screen candidates.[3]

Maultsby underwent as many as thirty laboratory tests in which doctors gathered chemical and cardiographic data. His entire body was thoroughly mapped by X-ray and his eyes, ears, and throat checked for any abnormalities. Technicians determined the water ratio of his body and screened him for radiation. To test his endurance, stamina, and mental toughness, he blew up balloons until exhausted and spent hours running on a treadmill; he was exposed to heat and loud noises and subjected to written and oral tests to evaluate special aptitudes and intellectual functions. The CIA was looking for a special breed of airman, one who loved his country without reservation and would not reveal the agency's secrets if he fell into enemy hands. Maultsby's mettle had been tested every day for two-and-a-half years as a pris-oner of war in Korea, and the most brutal methods of torture had not bent, let alone broken, him. This fact was not lost on men like Dick Bissell and Richard Leghorn. Maultsby passed both the physical and

mental evaluations with relative ease and then headed to March Air
Force Base in Riverside, California, to begin the next crucial phase of
his training.

On arriving at base, Maultsby and the other candidates were not
told what type of aircraft they would be flying; they learned only that
training would take place somewhere in the desert. The pilots were
then ushered onto a C-47 Globemaster without any knowledge of
their destination. They flew east for about an hour before landing near
a large, dry lake bed. Gazing out the small windows of the C-47, the
pilots could see a paved runway, hangars, a host of trailers, and—most
vital to their mission—six silver gliders with jet engines.

Maultsby and the other pilots were whisked off the large plane and
escorted into a small mess hall for an introductory briefing and official
welcome to Groom Lake.

"No writing home about where you are working and absolutely
no photos will be taken here," the U-2 commander told them.[4]

The pilots were ordered to forget everything they saw. Their mail
would be inspected, and each day the garbage cans would be checked
and scrubbed for any discarded material that could jeopardize the secrecy of the project. One security breach almost landed an airman in
prison. During leave, the pilot mentioned the U-2 project to a couple
of women, hoping to impress them. A fellow pilot immediately turned
him in as a security risk. The braggart was threatened with jail time
but reduced in rank and drummed out of the program instead. Airmen
were not confined to the base, however. Though ordered to spend
weekdays at Groom Lake, they were offered flights to civilization on
weekends. Those men who chose to stay on base during their off time
could entertain themselves with billiards and movies in the recreation
building. Pilots who wanted to hike and explore the mountain ranges
surrounding the base did so under the watchful eye of armed guards,
who followed their movements through binoculars.

CHAPTER TEN

Cloak, Dagger, and Danger

AT AREA 51, Chuck Maultsby was following in the footsteps of an elite cadre of airmen who had completed the program before him. Over one hundred American pilots and a few more from the British Royal Air Force and the Taiwanese Republic of China Air Force had already trained on the U-2, including Major Rudy Anderson, Major Steve Heyser, and Captain Jerry McIlmoyle.

Richard "Steve" Heyser grew up in Apalachicola, Florida, spending much of his free time hunting and fishing in the Gulf of Mexico. His father had served as a pilot in the US Coast Guard Auxiliary, and Heyser basically grew up around pilots and their planes at nearby Tyndall Field. Upon graduating high school he enlisted in the army and, after serving his hitch, went to college, graduating from Florida State University. Heyser was smart and witty, with a high forehead and receding hairline that made him look older. A detail-driven young man, he eventually joined the air force and flew combat missions during the Korean War. His training with U-2s had begun in 1957 alongside Rudy Anderson.

Anderson was an equally impressive pilot and extremely focused on his air force career. Captain Jerry McIlmoyle later reported directly to him and found him as dedicated a flyer as he had met and a smart decision-maker. Sometimes Rudy seemed a bit too intense and gung ho, but Jerry knew that genuine love of his job and country drove him. Rudy was ambitious, and his career was on an upward trajectory.

Before climbing into the cockpit of the strange bird called the U-2, all the "drivers" at Groom Lake went through ten days of ground school, where they learned, among other things, celestial navigation, a technique, perfected seven hundred years before, in which sailors had measured distances between celestial bodies, like stars or planets, and a visible horizon to locate their exact position. Now, centuries later, modern-day explorers would do the same thing in their space-age aircraft. The U-2 drivers learned to use a small sextant, as it would be their main navigation instrument for making celestial fixes during long overflights where cloud cover prevented them from locating their navigational points through the plane's periscope. The airmen proved good students, and most learned to navigate by dead reckoning with an error of less than one nautical mile over a thousand-mile flight.

After completing ground school, the airmen were taken to the heavily guarded hangar for their first up-close-and-personal view of the U-2. The aircraft, with its unusual design, pogo sticks, and condor-like wingspan, was a bizarre sight. The pilots got accustomed to the U-2's low-altitude flights and touch-and-go landings with instruction from Groom Lake's mobile control officer, who taught them when to add power, when to level off, and how to land. Exercising their final days of bodily freedom before donning the uncomfortable, partially pressurized flight suits that would keep them alive at ultra-high altitudes, most of the pilots made these initial flights wearing their favorite Levi's and a pair of street shoes. Like everything else in this program, the flight suits were a government secret worthy of James Bond.

For their fittings, the pilots were flown not to a military base but to the small city of Worcester, Massachusetts, where a driver delivered them to the David Clark Company, a huge factory that manufactured women's underwear. Jerry McIlmoyle, who went through the process in 1958, was ordered to wear only civilian clothes during the trip. No military uniforms were allowed—not even GI-issue underwear. He was also to travel with no military documents or identification. Upon arrival, McIlmoyle remembers that a man who did not identify himself but was most likely an employee of the CIA awaited him and another pilot at the terminal. The man simply said, "Follow me," and led

McIlmoyle and his fellow airmen into an old factory where women worked at sewing machines in an open room as big as a football field, making bras and corsets. Next, the "host" took them to a green door, down a series of steps, and through a basement where he handed the two pilots off to a new man who escorted them to a black door. They knocked, and a wizened old man pointed them inside.

"Take off your clothes, all of them," he barked. This was the "tailor," and he had the pilots climb a two-step platform where he took their measurements. He said not a word until he was finished, then simply grunted, "Go to your hotel."

The next morning the pilots were taken back to the bra factory basement and behind the black door where the tailor waited with two pressure suits. The suits were skin-tight, similar to a wet suit, and the pilots helped each other get into them. Once the suits were on, the pilots realized they fit perfectly. McIlmoyle was amazed that the old man and his team of seamstresses had achieved a flawless fit in just one night. He could only imagine how quickly they could create custom bras, corsets, and whatever else the factory produced.

The pilots knew the partial pressure suits could be vital for their very survival when flying at altitudes upward of 70,000 feet. Every opening in the suit had to be sealed airtight and the suit hooked to an air hose. Should the cockpit lose pressurization during flight, the flight suit would fill with air and become tight enough to simulate the air pressure per square inch on the surface of Earth: 14.5 pounds. The closed environment in which the pilots flew was also pressurized for this reason. A New York–based company was contracted to pressurize the cockpit of the U-2 to create an atmosphere equivalent to the air pressure at 28,000 feet. If the cockpit pressure fell below that threshold, the pilot's suit would immediately inflate, allowing him to breathe oxygen through his helmet only.

The suits were designed for survival—not comfort. In fact, many airmen became claustrophobic and hyperventilated after putting them on. Along with their partial pressure suit, the U-2 airmen had to wear gloves and a cumbersome helmet that was prone to fogging when pilots performed their prebreathing exercises in the cockpit. Technicians suggested covering the face shield of the helmet with red plastic so the U-2 drivers could see more clearly. Although training flights were conducted during the day, most real missions would occur under the cover of night, so the red plastic idea was scrapped at Groom Lake. Urination was also a major issue for pilots in the skin-tight suits. The original models did not account for natural body functions. As pilots complained, designers devised an external bladder arrangement that allowed for release, but sometimes the device malfunctioned. One pilot was forced to "hold it in" during a long flight and, upon landing, grabbed a knife and cut a hole in the crotch of his pressure suit to relieve himself. The knife also nicked his private parts. It was a particularly bloody wound but the airman refused medical treatment. He simply wiped away the blood, slapped on a bandage, and limped back to his barracks. In any case, urination was infrequent, since pilots lost most of the water in their bodies by sweating heavily in the pressure suits. To prevent the need for defecation, pilots were fed meals high in protein, like steak and eggs, before each flight to slow their bowels. If they got hungry during long missions, they had readymade foods in squeezable containers. They could sip the bacon- or cheese-flavored mixtures through a small straw inserted through a self-sealed hole in the pilot's face mask.

Air suit designers and aircraft engineers considered increasing pilots' comfort and safety at ultrahigh altitudes the top priority. But there was no way to eliminate the danger posed by flying the U-2. In May 1956, the program lost its first pilot when Wilburn S. "Billy" Rose could not drop the plane's pogo sticks during takeoff from the base at Groom Lake. Once airborne, he buzzed the airstrip and managed to drop the left-hand pogo. Rose tried another maneuver to shake the remaining pogo loose, when suddenly the plane stalled and plunged toward Earth. The aircraft dove into the ground and disintegrated, killing Rose instantly. Just three months later, Rose's squadron mate Frank Grace, a thirty-year-old married man and father of four young children, stalled shortly after takeoff. He had climbed too quickly during a nighttime training mission and was only fifty feet off the ground when the plane's engine stopped and would not restart. The aircraft dropped out of the sky and landed hard on the ground, then cartwheeled on its left wing and slammed into a power pole near the runway, killing the pilot. In all, three spy plane pilots would die in training accidents in 1956. The third man lost, Howard Carey, was just weeks away from his thirty-fourth birthday when his U-2 broke up mysteriously upon takeoff from Lindsey Air Force Base in Wiesbaden,

Germany. The plane lost part of its right wing as it climbed, and officials later determined that the U-2 had been caught in the wake turbulence of four American fighter planes training nearby.

With every training crash, engineers and flight commanders went to work immediately to determine the exact cause and how best to improve design and train pilots to prevent a recurrence.

At Groom Lake, Rudy Anderson, Steve Heyser, Jerry McIlmoyle, and later Chuck Maultsby learned to cut back abruptly on the throttle as the pogo sticks fell away to avoid stalling and a potential disaster.

During his very first flight in the U-2, Chuck Maultsby realized why it took a sturdy pilot to man the fragile aircraft. Takeoff was the only part of the flight he enjoyed. During the initial sensation of ascending at a sixty-five-degree angle, he felt like he was piloting a rocket ship. Once at the desired altitude of 70,000 feet, he could scan the terrain from horizon to horizon and identify checkpoints miles away through the U-2's drift sight.

His first flight was scheduled to take six hours. It was a round-robin mission, meaning that he would leave from and return to the same airfield. During the flight, Maultsby could feel the air suit constricting tighter around his body. He tried not to think about it. Instead, he busied himself with taking observations with his sextant. Despite his best efforts, anxiety continued to creep in. It resembled the claustrophobia he had experienced as a POW. By the time he finally made the approach to land, the feeling was overwhelming.

"Get me out of this thing," he growled to himself.[1]

He touched the plane down smoothly on the runway—a perfect landing. Maultsby maintained a calm demeanor as ground crew technicians surrounded the spy plane and helped him out of the cockpit. When they removed his helmet, a torrent of sweat poured out of his neck seal. He had lost four pounds during the flight.

CHAPTER ELEVEN

Secrets Revealed

AFTER TRAINING AT Groom Lake, the U-2 pilots were reassigned to the 4028th Strategic Reconnaissance Weather Squadron at Laughlin Air Force Base in Del Rio, Texas, just eight miles east of the Rio Grande. The "weather squadron" designation was just a cover for the unit's real mission, which was to spy on the Soviet Union. This was Dick Bissell's idea. He thought that, should one of the U-2 pilots be killed or captured behind enemy lines, the CIA could sell the story that they were conducting high-altitude weather research, which included studies of the jet stream, convective clouds, and cosmic ray effects, on behalf of the National Advisory Committee on Aeronautics.

If Area 51 was a barren wasteland in the middle of the desert, Laughlin Air Force Base was no great improvement. There, pilots were reunited with their families and tasked with building happy homes from scratch under the blistering Texas sun. Hundreds of miles of cacti, sage, and stones surrounded the base on all sides. The first families to arrive had to rent temporary housing in town, as family quarters were still under construction. Some pilots found small homes, apartments, and even screened-in porches and garages to rent. Families later moved into rows of newly built duplexes, and a tight-knit community was formed.

New inhabitants were unfamiliar with the climate, where temperatures could soar to 110 degrees during the day and plummet to 40 degrees at night. The wives of pilots, raising families while their

husbands were on duty, also had to deal with all sorts of desert crit-
ters crawling into their tiny homes. The women complained of field
mice giving birth under their couches, rattlesnakes slithering along the
sidewalks, and even black widow spiders nesting in the children's bed-
rooms. Backyards were nothing more than a patch of dirt where wild
pigs and jackrabbits roamed freely. Families planted grass and trees on
their lots, but sporadic, heavy rains often washed the seeds and shrubs
away. Such was life on the atomic frontier.

Jane Anderson made the best of her situation. Rudy was not home
much, so she and the other base wives looked after their children together. The Andersons now had two young boys, Tripp and Jim, and
hoped to grow their family. When Rudy was not working, he was a
doting father to his young sons.

"Dad was always playing with us and swinging us around," recalls
the eldest, Tripp Anderson. "We spent a lot of time outside and taking
day trips across the border to Mexico."[1]

Anderson's mischievous side shined brightest around the children.
The same man who had chased a pigeon down the hallway while in
college entertained his boys with fantastic stories of wonder.

"There was a wall near the front door of our home that created an
illusion of a secret door," Tripp Anderson remembers. "When I asked
my dad why it was there, he told me that it was a magical door that
could take me to another dimension."

Rudy Anderson was a fun dad, but he was also caring. When
young Tripp cut his finger after breaking some glass on the street outside their home, his father rushed him to the emergency room and
comforted the frightened child while a doctor applied stitches and a
bandage to the wound. The Andersons regularly attended church together on base and enjoyed cookouts, dinners, and bridge games with
their neighbors. During these occasions, the pilots could not discuss
their work in front of their wives. Higher-ups routinely pounded this
into the pilots' brains with the sexist mantra "If the women know, it
won't be classified for long."[2]

This secrecy became a point of frustration for Jane and other
wives, who wanted to better understand why they had all sacrificed
normal lives to support their husbands at the remote Texas outpost,
while other military families enjoyed relative comfort at other bases

across the country and overseas. Regularly, the base commander gathered the wives together in the base theater to explain to them that their husbands' work was classified top-secret and to reinforce the importance of their missions to the security of the United States. The commander also stressed the value of the wives' own contributions to the overall mission by taking care of the home front.

Maintaining total secrecy over the program was a constant struggle as situations often arose that required quick thinking and immediate action. During one nighttime training mission, a U-2 pilot was forced to perform a deadstick landing after losing power over New Mexico. He touched down safely at Kirtland Air Force Base in Albuquerque, climbed out of the cockpit, and rushed over to the officers' club, where the base commander was attending a formal event. The pilot pulled the commander away from the party and shoved a letter into his hand. Signed by President Dwight Eisenhower himself, it gave orders to cover the U-2 with canvas immediately and place armed guards at the nose, tail, and each wingtip while the aircraft was grounded. The base was then completely evacuated while a Lockheed technician was flown in to fix the spy plane. The U-2 took off hours later without its secrets revealed.

PRESIDENT EISENHOWER REINSTITUTED U-2 flights over Soviet border regions after his landslide reelection victory in 1956. This part of the world had become a powder keg over the past several months with Russia's violent suppression of the Hungarian uprising that fall. Carmine Vito, the last U-2 pilot to have flown over the Soviet Union, made the first flight over Bulgaria in December. Vito's fellow pilots called him "The Lemon Drop Kid" because he favored lemon drops during long flights. He kept the hard candies in the right knee pocket of his flight suit. Before takeoff over Bulgaria, a member of the preflight crew placed a poison L-pill in Vito's knee pocket, for use should he be shot down and captured by the enemy.

Halfway through the mission, Vito lifted his faceplate and reached into his pocket for a lemon drop. He placed one in his mouth and began sucking on it. The object had no flavor and felt smoother than a lemon drop as he rolled it around his tongue. Vito spit it into his hand

and was horrified to see that he had been sucking on a capsule filled with liquid potassium cyanide. Had he bitten down, he would have been dead within fifteen seconds.

When Vito described his near-death experience upon landing, the CIA went to work to prevent a similar mistake from happening again. The L-pill was soon replaced with a needle tipped with a deadly shell-fish toxin called algal. The CIA hid the needle in a tiny hole in a silver dollar handed out to the U-2 pilots before each flight.

The CIA had also begun to coat the needles with a sticky brown substance called curare, a poison first used by tribesmen in South America on arrows and blow darts to paralyze and kill an enemy. This lethal fail-safe device was placed in the hand of pilot Francis Gary Powers before a surveillance flight on May 1—May Day—1960.

By now, President Eisenhower had reluctantly agreed to allow overflights of the Soviet Union itself, but only over marginal areas such as Russia's atomic testing location in Semipalatinsk and the Kamchatka Peninsula. In Operation Grand Slam, Powers would be the first U-2 pilot to fly across the Soviet Union from south to north on a route that would take him over suspected Russian missile sites.

Powers would make the flight from a secret air base in Peshawar, Pakistan. A native of Kentucky, Francis Gary Powers had become a legend in the U-2 program, having flown twenty-seven operational missions, including one over the Soviet Union, one over China, and six along the Soviet border. Powers was to fly across 2,900 miles of Soviet airspace before landing at a base in Norway. Like all U-2 pilots, he received survival gear in case something went wrong. Tucked into his seat pack was a kit that contained a collapsible life raft, a compass, signal flares, a first aid kit, matches, and chemicals to start a fire with damp wood. The kit also included heavy-duty winter hunting gear, food, and funds that would help him bribe his way to safety, including 7,500 Soviet rubles, two dozen gold Napoleon francs, wristwatches, and gold rings. If all else failed, he was also armed with a hunting knife and a .22-caliber pistol with a long barrel and a silencer.

Powers woke up at 2 a.m. on Sunday, May 1, and enjoyed a hearty breakfast of three eggs, bacon, and toast. He savored the meal as it would be his last until he landed in Norway thirteen hours later. Powers met with his mobile control officer to go over the radio code. A single click meant he should proceed as directed, while three clicks

meant that he should abort the mission. They also discussed existing problems with the plane. This particular U-2, called Article 360,
had known issues with its fuel tank. All U-2s were custom-built, not
mass-produced like other aircraft, and this often led to problems with
flying, landing, and fuel consumption. The mobile control officer suggested that if he was running low on fuel, Powers should take a short-
cut across Finland and Sweden and look for alternate landing fields, as
anything was preferable to "going down in the Soviet Union."[3]

Takeoff was scheduled for 6 a.m., but there was a long delay as
the White House still had not given its approval for the flight. Francis
Gary Powers sat on the runway in his partial-pressure suit, sweating
buckets, his long underwear soaked with perspiration. He could not
wait to get out of the suit and thought the mission would be cancelled
as all preflight calculations were based on a 6 a.m. start time. Instead,
he was cleared for takeoff at 6:20 a.m.

Powers ascended quickly, reaching a penetrating altitude of 66,000
feet. He switched on the autopilot and recorded in his flight log "Aircraft Number 360, Sortie Number 4154." He wrote down "6:26 a.m."
as his takeoff time and noted that the flight was delayed by half an
hour.

He heard a single click from the mobile control officer to proceed
and then broke off all radio contact. Powers entered the Soviet Union
and soon passed the Tyuratam Cosmodrome, a Russian missile-launch
site thirty miles east of the Aral Sea. He flipped on the U-2 camera
switches and went to work gathering whatever intelligence he could
through large thunderclouds blanketing the area. The clouds disappeared as Powers reached the Ural Mountains. Just as his view became
clear, the U-2's autopilot went haywire, and the plane pitched nose up.
He disengaged the mechanism and flew manually before switching to
autopilot a second time. Again, the plane went nose up. It would be
almost impossible and at best grueling to finish the long mission without autopilot, and Powers could have turned back. But he was already
1,300 miles inside Russia, so he decided to complete the mission.

He continued to fly manually while paying close attention to his
instruments and making notations on his map when he spotted a field
of Soviet tanks or a large building complex.

The timing had been all wrong for such a flight. Because of the
May Day holiday, Soviet military and civilian air traffic was slow.

Without an abundance of planes in the air, Soviet radar easily identified and tracked the U-2. The Russians scrambled as many as thirteen MiG-19s to intercept Powers.

Now four hours into his flight, Powers neared the city of Sverdlovsk Oblast, nine hundred miles east of Moscow, and spotted an airfield that did not appear on his map. He marked it down and flipped on the camera switches once more.

Suddenly, he felt a dull thud, and the aircraft lurched forward. A bright orange flash in the sky illuminated the cockpit. An SA-2 surface-to-air missile had exploded somewhere behind the plane. The force of the near miss caused the U-2's right wing and nose to drop. Powers pulled back on the wheel to bring the plane back up, but it was no use. He had no control over the aircraft, which shook violently and began spinning upside down with its nose pointed to the sky.

As the U-2 spiraled out of control, Powers pulled his legs back into the proper position to use the ejection seat. His next move should have been to activate the plane's self-destruct mechanism, as he had been trained to do, to prevent the top-secret camera equipment and other sensitive instruments from falling into enemy hands. The mechanism was operated by two switches. The first, marked "Arm," activated the circuits. The second, marked "Destruct," started the timer and would allow the pilot seventy seconds to bail out before the plane exploded in midair.

Instead of reaching for the switches, Powers focused on exiting the doomed aircraft. He managed to get both heels into the seat stirrups, but because his torso was thrown forward, Powers realized, if he hit the eject button his legs would be severed. *Stop and think*, he told himself, and for a second his fear abated enough for him to consider a different escape. He decided to try to climb out of the plane.

Powers unlocked the canopy, and it flew off in a flash. Somehow he got a read off the altimeter and realized he and the crippled plane had already fallen 38,000 feet. Time was running out. He thought of the destruct switches but did not reach for them; instead he released his seatbelt.

Powers later wrote, "The centrifugal force threw me halfway out of the aircraft."[4] He remained attached to the plane by the oxygen hoses, which he had forgotten to unfasten and now served as an umbilical cord to the out-of-control aircraft. Powers tried get his entire body back into the aircraft, but the g forces were too great. Then he attempted to reach the destruct switches, but they were just out of reach.

Knowing that his chances of survival were fading with each passing second, Powers struggled free of the oxygen hoses and the doomed spy plane. Suddenly he was in free fall.

His parachute opened automatically at 15,000 feet. He looked down at the ground below and the rolling hills, which reminded him of the Virginia-Kentucky border country he had hiked as a kid. Powers reached into the pocket of his flight suit for his map, which he tore to pieces and scattered into the air. Next, he reached for his silver dollar, unscrewed the loop at the end, and let the coin flutter off his fingertips.

Powers parachuted to the ground with his poison pin in hand.

He landed safely, narrowly missing some power lines, and was met immediately by four Russians, who collapsed his parachute, took his pistol, and ordered him into a car. Powers was driven down a long, muddy road into the city of Sverdlovsk, where buildings were draped with bright red banners and flags to celebrate May Day, Russia's most important Communist holiday. He was then escorted into an imposing three-story government building for interrogation. Before any questions were asked, state security agents searched him and found the poison pen, which they placed in a briefcase. Through a translator, Powers admitted he was American but claimed that he had simply lost his bearings and flown over Russia by mistake. The evidence in the wreckage of the U-2, such as maps, Powers's survival pack filled with Russian rubles and gold coins, and a reel of seventy-millimeter film, told a far different story.

CHAPTER TWELVE

High Crimes

INITIALLY, THE PLIGHT of pilot Francis Gary Powers was a mystery to those in the U-2 program. The CIA's Operations Center received information that Soviet radar had tracked his plane a couple hours earlier in the skies over Sverdlovsk, but for some unknown reason, the Russians had discontinued tracking. When Dick Bissell arrived at the Operations Center later that afternoon, his top personnel had plenty of questions but no answers. Did the U-2 crash somewhere in the Ural Mountains, or was it shot down? Regardless, Bissell and others believed there was no way the pilot could have survived the crash, so they developed a cover story. Two days later, the National Aeronautics and Space Administration (NASA) released a statement that one of its high-altitude weather planes had gone missing during a flight inside Turkey and that the pilot had reported experiencing oxygen difficulties. If the plane's wreckage was discovered inside the Soviet Union, US government officials could simply claim that he had lost consciousness and drifted across the border before crashing.

The Soviets did not respond right away. Cunningly, Premier Nikita Khrushchev allowed the Americans' claim to go unchallenged until May 5, 1960, when he announced that a US spy plane had gone down near Sverdlovsk. The State Department then received word from the US ambassador to Moscow that the pilot might have survived the crash. Still, the Eisenhower administration continued to deny that an American pilot had deliberately violated Soviet airspace. On Saturday,

May 7, Khrushchev offered the world proof of the American deception. He showed reporters an aerial photograph taken from Powers' U-2. After further examination analysts in Washington determined that the photograph had the same unique nine-by-eighteen-inch format used by the CIA's high-performance B camera. The Soviet leader then stunned everyone with his announcement that the U-2 pilot was alive and in Russian hands.

President Dwight Eisenhower's worst fears for the U-2 program had been realized. Dick Bissell and the CIA had failed to ensure the secrecy of the program. Now world leaders knew about America's clandestine activities against the Soviet Union, and some called into question the president's ongoing pledge to strengthen relations with Russia and bring lasting peace to the world.

In an attempt to cauterize the deepest wound to his presidential administration and his legacy, Eisenhower went before the American public on May 11 to explain the deception while also reinforcing the need for intelligence-gathering activities against the Soviets.

"No one wants another Pearl Harbor," President Eisenhower said. "This means that we must have knowledge of military forces and preparations around the world, especially those capable of surprise attack."[1]

Eisenhower recalled his proposal from 1955, written by Colonel Richard Leghorn, which would have called for both the United States and the Soviet Union to exchange maps pointing to the locations of all military installations in their respective countries. Khrushchev had rejected this so-called Open Skies plan. The president stressed that Russia's "fetish of secrecy and concealment" made spying essential—in fact it was a "distasteful but vital necessity."

The president showed no contrition and offered no apology.

Both Eisenhower and Khrushchev traveled to Paris later that month to attend the Four-Power Summit Conference along with French president Charles de Gaulle and British prime minister Harold Macmillan. Khrushchev used the opportunity to blast the United States for what he called its "inadmissible and provocative actions" in sending a spy plane over the Soviet Union. He also stated that President Eisenhower would not be welcome in Russia for his planned visit in June 1960, which had been postponed from the previous year, and demanded a formal apology from the American leader. Khrushchev then called upon Eisenhower to ban future surveillance flights over the Soviet Union and punish all those involved in the May 1 incident.

Following Khrushchev's tirade, President Eisenhower told both Macmillan and de Gaulle, "I don't care. My hands are clean. My soul is pure."[2]

Again, Eisenhower refused to offer any apology or to punish any member of the U-2 program. He also stated that the United States would suspend spy plane flights over the Soviet Union but would not yield to an all-out ban on such missions. Outraged, Khrushchev and the Russian delegation walked out of the summit with no discussion of a nuclear test ban, disarmament, or growing tensions in Berlin. In 1958, Khrushchev publicly demanded that the United States, Great Britain, and France remove their forces from West Berlin in six months. When the Western powers did not comply, the Soviet premier threatened to cut off all access to West Berlin from West Germany, just as Russia had done during the Berlin Blockade a decade before. Although the Allies successfully airlifted much-needed supplies to the people of West Berlin, the city's population had ballooned over ten years, and the Western powers could not sustain another effective campaign. Another blockade would lead to a humanitarian disaster. The Soviet leader proposed that the summit be suspended up to eight months, indicating that he would rather negotiate with the next administration.

The two men vying to succeed Dwight Eisenhower in the Oval Office were Vice President Richard Nixon and Senator Jack Kennedy, who was now just weeks away from officially accepting the Democratic nomination for president.

After the summit collapsed, Kennedy expressed deep concern about Eisenhower's handling of the situation. He told reporters in Oregon that the president should have offered some kind of apology for or regret over the U-2 incident to get Khrushchev back to the negotiating table.

Kennedy's opponents seized on the comments and tried to spin them as proof that the Massachusetts senator was soft on communism. He tried to explain his stance on the issue during the second televised presidential debate against Nixon, the Republican nominee.

"The U-2 flights were proper from the point of view of protecting our security but they were not in accordance with international law,"

Kennedy stated. "Rather than tell the lie which we told, rather than indicate that the flights would continue . . . it would have been far better . . . if we had expressed regrets, if that would have saved the summit."[3]

If elected president, Kennedy said, when dealing with the Russians he would take a page from Teddy Roosevelt's playbook: be strong; maintain a strong position; but also speak softly.

Global criticism of the U-2 program spread not through gentle murmur but with a thunderous echo. Britain pulled back the bulk of its support for the clandestine project, and surveillance flights were suspended in Turkey and Japan, where the U-2s were dismantled and returned to the United States. Even NASA, which had been instrumental in the overall concealment of the program, refused to allow the CIA to use the space agency in its cover story.

Morale among the pilots and their families hit an all-time low. Francis Gary Powers's fellow U-2 pilots and their wives read in the daily newspaper and watched on small black-and-white television screens as he was paraded before the world press and the public and labeled both a spy and a traitor during a dramatic show trial.

A pall had been cast over Laughlin Air Force Base as pilots whispered among themselves, wondering what they would have done in Powers's boots. Would they have stuck themselves with the poison pin? Each man had resigned himself to the risk of being shot down and killed or dying under the unmerciful duress of physical torture. But the pilots prayed they would never face the decision to give up their own lives freely and without last resort. Chuck Maultsby understood what Powers was going through, as he had also ejected from his plane and been captured behind enemy lines. Maultsby prayed that the Soviets would treat Powers more humanely than the Chinese had treated him.

Most pilots did not see Powers as a traitor at all for simply wanting to live. The hawkish military personnel in high-ranking positions at Strategic Air Command headquarters in Nebraska did not share these feelings, however. Some considered Powers a traitor deserving of death for the embarrassment he had caused the United States and for the secrets they believed he would reveal to the Soviets in a desperate attempt to save his own skin.

When interviewed in the fall of 2016 at his Cape Cod home, more than fifty years after the incident, legendary Cold Warrior Richard Leghorn said he had no sympathy for Francis Gary Powers.

"He should've killed himself," said the ninety-seven-year-old Leghorn without hesitation. "His death would have saved us and the program from a lot of problems."[4]

Powers insisted that he only revealed trivial information to his Soviet captors during hundreds of hours of interrogation at Moscow's notorious Lubyanka Prison. Sitting in his dank cell and subsisting only on yogurt and foul-smelling fish soup, Powers lost up to fifteen pounds during the initial weeks of his imprisonment. He was alone, unarmed, and very afraid. His initial hope that he would be handed back over to the US government as a show of Soviet compassion and goodwill soon gave way to the dark reality that he would remain a prisoner behind enemy lines.

In mid-August 1960, a military tribunal of the Supreme Court of the USSR convicted Powers of espionage and sentenced him to ten years, three to be served in a Russian prison and the remaining time to be served in a Soviet labor camp.

CHAPTER THIRTEEN

Dawn of a New Era

AT NOONTIME ON January 20, 1961, forty-three-year-old John Fitz-gerald Kennedy placed his left hand on a frayed Bible chronicling the births and deaths of three generations of Fitzgeralds, his mother's family. With his right hand raised, the youngest man to be elected president of the United States took the oath of office administered by Chief Justice Earl Warren. After pledging to preserve, protect, and defend the US Constitution, Kennedy shook hands with Warren, new vice president Lyndon Johnson, vanquished rival Richard Nixon, and President Dwight Eisenhower before addressing thousands of Americans who had trudged into the nation's capital on the tail end of a nasty winter nor'easter that had dumped eight inches of snow on the parade route and dropped temperatures to a windchill of only seven degrees. Most attendees had dressed smartly—bundling up against the bitter cold. But President Kennedy decided against wearing an overcoat or a scarf. Instead, he sported a stylish but simple morning suit in yet another attempt to showcase his strength and youthful vitality. Kennedy's choice worked for the television cameras, but some standing just feet away from the new president were alarmed by what they saw. General Howard Snyder, White House physician under Eisenhower, noticed that Kennedy was sweating despite not wearing a topcoat in the brutally cold January weather.

"He's all hopped up," Snyder confided to his Washington friends. "I hate to think of what might happen to the country if Kennedy is required at three a.m. to make a decision affecting the national security."[1]

Serious questions about his health had surfaced during the often-bitter presidential campaign. While traveling across the country to elevate his national profile, Kennedy always brought with him a special black bag that held his "medical support." So secret were its contents that panic set in when the candidate misplaced it during a campaign swing through Connecticut. Kennedy himself called Connecticut governor Abe Ribicoff to warn him of the gravity of the situation. "There's a medical bag floating around, and it can't get in anybody's hands. You have to find that bag," he told Ribicoff. "If the wrong people get hold of it, it will be murder."[2]

The bag was found and returned to Kennedy without incident. The candidate's medical condition remained tightly under wraps until he went head-to-head with Lyndon Johnson, then a Texas senator and political opponent, for the Democratic nomination. Two of Johnson's surrogates, Texas governor John Connolly and India Edwards, former vice chairwoman of the Democratic National Committee, leaked a story to the press that Kennedy suffered from Addison's disease. The Kennedy campaign firmly denounced this rumor, despite its truth. JFK's doctors countered with a letter falsely describing his health as "excellent" and asserting his fitness to serve as president. Just before the fall election, burglars attempted break-ins at the offices of two of Kennedy's New York doctors. Fortunately for Kennedy, his advisors had planned for such a scenario and kept his medical records on file under a false name. Before agreeing to join the Kennedy campaign, Harvard-educated historian Arthur M. Schlesinger Jr. asked him point-blank about the rumor that he had Addison's and was taking regular doses of cortisone to manage the condition. Kennedy said that talk about his health had stemmed from wartime bouts with malaria and that he displayed none of the symptoms associated with Addison's disease, which included black spots in the mouth and yellowed skin.

"No one who has the real Addison's disease should run for president, and I do not have it."[3]

Kennedy apparently defined Addison's disease in his own way and successfully managed to dodge and parry questions about his physical ability to serve in the White House. Health posed just one of the formidable obstacles that Kennedy had to overcome to be standing at the east portico of the US Capitol and addressing the world as the nation's thirty-fifth president.

As a Roman Catholic, Kennedy had to convince fearful voters in the Midwest that he would not take any guidance from the Vatican, while also standing up to political forces in the southern states by running on a strong civil rights platform.

Liberals had also roundly criticized Kennedy for doing nothing to stem the tide of the Red Scare during the early 1950s. Jack Kennedy's father had been a friend of Senator Joe McCarthy, and younger brother Bobby had served under McCarthy on the Senate Permanent Subcommittee on Investigations before losing a bid for appointment as staff director in favor of McCarthy's top henchman, Roy Cohn. But Jack Kennedy had always been indifferent to McCarthy. They did not share the same voting record, and Kennedy had agreed to vote for Joe McCarthy's censure in 1954, but was then hospitalized for a life-threatening back surgery.

Many vocal Democrats saw Kennedy's delicate treatment of McCarthy as the same kind of appeasement Joseph Kennedy had recommended as US policy with regard to Adolf Hitler's Germany in 1940. But Republicans had a different view. Vice President Nixon, the GOP nominee, wanted to paint Kennedy as soft on communism. The Nixon campaign pointed specifically to Kennedy's comments about Eisenhower's hard line against the Soviets after the downing of Francis Gary Powers's U-2.

But in 1960, what Kennedy had going for him was a sense of youthful idealism as well as courage, as defined by Ernest Hemingway— grace under pressure.

The Nobel Prize–winning writer was now among the invited guests waiting to hear President Kennedy usher in a bold new era for American politics. It was an era that would acknowledge the sacrifices and triumphs of those who had stormed the beaches of Normandy and sailed into the deadly waters of the Pacific but not become trapped by history. The new president had even invited the surviving members of his PT-109 crew to witness their skipper's inauguration. Pappy McMahon was there. He owed Kennedy his life for swimming for hours with Pappy's charred and broken body on his back. During McMahon's long and grueling hospitalization with third-degree burns, Kennedy had written a letter to Pappy's wife, Rose, back home.

"Your husband is alive and well," Kennedy wrote on August 11, 1943. "He acted in a way that has brought him official commendation—and the respect and affection from the officers and crew with whom he served."[4]

Later, on Inauguration Day, McMahon would ride a float modeled after PT-109. It was meant as a surprise for the new commander in chief. Kennedy stood up on the reviewing stand, tipped his silk top hat at his former crew, and gave them the skipper's signal: "Wind 'em up, rev 'em up, let's go!" Two men were not on the float that day—those lost under his command: Harold Marney and Andrew Jackson Kirsey.

Kennedy had also penned a letter to Kirksey's widow, Kloye Kirksey, during the war, telling her that her husband had done a "superb job" and had talked about her and their infant son often and with tremendous pride. The widow wrote back, and the two continued to correspond for several years as Kennedy made sure she received all veterans' benefits available to her. During the campaign for the presidency, Jack Kennedy and Kloye Kirksey came face-to-face during a stop in Warm Springs, Georgia. Kennedy also met Kirksey's son, also named Jack. Kennedy asked about the young man's education and plans for the future. It was a fatherly discussion with a boy who did not have one. Kennedy had just recently learned about the joys of parenthood himself. His daughter, Caroline, was now three years old, and his wife, Jacqueline Kennedy, would give birth to a son, John Jr., seventeen days after the election. Caroline's precocious charm and the arrival of a healthy baby boy helped ease the couple's pain over past pregnancies. Jackie Kennedy had suffered a miscarriage in 1955 and a year later had given birth to a stillborn daughter they had planned to name Arabella. Two healthy children marked the dawn of a new era for the couple themselves.

Young Caroline told her father that he had beaten Richard Nixon by walking into his bedroom at the Kennedy family compound in Hyannis Port the day after the closest presidential election on record at the time and announcing, "Good morning, Mr. President."

As a father of two young children and now leader of the free world, JFK evoked hope and progress in his inauguration speech and called upon all American citizens born in the twentieth century—a new generation—to protect human rights while standing together to defend freedom in its hour of maximum danger.

Kennedy's new political era would focus on the United States' responsibility to lead a different world, one where mortals held the power to abolish all forms of human poverty and all forms of human life.

"To those nations who would make themselves our adversary, we offer not a pledge but a request; that both sides begin anew the quest for peace, before the dark powers of destruction unleashed by science engulf all humanity in planned or accidental self-destruction," President Kennedy stated during his inaugural address. "We dare not tempt them with weakness. For only when our arms are sufficient beyond doubt can we be certain beyond doubt that they will never be deployed."[5]

In both the development and delivery of his inaugural address President Kennedy hoped to build a new bridge of cooperation and friendship between the United States and neutral governments of the third world and to show Allied leaders such as Charles de Gaulle of France, Konrad Adenauer of West Germany, and Harold Macmillan of Great Britain that despite his youth, Kennedy would not shrink in his new role. Most importantly, he wanted to show Soviet chairman Nikita Khrushchev that he was willing to negotiate for peace but would also defend the United States and its allies against armed aggression and any encroachment on freedom.

Khrushchev read the text of President Kennedy's speech the following morning in Moscow and ordered Soviet newspapers *Pravda* and *Izvestia* to reprint it without comment. US ambassador to the Soviet Union Llewellyn Thompson had also assured him that President Kennedy would not resume American overflights of the USSR, suspended since May 1960.

Perhaps, thought Khrushchev, the dark days of the Eisenhower administration, the U-2 program, and the Cold War were coming to a close as a new dawn emerged for the world's two superpowers.

CHAPTER FOURTEEN

Castro Must Go

DESPITE THE INTERNATIONAL uproar and embarrassment caused by the downing of Francis Gary Powers's U-2 in May 1960, many still considered Dick Bissell, the program's architect, "the most brilliant man in Washington." Two months before the U-2 debacle, CIA chief Allen Dulles had placed Bissell in charge of covert operations for the agency.

Bissell shifted his focus away from the U-2 project and concentrated his efforts on thwarting Soviet encroachment in Latin America—primarily the island of Cuba. The Russians had found an ally in bearded dictator Fidel Castro, a former lawyer and the son of a wealthy sugarcane farmer who had successfully waged a two-year guerrilla war against General Fulgencio Batista, Cuba's US-backed president. Batista had defined his role as "president" very loosely. In reality, he was a cold-blooded despot who had suspended elections along with his citizens' constitutional rights, carried out widespread terror campaigns, and executed political adversaries—namely, suspected Communists. Batista was a brutal tyrant, but he was America's brutal tyrant, having aligned himself with the US government and American business interests.

Such support could not guarantee Batista's political survival, however. He fled the island after Castro's ragtag army of revolutionaries seized the city of Santa Clara in late December 1958. In February 1959, Castro declared himself prime minister of Cuba and entered into an agreement to purchase oil from the Soviet Union. When the

American-owned Standard Oil refused to process it, Castro seized and nationalized the corporation's refineries on the island. The Eisenhower administration responded by halting US import of sugar, the product that fueled Cuba's economic engine. Castro immediately turned to the Soviet Union for financial and military support. At first a bit skeptical of Castro, viewing him as a socialist and not a staunch Communist, the Russians were all too willing to build a relationship with this new thorn in America's side.

For this reason, Allen Dulles and Dick Bissell decided that Fidel Castro had to be removed from power by any means necessary.

Bissell oversaw a clandestine plan to recruit and train Cuban exiles to infiltrate the island and spark a revolution that would lead to the overthrow of Castro and his government. Presented to President Dwight Eisenhower in March 1960, the plan was finally approved in August with an operational budget of $13 million. Eisenhower knew this bold operation would not be carried out under his watch and that the next president would reap the benefits of its success or bear the heavy burden of its failure.

The plan did not remain top-secret for long. In October 1960, Fidel Castro received intelligence that Cuban exiles were drilling and training in CIA-funded camps in Guatemala. Instructors from the agency and Army Special Forces spent weeks teaching the recruits infantry and amphibious assault tactics, team guerrilla operations, and land navigation. Bissell wrongly presumed that all insurgents had been properly screened and vetted before the mission. Among the recruits were several double agents who were feeding information to Castro and his army.

The Cuban dictator was not the only person outside the Eisenhower White House to get briefed on the invasion plan. According to investigative reporter Seymour Hersh in his 1997 book *The Dark Side of Camelot*, John F. Kennedy met with Bissell before the election in a secret CIA safe house in Georgetown, where he learned about the plan to depose Castro.

Bissell's plan had three phases. The first and second called for insurgent pilots to destroy Castro's air force so that it could not respond to or retaliate against the impending land invasion. Phase three called for 1,400 armed Cuban exiles to storm the beaches of Trinidad, a colonial town in the heart of the island where counterrevolutionaries had established a strong presence.

Bissell was confident the plan would work. A month after Kennedy's inauguration, he attended a private dinner hosted by Dulles for key members of the new administration at the exclusive Alibi Club in Washington, DC. There the normally restrained Bissell downed a few cocktails and boldly introduced himself to the group of men as "a man-eating shark."[1]

Bissell calculated the odds of success as about two to one. He knew that nothing was certain in the fog of war. To increase his chances, Bissell ordered two U-2 overflights of Cuba on March 19 and then three days later on March 21, 1961. As the CIA's deputy director for plans, Bissell had relied heavily on his aerial reconnaissance pilots in the months leading up to the invasion. Airmen from Laughlin Air Force Base flew two long missions over Cuba in late October 1960. These flights stretched over nine hours and covered 3,500 miles. But because of heavy cloud cover, their missions netted poor results. A week later, three more flights were approved. These U-2 missions allowed Bissell and his team to assess Cuban troop strength and identify potential landing beaches. Additional flights were ordered in late March and early April 1961 as final preparations for the invasion were now under way.

President Kennedy had formally approved the plan but wanted it carried out under the cloak of deniability. It had to seem like an organic uprising by the Cuban people against a tyrannical despot—Castro. Otherwise, the operation would give the lie to all of Kennedy's inaugural pledges. The president voiced concern about the proposed landing site at Trinidad. Despite the town's defensible beachhead in close proximity to the Escambray Mountains, where exile fighters could flee if the invasion failed, Kennedy was leery of a spectacular invasion reminiscent of World War II. The president wanted something "quieter" to ward off charges of American military intervention in Cuba. Bissell and his team scrambled for an alternative. They chose the Bay of Pigs, an isolated beach one hundred miles west of Trinidad on the Zapata Peninsula. The landing zone had an airstrip at Playa Giron but little else to support the brigade of Cuban exiles. Bissell's confidence in the mission diminished, but he failed to alert President

Kennedy of the risks of the new landing site. For one, it lacked port facilities, and rugged coral reefs edged its shark-infested waters. Uninhabitable swampland surrounded the beaches, making it virtually impossible to mount a mass insurrection.

Launched just after midnight on April 17, 1961, the invasion was an immediate and spectacular failure. The Cuban exiles struggled to make it to the beach as boat engines stalled and razor-sharp coral reefs shredded the bottoms of their landing crafts. Soon after, Castro's planes bombed the secret brigade's ammunition ship, which also stored medical supplies, and Cuban soldiers began to bear down on the landing beaches. In the early hours of the invasion, the White House received only scant information from Bissell and the CIA. President Kennedy had put his faith and trust in the agency and now felt duped. He sought out his most trusted advisor—his brother Bobby, now the US attorney general.

"I don't think it's going as well as it should," said the president.[2]

The aerial reconnaissance photos taken by U-2 pilots, ordered over the skies of Cuba to capture the carnage on the ground, supported Kennedy's fears. Spy pilots flew two missions over the island on the day of the invasion and two more the following day.

"The shit has really hit the fan," the president later told close friend and former Senate colleague George Smathers of Florida.[3]

Smathers suggested sending in the US Marine Corps, but that was the last thing Kennedy wanted to do. He still felt the exiles could disappear into the mountains and save their own lives and also save his administration embarrassment. At this point, Dick Bissell had to disclose that the mountains were eighty miles away and unreachable because of heavy swamp. The brigade was trapped.

In all, Castro's forces mowed down 114 Cuban exiles and marched more than 1,200 others off to prison.

For the first time since the PT-109 ordeal, Jack Kennedy had lost men under his command. The president contemplated this as he walked alone in the Rose Garden. When he finally went to bed in the early-morning hours of April 18, President Kennedy wept.

CHAPTER FIFTEEN

Vienna Waits for You

JUNE 1961

President John F. Kennedy took small bites from a breakfast roll and sipped a glass of orange juice as Air Force One navigated clear skies during the two-hour flight from Paris, France, to Vienna, Austria.

He was on the second leg of his first visit to Europe as the leader of the Western world. The crew of Air Force One departed after a slow start on the morning of Saturday, June 3, 1961, as the plane was delayed at Orly Field by the late arrival of First Lady Jacqueline Kennedy's social.secretary, her maid, and a mountain of luggage. The president was glad to have a few more precious moments to review the briefing books for his first summit with Nikita Khrushchev.

Kennedy leafed through the leather-bound dossier describing Khrushchev's complicated psychological profile, compiled by American intelligence analysts. The president had met Khrushchev only briefly in Washington, DC, in 1959, just long enough to jot down descriptions of the premier's dress and vodka consumption during his meeting with the Senate Foreign Relations Committee.

Intelligence experts warned that the Russian leader's manner ranged from cherubic to choleric and that he often became visibly angry before abruptly switching to more amiable topics during meetings. But their report also stated that a softer side to the sixty-seven-year-old Khrushchev's volcanic personality had begun to emerge in his advancing years. The CIA believed that the Soviet leader's pace had slowed and that he was now prone to taking frequent vacations. The dossier revealed that Khrushchev had made frequent mention of his age and health and was concerned about possible problems of succession should he decide to step down.

Which side of Nikita Khrushchev's personality would the American president encounter in Vienna?

Kennedy's youth and his recent handling of the Bay of Pigs fiasco had put him at a disadvantage on the world stage. This European tour had begun with a courtesy call to French president Charles de Gaulle. The meeting with de Gaulle was set up as a tune-up bout for the young American president before his showdown with Khrushchev in Vienna.

"De Gaulle likes fighters," explained Pierre Mendes-France, France's former minister of foreign affairs, during a conversation with an American intelligence source one month prior to Kennedy's meeting. Mendes-France had served with de Gaulle in the Free French forces during World War II but now considered him a political adversary.

"[He] may become huffy, but he respects candor," Mendes-France went on to say.

He urged Kennedy to stand his ground with the six-foot-five French leader.

"During the war, he had one fight after another with Winston Churchill, but these were argued in the open, and in consequence, de Gaulle respects Churchill more than any other statesman of our time."[1]

AFTER AN AWKWARD greeting at the airport in Paris, at which Kennedy failed to acknowledge a waiting color guard performing in his honor, the president was escorted to the Quai d'Orsay, where he freshened up before his lunch with de Gaulle at the Élysée Palace. While Kennedy's young wife dazzled Parisians in the City of Light, he was sequestered at the French president's palatial residence discussing de Gaulle's commitment to Western unity and Kennedy's obligation to France, "America's oldest friend."

De Gaulle wanted to pull his country away from the North Atlantic Treaty Organization (NATO) and establish his own nuclear-armed defensive perimeter against the Soviet Union.

"[The Soviet Union] has perhaps ten times the killing power of France," he told Kennedy. "But she might not attack if she knew that France could tear an arm off Russia."[2]

Kennedy was direct with his counterpart. He asked de Gaulle to suspend his goals for a greater France until the fate of Berlin was settled or at the very least tension had died down. The American president reiterated his predecessor Dwight Eisenhower's pledge to retaliate with nuclear weapons should the Soviet Union wage an attack on Western Europe.

"I regard European and American defense as the same," Kennedy told de Gaulle.

"Since you say so, Mr. President, I believe you," he replied.

De Gaulle assured Kennedy that France would follow America's lead during the crisis over Berlin but would move ahead with its plans to build a nuclear arsenal in the future.

Kennedy saw this as a victory over the French leader, whom he considered "selfish."

That evening at a formal dinner in the Hall of Mirrors at Versailles, President Kennedy used a touch of humor to reinforce America's commitment to its longest-standing ally. "It is not difficult for this President of the United States to come to France," Kennedy said as he raised a glass to de Gaulle, his host. "I sleep in a French bed. In the morning, my breakfast is served by a French chef. . . . I am married to a daughter of France."

As talks ended between the two leaders at the close of Kennedy's visit, de Gaulle told him, "I have more confidence in your country now." Despite a thirty-year age difference between the two men, Kennedy had earned the French president's respect.

The young president had used a combination of guile and tact to win over de Gaulle, the last great figure from World War II. On the short flight from Paris to Vienna, Kennedy met with his advisors to go over the final game plan for the summit with Khrushchev.

"Avoid ideology," warned Llewellyn Thompson, former US ambassador to the Soviet Union. "Khrushchev will talk circles around you."

Averell Harriman, who had served as US ambassador to the Soviet Union during World War II, urged Kennedy to relax and take it easy. "Be humorous, open and funny," he advised.

But Kennedy's first visit to Europe as commander in chief was as much about style as about substance. He remained under constant care by a team of doctors for excruciating back pain compounded by Addison's disease but would not allow a physician even to be photographed in his presence.

Advisors had urged him to use crutches during meetings with de Gaulle in Paris and later with Khrushchev in Vienna. The president refused, saying he was not going to meet the Soviet premier "as a cripple." He believed that signs of Franklin Roosevelt's physical weakness at the Yalta Conference in 1945 had infused Soviet leader Joseph Stalin with the confidence to act boldly and pry Eastern Europe and Northeast Asia from Western influence and control.

As he had during the campaign, Kennedy ingested a cocktail of prescription drugs to help him project an image of youthful vigor and steely resolve. Each morning while in Europe, he received a shot of cortisone to keep him upright. The young leader had become dependent on the drug, which concerned Admiral George Buckley, the White House physician, who knew that Kennedy's mood could swing from high to low when the effects of the medicine wore off. President Kennedy received procaine injections as many as three times a day to help numb the pain. But still it wasn't enough. Also accompanying Kennedy on the trip, but kept out of public view, was Dr. Max Jacobson, an eccentric New York physician who injected the president with formulas that contained amphetamines, steroids, and even animal organ cells. Once, when confronted by his brother Bobby about the potential dangers of Dr. Jacobson's "cocktail," the president reportedly replied, "I don't care if it's horse piss. It works."[3]

But no one was overseeing the variety and amount of drugs the president was taking, and that meant no one understood the potential side effects.

Kennedy stared out a window of Air Force One as it landed and taxied down the runway in Vienna. Hundreds of well-wishers stood in the late-spring rain awaiting the young president and his beautiful wife. Supporters waved signs reading "Give 'em hell, Jack!," "Lift the Iron Curtain," and "Jackie . . . Ooh, la, la." The president was not the only one with Roosevelt's past mistakes fresh in mind. Austrian activists were also on hand at the airport passing out leaflets reading, "Mr. Kennedy, Europe does not forget Yalta."

Despite the pain in his lower back, Kennedy descended the stairway of Air Force One with confidence and strode across the tarmac smiling, before climbing into a waiting limousine. By contrast, Soviet premier Khrushchev nearly stumbled off his train after it pulled into Austria's capital city, where he was greeted by a small crowd that included four young Austrian girls wearing flowery dresses and frightened expressions, holding bouquets of flowers for Khrushchev's third wife, Nina.

President Kennedy's motorcade carved its way through Vienna's winding roads and regal boulevards before arriving at the US embassy residence at Weidlich Gasse. The embassy lacked the grandeur of the Vienna Opera House and the nearby Schönbrunn Palace. The mansion was a foreboding place surrounded by a high barbed-wire fence and patrolled by military guard dogs. Despite the American seal over the entrance and Old Glory waving atop the flagpole, the estate looked very much as it had when it served as headquarters for Hitler's Schutzstaffel (SS) during World War II. Vienna had once housed the largest Gestapo headquarters outside Berlin; an estimated 50,000 people had been questioned and tortured there, then marched off to concentration camps. The president and First Lady were escorted to the second floor of the residence, where they would be staying along with Dean Rusk, Kennedy's secretary of state, and Kenny O'Donnell and Dave Powers, two close friends and advisors since JFK's Harvard days. As the delegation settled in, Kennedy paced the hallways with arms folded. He was nervous, and it showed. He turned to his "Dr. Feelgood" for help.

Max Jacobson administered an injection to relieve Kennedy's back pain, and the president was then fitted with a tight corset to keep him from stooping over. Jack Kennedy appeared tall and presidential as he greeted his Cold War rival on the front steps of the American embassy. The two world leaders shook hands and exchanged pleasantries as news photographers snapped pictures that would appear on the front pages of newspapers and magazines around the world.

After formal introductions to Kennedy's staff, Khrushchev was escorted into the embassy's music room, which happened to be built directly over an escape tunnel once used by the Nazis. When they were seated together on a sofa, Kennedy reminded the Soviet leader that the two had met once before.

"As I recall, you were late for that meeting," Khrushchev reminded his young adversary.

Kennedy responded with charm. "As I remember, you said I looked too young to be a senator, but I've aged a lot since then."

Khrushchev returned the serve with equal charm. "The young always want to look older and the old to look younger."

Polite smiles soon gave way to politics as the leaders addressed the big white elephant in the room—the divided city of Berlin. For the Soviets, the gaping wounds of World War II had not fully healed.

"Sixteen years have passed since the war," Khrushchev reminded Kennedy. "The USSR lost 20 million people in that war and many of its areas were devastated. Now Germany, the country that unleashed that war, has again acquired military power and has assumed a prominent position in NATO."[4]

Khrushchev told Kennedy that German military strength "constituted a threat of World War III which would be even more devastating than World War II." The stockpile of nuclear weapons now available to NATO and the Soviet Union made this a reality easy for all to grasp. The Russian leader urged his American counterpart to sign a peace treaty under a myriad of conditions, including the recognition of two separate Germanys—East and West—and, most importantly, the evacuation of most US troops from Berlin.

"A united Germany is not practical because the Germans themselves do not want it," Khrushchev claimed.

"We are in Berlin not because of someone's sufferance," Kennedy replied. "We fought our way there, although our casualties may not have been as high as the USSR's. We are in Berlin not by agreement of East Germans but by contractual rights."

The president stressed that Western Europe was vital to the national security of the United States and that American servicemen had supported it through blood and sacrifice in two world wars. Kennedy also told Khrushchev that if the United States left Berlin, Europe would feel abandoned also.

"Loss of a drop of blood equals the loss of a pint of blood by those who shed that blood," said Khrushchev, whose son Leonid, a Soviet fighter pilot, had been shot down and killed in 1943. "The U.S. lost thousands and the USSR lost millions, but American mothers mourn their sons as deeply as Soviet mothers shed tears over the loss of their beloved ones."

These painful losses and Khrushchev's belief that Hitler's generals now held high positions in NATO were reason enough for the USSR to sign a separate peace treaty with East Germany that could block American access to the city of Berlin.

Kennedy reminded his rival that he had also lost a loved one in the war—his brother Joe.

"I didn't come to Vienna to talk about a war of twenty years ago," President Kennedy said in frustration. "The decision to sign such a peace treaty is a serious one. The USSR should consider that in light of its national interests."

Khrushchev would not budge. During a walk together in the residence gardens and later back in the music room of the mansion, the Soviet leader continued to take a hard stance on Berlin. Kennedy had grown tired, and his mood most likely shifted as his body felt the effects of the drugs wearing off. He let his mental guard down and Khrushchev seized the opportunity. The Soviet leader slowly lured Kennedy into a classic struggle of ideas, where the American president, a realist, proved no match for Khrushchev's impassioned rhetoric. JFK had failed to heed Llewellyn Thompson's warning not to fall into this political trap.

When it came to the virtue of each political system—communism versus capitalism—Khrushchev felt that history would prove the fairest judge. "If capitalism ensures better living for people, it will win," he lectured Kennedy. "If communism achieves the goal, it will be the winner."

The Soviet leader said that his country did not spread its influence through the barrel of a gun but instead supported "the aspirations of the people" for a better life—a better way. The United States, not the USSR, was focused on world domination, according to Khrushchev. The case in point was the continued US meddling in Cuba. Kennedy's counterpart reminded him that the United States had supported corrupt Cuban dictator Fulgencio Batista before Castro overthrew him.

Khrushchev then said the three words Kennedy had been expecting and dreading: Bay of Pigs.

The pain and embarrassment were still fresh in Kennedy's mind, and his closest confidants had urged him to postpone the summit in Vienna until the United States had regained the ideological and moral high ground against the USSR.

The Bay of Pigs invasion "only strengthened the revolutionary forces and Castro's own position," Khrushchev eagerly pointed out.

"The people of Cuba were afraid they would get another Batista and lose the achievements of the revolution."

"Castro is no communist," he argued. "But you are well on your way to making him a good one."

The words stung Kennedy, who knew they were accurate. Fidel Castro's victory at the Bay of Pigs had buoyed his popularity and his stranglehold on Cuba.

When the conversation later turned to the turbulent situation in Laos, Khrushchev continued his verbal attack, saying that he believed Kennedy knew full well that the United States had manufactured the coup that ousted the small country's leader, Prince Souvanna Phouma, in December 1960, a month before the American president's inauguration. A year later, both countries were infusing Laos with armaments in its civil war. The Soviet premier warned that this conflict on the far side of the world could trigger a clash between the USSR and the United States.

Once again, the short, pudgy former metalworker from Ukraine had the Ivy League–educated Kennedy at a loss for words. When he did respond, the young president opened a door that would lead to possible Armageddon.

"We regard Sino-Soviet forces and the forces of the United States and Western Europe as being more or less in balance," Kennedy admitted.

Although the president did not fully realize it, his words marked the first US admission that Soviet military strength was on par with its own. This statement only reinforced Khrushchev's view that Kennedy was both inexperienced and weak. JFK, Khrushchev thought, was certainly not ready to take decisive action during a crisis. The world was now up for grabs, and the Cold War was about to come to a boil. When the young president returned to Washington, he sat down for an off-the-record conversation with *Time* magazine reporter Hugh Sidey, who asked what Khrushchev was like.

"I never met a man like this," President Kennedy told him. "I talked about how a nuclear exchange would kill seventy million people in ten minutes and he just looked at me as if to say, 'So what?' My impression was that he just didn't give a damn if it came to that."[5]

CHAPTER SIXTEEN

Trouble at Home

JUST AS HE was finally getting acclimated to the searing heat of Del Rio, Texas, Chuck Maultsby received orders to replace another U-2 pilot at the spy program's operating location at Eielson Air Force Base in Alaska. The Soviet Union was preparing to test its most powerful nuclear weapon, a hydrogen bomb with a yield of fifty-seven megatons—1,570 times the combined energy of the atomic bombs dropped on Japan at the end of World War II.

Maultsby's mission, sponsored by the Defense Atomic Support Agency, was to determine the quantity of radioactive material released into the atmosphere following a nuclear explosion such as the Soviet test conducted in Mityushikha Bay north of the Arctic Circle. Heat from that megablast caused third-degree burns more than one hundred kilometers away from ground zero.

Maultsby flew eleven missions over a three-month period beginning in late summer 1961. Temperatures in Alaska were cooler than in Texas, but he never got used to the perpetual sunlight. He had a difficult time sleeping between missions, and the night terrors from his time as a POW came creeping back. Maultsby had kept his posttraumatic stress disorder under wraps, and it did not affect his performance. He was always cool in the cockpit. During those quiet moments alone in his barracks, however, his past returned to haunt him.[1]

He found solace in the letters his wife, Jeanne, wrote him each week. The past few months had been trying ones for his family.

Maultsby was grieving the recent passing of his aunt Inez, the only true parent he had known since his mother's death when he was a child. After the funeral, Maultsby brought his uncle Louie to Laughlin Air Force Base to live with them, which proved a disaster from the start. Louie drank away his days, and military police escorted him home numerous times. When he got in trouble for impersonating a senior CIA agent, that was the last straw. Family or not, Uncle Louie was sent packing home to Virginia.

RUDY ANDERSON'S WIFE, Jane, loved her husband, but she hated his job, or at least the secrecy surrounding it. His missions were always classified, so he could not discuss them with her.

"This was the one thing that would drive my mother nuts," recalled James Anderson, the couple's second son. "She was always worried because what he did on a *good day* carried risks for misadventures."

When Anderson flew missions that required his absence for any length of time, he always found a way to call her. Since every aspect of his job was classified, he and Jane spoke in their own special code. Anderson never broke rules by sharing secret information with her, but he told her indirectly that all was going well and that he would return to her and the boys soon.

The couple spoke by phone one evening in early March 1962 while Anderson was flying missions out of Edwards Air Force Base in California. Their conversation went the usual way. He told Jane that he was fine and that he loved and missed her and the kids. Hearing her husband's voice on the telephone always comforted Jane. She did not know where he was or what he was doing, but at least she knew he was safe. Jane could put her worries to rest and focus on running their small household and raising two little boys.

The next day a big dark automobile drove slowly through the base. It had official air force markings, and the wives warned each other about it. There was only one reason for such a car to be on base—to deliver the terrible news that an airman was dead. Many of the wives were outside hanging clothes when the big car motored by. Each held her breath and prayed the vehicle would not stop in front of her residence. The wives watched as it continued on to Arantz Street, where it pulled to the curb outside the Andersons' home. Two air force notification officers stepped out of the vehicle, walked slowly to the front door, and knocked. Jane approached the front door and stood at the entrance of her home with her arms folded.

"Mrs. Rudolf Anderson?" one of the men asked.

Jane nodded.

"We are sorry to inform you that your husband was killed in a training accident on March 1st."

Jane paused and processed the words slowly.

"I am sorry but you are seriously mistaken," she replied.

The notification officers looked at her and then each other.

"No ma'am, unfortunately we are quite sure of this."

"He's not dead," Jane said.

The officers thought she was hysterical. There was no way to know how a family member would react on learning about the death of an airman—sometimes with anger and screaming, other times with stunned silence or denial.

"What date did you say the pilot was killed?" she asked.

"March 1st."

"Well that's a couple days ago," Jane said. "I just spoke with my husband last night and he is very much alive."[2]

It was the officers' turn to react with disbelief. They made several phone calls to check and recheck their information. Finally, the officers learned they had made a grave mistake. Jane felt no elation with the confirmation as she had known both in her heart and in her head that Rudy was alive. Instead, she felt a wave of dread wash over her with the realization that another woman would learn she had become a widow that day.

That woman was the wife of Captain John Campbell, a U-2 pilot killed when his plane crashed during aerial refueling training near Edwards Air Force Base. The flight plan filed with the Federal Aviation Administration showed the pilot as Anderson rather than Campbell. Training can be as difficult and every bit as dangerous as combat or surveillance missions. During a night refueling maneuver, Campbell and his spy plane somehow entered the slipstream of a Boeing KC-105 Stratotanker, and the U-2 started tumbling toward Earth, with Campbell unable to regain control. He tried to eject—his altitude was low enough that he didn't need oxygen—but something went horribly wrong. When the plane was later found crumpled on the ground,

Campbell was dead inside. Apparently he had tried to escape up to the last second because he had manually opened the canopy, and his body was halfway out of the cockpit.

BY THIS TIME, imprisoned U-2 pilot Francis Gary Powers had returned to the United States, exchanged for convicted Soviet spy Rudolph Abel. Powers was debriefed extensively as many in the intelligence community remained skeptical of his actions. The CIA and Senate Armed Services Select Committee put him under investigation, and after eight days of hearings, both groups determined that Powers had followed orders and acted appropriately during and after the shoot-down. The CIA even awarded him an Intelligence Star, but that honor remained confidential. But one man whose star had dimmed at the CIA was its longtime director Allen Dulles. President Kennedy laid the blame for the Bay of Pigs debacle at Dulles's feet and immediately began work to reorganize the spy agency. Dulles was forced out in favor of John McCone, a Republican millionaire from California who had served under President Harry Truman as undersecretary of the air force and under Dwight Eisenhower as chairman of the Atomic Energy Commission. The new director was considered more cautious and less of a risk taker than his predecessor. Dick Bissell was also pushed out. JFK offered him the directorship of a new science and technology department, but he turned it down and instead went to work for a Pentagon think tank. Once a certified superstar within the ranks of America's intelligence community and a self-proclaimed "man-eating shark," Bissell left the CIA a beaten and defeated man.

He could not know at the time that the U-2 program he had fought for, built, and cultivated for nearly a decade was about to take center stage in a game of global brinksmanship that would bring the world's two superpowers to the edge of nuclear war.

CHAPTER SEVENTEEN

Soviets Pour into Cuba

IN THE LATE summer of 1962, President John F. Kennedy found himself under increasing pressure to take action regarding the Soviet Union's military buildup in Cuba, and his opponents were calling him weak and ineffective. The US government knew that Soviet ships had delivered all manner of military equipment and advisors to Cuba starting in July. Before then, based on Russia's training and practice in other countries like Indonesia and Egypt, the CIA had estimated that the Soviets had about five hundred advisors and technicians in Cuba. That number had ballooned to approximately 4,000 in late summer. As the buildup of Soviet military personnel and weapons continued, so did US surveillance of the island. The CIA had ordered five U-2 overflights of Cuba in June and July.

When confronted, the Russians responded that the weapons were entirely for the purposes of defending the island. Through surrogates, Nikita Khrushchev also let President Kennedy know that the Soviet Union would take no action in any of the Cold War pressure points around the globe before the American congressional elections to be held in November; he even floated the idea of an official state visit to Washington later in the year. This was a clear deception as the Soviets had installed several surface-to-air missile (SAM) and radar-tracking sites, transforming Cuba from a low-tech adversary to one with sophisticated weaponry and warning systems. They were even at work creating what they called a major fishing port that the United States considered a naval base, all within one hundred miles of Key West, Florida.

The first SAMs were definitively identified on August 29, when a U-2 overflight of Cuba produced film examined at the National Photographic Interpretation Center. The eight missiles detected in the western half of the island were SA-2s, the same model that brought down U-2 pilot Francis Gary Powers over the USSR in 1960.

On August 30, a U-2 flew for nine minutes high above Soviet-controlled Sakhalin Island in the North Pacific Ocean. The Pentagon claimed the plane had simply blown off course. In an attempt at the transparency lacking in the Eisenhower administration's handling of the Powers situation, Kennedy's White House immediately acknowledged the mistake. Khrushchev didn't believe the American story that a U-2 pilot had accidentally flown over an island of vital importance to Russia's Pacific fleet. The Soviet Union issued a formal protest, stating, "What is this, a rebirth of the former government's bandit practice, which President Kennedy himself condemned?"[1]

A September 5 overflight of Cuba discovered more SAM sites as well as Soviet fighter aircrafts (MiG-21s). President Kennedy ordered that the information be "nailed right back into the box"[2]—that is, not made public—to give him more time to monitor the situation and consider how to respond. Kennedy also worried that a U-2 might be shot down, exposing US incursions over Cuban airspace. His fears grew on September 9 when a Taiwanese pilot, as part of a CIA reconnaissance program, was shot down over the People's Republic of China and captured. The pilot, who was never heard from again, flew an American-made U-2, and the missile that crippled the aircraft was a Soviet SAM SA-2. Any illusion on the part of Kennedy and his military advisors that a lucky shot had brought down Gary Powers's U-2 gave way to the reality that the Soviet SAMs were indeed accurate even at thirteen miles above the earth.

The U-2s were vulnerable, but they were still essential: no other aircraft could cover such large geographic areas, searching for missiles across the 110,000 square miles of Cuba. A U-2 could travel over the entire length of the island and come away with enough photographs to cover a 125-mile-wide strip. The photographs could then be enlarged with enough clarity to show people on the ground. The United States had another reliable reconnaissance aircraft, the Crusader, but it could not cover as much territory as a U-2. The Crusader would play the useful role of securing close-up photos of sites that the U-2s had already discovered. Flying at 480 knots, sometimes just above the tree-tops at 350 feet, the Crusaders were an excellent low-level companion to the high-flying U-2s, but first the U-2s had to locate the target. And like the U-2s, the Crusaders had their vulnerabilities. They could be destroyed by traditional antiaircraft. (Despite this risk, pilots flew the streaking jets around the periphery of the island and then, beginning on October 23, performed surveillance by swooping directly over heavily defended Soviet sites.)

Although the United States did have spy satellites, designed by Colonel Richard Leghorn's new company, ITEK, and code-named CORONA—the first one launched in August 1960—they could not capture photographs with nearly the clarity and definition of those taken by U-2s, nor could drones or balloons. Only the high-flying spy plane could give Kennedy the information he so desperately needed. Yet the president was in an uncomfortable position: should one of the U-2s be shot down over sovereign Cuban airspace, the world of public opinion might focus on the United States as the provocateur and view the Soviet buildup as secondary.

Concerned about international blowback, the Kennedy administration—over the objections of John McCone, the new CIA director—began discussing implementing a more cautious approach to reconnaissance flights. In particular, Secretary of State Dean Rusk and National Security Advisor McGeorge Bundy advocated limited short and quick overflights of Cuba to reduce risk of a hit by a SAM. Rusk had not been Kennedy's first choice to lead State, but JFK's selection, Senator J. William Fulbright of Arkansas, had voted with segregationists on civil rights and was too controversial. Rusk, a career diplomat from Georgia, proved a safe and competent pick. He also had the support of the president's brother Bobby. "Mac" Bundy, a native Bostonian, had been the youngest Harvard dean in history.

Kennedy trusted both men, and each knew the critical importance of the U-2s as the United States' only reliable information source, but they worried that one shoot-down could jeopardize the whole U-2 program. McCone, on the other hand, argued that the SAMs were intended to "blind our reconnaissance eye,"[3] perhaps allowing the Soviets to install something more ominous than SAMs—nuclear missiles.

He advocated continued U-2 overflights as essential for detecting the presence of nuclear missiles that could easily reach most of the United States. But the Kennedy administration was inclined to believe the SAMs were there to defend the island after the Bay of Pigs fiasco. Although McCone was correct in his assumption, the Kennedys had grown to distrust the California Republican. McCone had not been JFK's first choice to replace Allen Dulles at CIA. The president initially wanted to slide his brother Bobby into the position, which would have required him to relinquish his post as attorney general. But RFK backed McCone for the position despite the millionaire's close relationship to Kennedy rival Richard Nixon. Director McCone had first warned the president that the Soviets might be installing nuclear missiles in Cuba in late August. But instead of continuing to press the matter, McCone, a sixty-year-old widower, decided to sail off to the south of France with his new wife for a three-week honeymoon—an ill-timed decision that incensed Bobby Kennedy and others.

"As far as ever putting anything in writing, as far as ever communicating his thought to President Kennedy or to anyone else, he [McCone] didn't," Bobby Kennedy later told an oral historian during a 1965 interview. "And to indicate the fact that he wasn't really concerned about it himself, he went to Europe for a honeymoon during that period of time. . . . He should have come home and worked at it, not be sending a letter from Cannes, France."[4]

On September 4, Bobby Kennedy met with Soviet ambassador to the United States Anatoly Dobrynin at the Justice Department to tell him that President Kennedy was deeply concerned about the amount of military hardware moving from Russia to Cuba. Dobrynin assured Bobby that the Soviets would place no offensive or ground-to-ground missiles on the island.

The administration could only call Moscow's bluff by sending more U-2s high over Cuba, a plan fraught with danger. There had to be a compromise. Four days later, on September 8, Dean Rusk, Mac Bundy, and CIA deputy director Marshall Carter (sitting in for the honeymooning McCone) agreed to advise President Kennedy to limit the amount of time any single U-2 was directly over Cuba. Kennedy concurred and ordered flights to stick to the island's periphery or make the briefest of in-and-out inland patrols rather than flying over the heart of the interior. They hoped this approach would still produce intelligence but minimize the danger of U-2s flying over known SAM sites.

Because of this precaution, the subsequent U-2 flights gathered far fewer useful photographs than in the past, slowing the entire reconnaissance process. In addition, pilots avoided some areas of the island completely because of known SAM sites. While the U-2s were safer (and Cuban/Soviet leaders could not prove to the world that US spy planes were entering their sovereign airspace), the photographs gathered were inadequate to ascertain if the Soviets were installing nuclear ballistic missiles. Though clearly establishing an arsenal of weapons on Cuba, the Kremlin maintained they were defensive only, and the United States could not prove otherwise. The CIA was in a bind, and in a sense it was a blind bind. To keep the spy planes relatively safe meant reduced monitoring of Soviet activity, at the very time McCone suspected medium-range missiles were being installed.

Besides a handful of U-2 peripheral and "in-and-out" flights, other aircraft, such as F8U Crusaders and F3D Skynights launched by the navy and RB-47s launched by the air force, also flew along the Cuban coast to gather photographs. The Crusader photos were too limited in scope, and the photos from the other aircraft were mostly blurry; in some cases even the shoreline was hardly visible. U-2s were by far the best aircraft for gathering visual intelligence over a broad area.

A scattering of reports coming out of Cuba from informants and spies indicated the potential presence of missiles, but nobody knew for sure. An eyewitness observed large trucks, their cargo covered in canvas, rolling out of ports in both Mariel and Casilda under the cloak of darkness. The observers noted the estimated length of the cargo, the incredibly tight security, and other factors that might lead the CIA to conclude they were witnessing the transportation of medium-range missiles, but the cargo on the truck could also have been other military equipment. One thing was certain: in September the Soviets were working around the clock, installing weapons, radar, and "advisors" in all parts of Cuba.

Compounding the intelligence-gathering challenge from the air was a period of rainy weather. The cameras on U-2s could not penetrate cloud cover, and flights were cancelled whenever the skies were more than 25 percent overcast. In fact, no missions were flown from

September 6 through 16. With decreased capacity for surveillance, the United States was basically in the dark during one of the most crucial periods in the country's history.

Further weakening the CIA's push for more overflights was the fact that McCone was still on his honeymoon rather than in Washington to press his case. He did not return to the nation's capital until September 24. Acting CIA director Marshall Carter lacked McCone's clout, and the limited surveillance flights continued.

When McCone returned to Langley, he viewed a map prepared by his staff showing the areas of Cuba photographed since implementation of the flight limits. Alarmed by the gaps in the map, McCone snapped, "I'll take this,"[5] and used it to make his case for more overflights in a meeting with Bobby Kennedy.

McCone was not alone in sounding the alarm. Republican senator Kenneth Keating of New York claimed to have information that the Soviets had indeed installed offensive weapons in Cuba. Keating had been ratcheting up his rhetoric since he first announced publicly on August 31 that the Soviets had rocket installations in Cuba, requiring "immediate action." He continued sounding the alarm throughout September but refused to divulge his sources. The president was in the awkward position of seeming to know less about Russian intentions than a senator.

The president did address the situation in a news conference at the State Department Auditorium on September 13. By now, some sixty-five Soviet Bloc ships had arrived in Cuba, at least ten of them known to have carried military equipment and troops. President Kennedy told members of the White House Press Corps that movement of Soviet military and technical personnel into Cuba had increased and was under America's "most careful surveillance."

"These new shipments do not constitute a serious threat to any other part of this hemisphere," Kennedy announced. "If the United States ever should find it necessary to take military action against communism in Cuba, all of Castro's communist-supplied weapons and technicians would not change the result. . . . However unilateral military intervention on the part of the United States cannot currently be required or justified. And it is regrettable that loose talk about such action in this country might serve to give a thin color of legitimacy that such a threat exists."[6]

That line in Kennedy's speech sent a warning to Senator Keating and others inside the US government who were beating the war drums. The president went on to stress that if at any time the military buildup threatened the United States in any way, he was prepared to do whatever was necessary to protect the nation's security and that of its allies. JFK had won congressional approval to call up 150,000 reservists to defend US interests if the Soviet military buildup in Cuba continued to escalate. US marines began training for amphibious landings in the Caribbean against a fictitious dictator named Ortsac—Castro spelled backward.

As September rolled into October, CIA director McCone's lobbying for U-2 overflights gained traction. Spies on the ground in Cuba reported seeing missile transports heading west from Havana toward San Cristobal. Other observations cited very secretive and "important work" in the area. In addition, the few peripheral U-2 flights made in the prior two weeks uncovered more SAM sites, bringing the total to nineteen. During an October 9 meeting of the Special Group Augmented (SGA) for Operation Mongoose (tasked with covertly overthrowing the Castro regime and including far-fetched plots to assassinate Fidel Castro with such things as exploding cigars and poisoned milk shakes), McCone bolstered his case with the chairman of the group, Bobby Kennedy. McCone, along with air force colonel Jack Ledford, explained that a vulnerability analysis indicated a one-in-six chance that the SA-2s in Cuba would shoot down a U-2. Not the best odds if you were the pilot, but McCone made a convincing case that the United States needed to find out about the installation of any ballistic missiles before they became operational. The SGA group concurred. Especially concerned about the lack of intelligence about western Cuba—and San Cristobal in particular—its members recommended to the president that a U-2 fly over this section of island. JFK agreed. Whatever the Soviets were doing in Cuba, they were going to extraordinary lengths to keep it a secret from US intelligence both from the air and from the limited spies on the ground. Only a U-2 pilot had a chance of discovering just what was going on.

Another discussion at the end of the October 9 SGA meeting concerned who would fly these high-risk U-2 missions. For prior reconnaissance flights over Cuba, the CIA had controlled the U-2 planes, and CIA employees had flown them. The cover story—should one crash or be shot down over Cuba—was that the pilots were employees of Lockheed (the company that manufactured the U-2) going to or coming from Puerto Rico. The story seemed weak to the SGA, and the air force suggested that its pilots, rather than the CIA's, should man the spy planes. A new cover story would state that the downed plane had gone off course during surveillance along the outer edge of Cuba. McCone agreed with the suggestion, but there was one problem—the air force's U-2s were not the latest models.

A dangerous mission over San Cristobal required the best planes, and those belonged to the CIA. Called U-2Cs, they had better electronic countermeasures and could fly a bit higher than the air force's models. The air force decided that only its elite pilots would undergo immediate familiarization training on the CIA aircraft. President Kennedy saw the wisdom of the plan and was more than happy to transfer control of the flights from the CIA to the air force. Still smarting from what he considered CIA deception and misinformation regarding the Bay of Pigs invasion, he felt more comfortable dealing with the air force and Department of Defense, despite knowing he would have to tame fiery and impulsive air force head General Curtis LeMay.

Not all agreed with this transfer. Deputy CIA director Marshall Carter thought the decision was purely political, orchestrated to get the air force "in the act,"[7] and said that a transfer at such a critical time was "a hell of a way to run a railroad." He had a point. A flight was needed right away to ascertain just what was happening at San Cristobal, and Carter objected that to "completely disrupt the command and control and communication and ground support" on such short notice made no sense. He suggested a much simpler solution: "Let's take one of my boys and put him in a blue suit," referring to the air force's uniform. But Carter was fighting a losing battle—the air force wanted complete control, and Kennedy had already consented to the reassignment.

Weather delayed the approved flight, but finally on October 14, with blue skies forecasted over Cuba, the mission was cleared for take-off. This was a high-risk overflight: several SAMs were known to be operational in the San Cristobal area. Would the Soviets or Cubans risk war by shooting down a U-2 to protect their secret?

CHAPTER EIGHTEEN

A Change in Strategy

ONLY THE HIGHEST-RANKING officers in the Soviet military knew the full extent of the mission in Cuba, which they called Operation Anadyr. Troops boarding ships had no idea of their true destination and received winter clothes and skis in an effort to heighten the deception. Even the captains did not know where they were headed until they left port and later opened a sealed envelope in the presence of a KGB agent. While the Soviets knew they could not keep the military buildup on Cuba a secret from the United States forever, Nikita Khrushchev was gambling that the Americans would not detect the nuclear missiles until they were operational. Whenever pressed about his military intentions regarding the island, Khrushchev merely stated that the United States had tried to invade Cuba at the Bay of Pigs and that Moscow was sending defensive weapons to the island. He assured the United States that the Kremlin would place no nuclear weapons in Cuba.

The first missiles, delivered inside the belly of two freighters, the *Poltava* and the *Omsk*, probably arrived in Cuba on September 8. Although US surveillance photos of the ships revealed oversized hatches and that the vessels were riding high (indicating their cargo was not bulk but rather lightweight and large), no one in the intelligence community could prove they carried ballistic missiles, and most US government officials thought the ships were bringing additional conventional military equipment. The Soviets were careful when unloading the ballistic missiles at the Mariel Naval Port. They did so at night and made sure they were covered in canvas. All civilian and nonessential Cubans and Soviets were prohibited from the area. And Soviet soldiers were directed always to wear civilian clothes in public.

Cuba was being turned into one big Soviet military base faster and more extensively than the CIA ever calculated. Approximately 40,000 Soviet troops were there by October.

RAUL CASTRO, FIDEL's brother, was instrumental in the alliance with the Soviets. Raul had flown to Moscow in July to hammer out the final details of the defense pact between the two nations. Raul, who was the Cuban minister of defense, was also Fidel's closest advisor along with the famed revolutionary Ernesto "Che" Guevara. Both Raul and Che were ardent Communists, even before Fidel had committed to that path. Raul was responsible for the protection of a large section of the island and, in the event of war, was also tasked with coordinating plans for the destruction of the US naval base at Guantánamo, on the southeastern end of Cuba. Raul worked closely with the Soviet military leadership in Cuba, and the plan to wipe out Guantánamo could potentially involve the tactical nuclear weapons the Soviets had brought to the island. Incredibly, the Americans at Guantánamo employed Cuban civilians for nonmilitary service work, and some of them were spies relaying information about the base and the activity there to Raul and the Ministry of Defense.

Fidel Castro believed he had every right to put missiles in his country and wanted to do so openly to avoid perception of the operation as underhanded. Khrushchev, however, thinking the United States would never stand for this, insisted it be done secretly, gambling that he could get the missiles in place and operational before the United States discovered them. And once they were up and running, the United States would put itself at great risk if it tried to destroy them. He would have nuclear missiles within ninety miles of Florida, ready to launch, if the United States attacked.

IF THE SOVIETS were installing nuclear missiles capable of reaching most or all of the United States, Kennedy, as commander in chief, needed proof to implement a plan to stop them before the weapons were ready for firing. But he and the military were operating in the dark: there had not been a single U-2 flight over western Cuba in a month and a half—perhaps enough time for the Soviets not only to mount the missiles on the launchpads but also to equip them with nuclear warheads. Thus the planned U-2 flight over San Cristobal was a matter of enormous national and international importance. Increasing the urgency was a recent opinion from image interpreter John White, who noticed an ominous detail that others had missed. In a photo taken weeks earlier, he discerned that the San Cristobal surface-to-air missiles (SAMs) were arranged in the same trapezoidal pattern as in the Soviet Union wherever they protected a ballistic missile site.

The air force and CIA worked out a plan to instruct three air force pilots on the U-2C, the CIA version of the spy plane, which had more thrust (a J-75 engine), allowing it to climb a little faster and about 3,000 feet higher than the standard U-2. The thinking was that this additional altitude just might save a pilot's life. Major Rudy Anderson, Major Richard "Steve" Heyser, and Captain Jerry McIlmoyle, all part of the 4080th Strategic Reconnaissance Wing at Laughlin Air Force Base in Del Rio, Texas, were chosen for this extra training to be conducted at Edwards Air Force Base. Heyser and Anderson had prior experience flying the CIA model but had not been in one in several months.

ON OCTOBER 11, 1962, with Cuba turning into a security nightmare, the three air force pilots were whisked to Edwards Air Force Base in California. Heyser and Anderson would refamiliarize themselves with the CIA model, and McIlmoyle would learn the differences between the CIA and air force U-2s. The pilots would then fly three of the CIA's spy planes to McCoy Air Force Base in Orlando, Florida, and fly over western Cuba as soon as possible. McCoy had several advantages over both Edwards and Laughlin with regard to the Cuba mission. With its close proximity to Cuba, pilots would not only be in the air for a shorter period but could also count on more up-to-date weather forecasts for the island at launch time. And once the mission was completed, the film could get to Washington, DC, for examination more quickly. To expedite the U-2's photo shipments to Washington, a T-39 aircraft would be standing by on the McCoy tarmac, engines running, to jet the photos to the National Photographic Interpretation Center for processing and analysis, before delivery to the White House.

Anderson, Heyser, and McIlmoyle felt they didn't need much training on an aircraft so similar to their own. After all, every U-2, whether CIA or air force, was built by hand, with patterns ("jigs" in aircraft jargon) used to cut the metal and shape the wings, tail, and body of the bird. Consequently no two aircraft were identical or flew exactly alike. But the CIA was taking no chances, and when the pilots arrived at Edwards, they attended a ground school on the differences between the two spy planes. Shortly after that session on October 12, it became apparent that one of the three U-2Cs needed maintenance and could not be flown to McCoy. McIlmoyle, being of lower rank than thirty-six-year-old Steve Heyser and thirty-five-year-old Rudy Anderson, was therefore sent back to Del Rio, while the other two air force pilots took orientation flights on the afternoon of October 12 and all the next day. The two men practiced mostly takeoffs and landings.

Heyser, outranking Anderson by date of rank, was chosen to make the critical first flight over San Cristobal on October 14 if the weather cooperated. Anderson was also battling bursitis after a recent fall that had bruised his shoulder. Ordered not to fly until at least October 15,[1] he would join Heyser for more interior flights the following day.

The original plan to have the pilots first fly the planes from Edwards to McCoy was quickly scrapped in the interest of time. Instead Heyser would launch from Edwards directly to Cuba, while Anderson rode as a passenger on an air force jet headed to McCoy, allowing him much-needed rest. CIA pilot James Barnes would fly the spy plane that Anderson would be guiding over Cuba to McCoy the day after Heyser's flight.

Future missions would require more pilots besides Heyser and Anderson to fly the two CIA aircraft loaned to Strategic Air Command (SAC). That problem was solved when McIlmoyle did an orientation flight a couple days later at McCoy, as did fellow air force pilot Buddy Brown. This meant four air force pilots were qualified to fly the two CIA U-2s. The remaining air force spy plane pilots would fly their own U-2s when needed.

AT 2:30 A.M. Pacific time on October 14, Steve Heyser launched from Edwards Air Force Base for the nearly five-hour flight to Cuba. There was minimal cloud cover during takeoff as Heyser, with his dark hair tucked away neatly into his helmet, propelled the aircraft into the sky. For flights in the U–2, he had to will his body to ignore the need for food and water or to relieve himself. Yet he remained hyperaware of his surroundings and his mission.

"Your mind never relaxes," Heyser later recalled. "If it does, you're dead."[2]

The pilot first approached the Yucatán Channel between Mexico and Cuba from a southeasterly direction. Then, after the channel, south of the western tip of Cuba, Heyser turned the plane in a north-northeasterly direction so that he would pass directly over San Cristobal and not have to turn the plane again until he was on the north side of the island on his way to McCoy Air Force Base. He planned to make a quick pass over the narrow width of the island to minimize his exposure to SAMs but allow for detailed photos of San Cristobal.

Alone in the cockpit, Heyser must have wondered about the danger he was in. He was penetrating Cuba's sovereign airspace, a violation of international law. The Soviets were likely following him on radar, pointing their SAMs directly at him. Would they fire? The Cubans certainly could claim they had the right, and the international community would agree: there was little tolerance for espionage. Even if Heyser somehow survived a SAM hit and then the parachute ride down through the thin air, the Cubans would likely try him as a spy and execute him.

Heyser could not dwell on this unpleasant subject for long. Approaching the island, he first scanned the sky for MiG jet fighters streaking toward him, but none appeared. As he was about to fly over land, at 7:31 eastern standard time, he flipped the camera switch on. The weather was crystal clear; the pilot need not worry about cloud cover ruining his pictures. Although he tried to view the flight as just another day's work, his mind raced. He focused on the task at hand but also knew that, as he piloted the first U–2 to cross the island in over a month and a half, anything was possible. He watched alertly for the contrail of a missile racing toward him. Nobody knew what the Soviets would do, and Heyser was aware he was putting his life on the line. But he had total confidence in his aircraft and his own capabilities.

Once he had passed San Cristobal, he glanced in his rearview mirror to see if SAMs were coming up. But this was a short flight, and after just fourteen minutes over Cuba, his U-2 was now over the ocean. Heyser knew the Soviets were highly unlikely to fire into international air space. He hoped the film in the belly of the camera turned out to be worth the risk.

Steve Heyser's flight all the way from California for a fourteen-minute photo shoot was one of the most important in history. That same day National Security Advisor Mac Bundy appeared on a Sunday talk show asserting there was no present evidence or likelihood that the Soviets and Cubans were planning to build a major offensive capability on the island. His outlook would soon change.

CHAPTER NINETEEN

"We've Got MRBMs in Cuba"

As SOON AS Steve Heyser touched down at McCoy Air Force Base in Orlando, technicians removed the film, all 6,000 feet of it, and sealed it in a special shipping container. Brigadier General Dale Smith, Strategic Air Command director of intelligence, then took control of it, boarded a waiting air force aircraft, and flew directly to Washington, DC. There, an armed guard drove Smith and the film to a used-car dealership on the corner of Fifth and K Streets, which secretly housed the CIA's National Photographic Interpretation Center (NPIC).

As the film was making its way to Washington, Heyser was being debriefed. He had no idea what the footage contained; his job was to fly the aircraft and manipulate the cameras. He described his mission most nonchalantly: "A piece of cake—a milk run."[1] Later, in an interview, he explained that although he was well aware of the significance and danger of his flight, his training and years of preparation allowed him to focus on the mission and not worry. And he gave credit to the spy plane itself, saying, "At least we weren't concerned about the basics, as to whether or not the airplane would perform. Over a period of months and years, several hundred hours of flying time, we've got an idea what our own capabilities are."

After the debriefing, Steve went to bed. He and Rudy Anderson would likely be flying again the very next day, and this time they would be covering a much bigger swath of Cuba, flying over even more of the surface-to-air missiles (SAMs) pointed skyward.

ON RECEIVING THE film, analysts at the NPIC in Washington immediately began the task of painstakingly reviewing every feature of 928 images. Led by Arthur Lundahl, director of the NPIC, the specialists needed hours to scrutinize the film. Several sets of eyes had to identify and confirm suspicious vehicles, equipment, buildings, and anything potentially related to the military; certain photos had to be enlarged and labeled. Special optical devices magnified the details, which, for film shot from thirteen miles up, were quite clear. You could make out objects as little as two feet wide.

However, the larger objects on the ground in San Cristobal first caught the analysts' attention and then took their breath away. Photo interpreters found what they were searching for and feared: hard evidence that the Soviets were installing medium-range ballistic missile (MRBM) sites. At approximately 4:30 p.m. on Monday, October 15, one of the interpreters announced, "We've got MRBMs in Cuba."

The analysts counted eight unmistakable missile transporters and four erector-launchers. Canvas covers on the trailers hid the missiles, but the cloaked cargo fit the length of SS4 MRBMs (sixty-seven feet), a missile more than capable of reaching Washington, DC, or New York City. The photos also showed long tents, large enough to accommodate more ballistic missiles. No one knew if the nuclear warheads were also there. (In fact, by October 15 some warheads were indeed in Cuba.) The launchers were in tentative firing position.

Surrounding the missile sites were several military vehicles and smaller tents to serve as barracks for the missile teams. SAM sites were spread further out. Analysts reviewed the images again and again, comparing the length of the missiles not only to photos of ballistic missiles taken by U-2s over the Soviet Union but also to photos smuggled out of the Soviet Union by a spy, Colonel Oleg Penkovsky. The colonel also gave the CIA field manuals and technical documents regarding the installation of ballistic missiles. This information was so useful that analysts could identify missile support equipment and even roughly determine the installation's readiness and status.

When all experts at the photographic center agreed that the images in fact showed ballistic missiles and their launch sites, Lundahl presented their findings to deputy CIA director Marshall Carter. (John McCone was now on the West Coast at the funeral of his stepson.) Carter asked the staff at NPIC to double-check all their work. More experts on nuclear missiles were marshaled to review the photos: if they were going to tell the president that the Soviets had offensive missiles in Cuba, they had to be absolutely sure. Analysts even compared the canvas-covered missiles at San Cristobal with those in the Moscow May Day parade. Finally, by early evening, every expert agreed: it was time to tell the White House what Steve Heyser's photos revealed.

National Security Advisor Mac Bundy received the startling news by phone while hosting a dinner party at his Washington, DC, home. CIA deputy director Ray Cline spoke cryptically over a secure line. "Those things we've been worrying about," he told Bundy. "It looks as though we've really got something."

"You sure?" Bundy asked.[2]

Cline assured Bundy it was true.

Marshall Carter then contacted Secretary of State Dean Rusk and Secretary of Defense Robert McNamara, a forty-six-year-old "whiz kid" from California and former president of the Ford Motor Company. On the evening of October 15, for the first time key Kennedy administration officials knew for sure that the Soviets were establishing a nuclear beachhead less than a hundred miles from the shore of the United States.

As bad as the situation was, it could have been worse. Had Heyser and his U-2 not undertaken the risky mission over San Cristobal, the United States might not have learned about the missiles until they were fully operational and equipped with the nuclear warheads. JFK would have been trapped. He could have done nothing, or if he tried to destroy the missiles, the Cubans and Soviets would have managed to fire some before all were destroyed. And that would have begun a nuclear war.

It fell to Bundy to alert the president, and in a controversial decision, he opted not to do so immediately. JFK had just spent a long day stumping for Democratic congressional candidates in New York State, and knowing the president would not make a spur-of-the-moment decision on his own, Bundy reasoned he needed a good night's sleep before being thrust into the eye of a storm that would surely consume him for days to come. Bundy later explained, "To remain a secret everything should go on as nearly normal as possible. In particular there should be no hastily summoned meeting Monday night. This was not something that could be dealt with on the phone."[3]

WHILE WASHINGTON PHOTO analysts were hard at work poring over the film on October 15, McCoy Air Force Base in Orlando was also a hub of activity. Two more missions over Cuba's interior had been ordered. There was no question which pilots would go: the two with the most experience, Heyser and Anderson. Heyser had only accumulated the minimal amount of rest between flights, but he was cleared to fly, and both men started their preflight preparation early in the morning. This included breathing pure oxygen for an hour to eliminate nitrogen bubbles in the blood. Just as a deep-sea diver can get the bends, the U-2 pilots would experience the same crippling pain if not for the prebreathing of oxygen.

At this time of year cloud cover could be expected over much of Cuba, but the pilots were fortunate; October 15 was a mostly clear day. Rudy Anderson took off in the late morning, and Steve Heyser launched just a few minutes later. These flights were even more dangerous than the one Heyser had just undertaken. Instead of crossing over a small section of Cuba, the two pilots would cover far more territory, greatly increasing their exposure to SAMs.

The Soviets tracked the flights but ordered the men on the ground who controlled the SAMs to hold fire. Khrushchev knew he was only days away from having the missiles operational and calculated he could have them completed before the young president made his move. In fact he predicted Kennedy would be indecisive, but the downing of a US plane might prompt him to act. Better to withhold fire and get the missiles up and running.

Steve Heyser later said of the flights, "With the two sorties, we made several passes back and forth across the island and covered pretty much all of it. It was an exceptionally good weather day."[4] Rudy's flight was the longer of the two, lasting five hours and fifty-five minutes, while Heyser's reconnaissance mission lasted five and a half hours.

The two pilots knew their assignments were important, but neither could guess the extent to which a group of the nation's most powerful men would use those photos in decision-making that could very well have led to the end of the world as we know it.

CHAPTER TWENTY

Grim Decisions

PRESIDENT JOHN F. Kennedy was in his private suite on the second floor of the White House, eating breakfast and still in his pajamas, when Mac Bundy knocked and entered on the morning of October 16. In Bundy's hands were select images from the film that Steve Heyser had shot on October 14. The national security advisor broke the news to the president that the Soviets had medium-range ballistic missiles (MRBMs) in Cuba. Kennedy remained calm. Nikita Khrushchev had lied to him, but he was already thinking about what came next.

Looking at the photos Kennedy must have wondered how the photo analysts could be sure. Even though the images had been significantly enlarged, the untrained eye would have difficulty surmising that they depicted a ballistic missile site. Arrows pointed to tiny objects labeled missile trailers, erectors, and tents. Bundy told JFK that Art Lundahl was available to explain in detail exactly what they were looking at.

The president wisely wanted the news limited to as few people as possible and decided to inform only certain members of the National Security Council, along with a core group of advisors and leaders of governmental and military departments. This handpicked working group became known as the Executive Committee of the National Security Council, or ExComm, and would advise Kennedy throughout the crisis. Its primary members included (in alphabetical order)

Dean Acheson, former secretary of state
George Ball, undersecretary of state
Charles Bohlen, former ambassador to the Soviet
    Union
McGeorge Bundy, national security advisor
C. Douglas Dillon, secretary of the treasury
Roswell Gilpatric, deputy secretary of defense
Lyndon Johnson, vice president
Robert F. Kennedy, attorney general
John McCone, director of central intelligence
Robert McNamara, secretary of defense
Kenneth O'Donnell, special assistant to the president
David Powers, special assistant to the president
Dean Rusk, secretary of state
Theodore Sorensen, special counsel to the president
General Maxwell Taylor, US Army, chairman of the
    Joint Chiefs of Staff
Llewellyn Thompson, ambassador to the Soviet Union

Often in attendance were U. Alexis Johnson, deputy undersecretary of state; Edwin Martin, assistant secretary of state for Latin America; Paul Nitze, assistant secretary of defense for international security affairs; and Walter Rostow, State Department policy planner.

Other officials would attend the meetings as needed. Air force chief of staff General Curtis LeMay became a frequent member of Ex-Comm because he controlled all aircraft reconnaissance involvement as well as the Strategic Air Command (SAC) in charge of ballistic missiles.

Ironically, CIA director McCone, who all along thought the Soviets were installing nuclear missiles in Cuba, was not in Washington, DC, when his fears materialized and the president called for an emergency meeting. He was in Seattle with his wife. To notify him without spilling secrets over an unsecured phone line, an assistant called the director and simply said, "That which you always expected has occurred. The President will need all the help he can get. An Agency plane is on the way to pick you up."[1]

DESPITE RECEIVING THE bitter news from Bundy at 8:30 a.m., the president decided to keep all his morning appointments and not convene the ExComm group until 11:45 a.m. He wanted the press to see him sticking to his previously distributed schedule so as not to tip them off about the unfolding crisis. In his mind it was imperative that he have time to weigh options without the additional pressure of the media, politicians, and the public clamoring for a decision.

Before the meeting even started, Bobby Kennedy, told about the missiles directly by the president, rushed to Bundy's office to see the evidence. Lundahl was also there. He knew that as soon as Bundy broke the news to the president, he would need to explain just what the grainy shapes in the photos were. When Lundahl pointed the missiles out to Bobby, the attorney general exploded, saying, "Oh shit! Shit! Shit! Those sons of bitches Russians."[2] Moscow's assurances that it would place no nuclear missiles outside the Soviet Union had been pure deceit, and the attorney general was furious.

Once Bobby had calmed down and peppered Lundahl with military questions, he asked, "Will those damn things reach Oxford, Mississippi?" He was joking, referring to racist officials at the University of Mississippi (in Oxford) who refused to enroll a black student. This attempt at humor would not be the last by him or the president as they tried to defuse the incredible tension with a joke or wit.

President Kennedy was agitated when he entered the Oval Office and took his seat behind the Resolute Desk. Made from the wood of the abandoned British ship HMS *Resolute* and presented as a gift from Queen Victoria to President Rutherford B. Hayes in 1880, the desk had been used by every president since. On its surface sat a vivid reminder of the president's past—a paperweight made from the coconut shell he had used to help save his men in the Solomon Islands. Carved into it was his message: "NAURO ISL . . . COMMANDER . . . NATIVE KNOWS POS'IT . . . HE CAN PILOT . . . 11 ALIVE . . . NEED SMALL BOAT . . . KENNEDY." It was a potent reminder and a symbol of young lives saved and young lives lost. JFK was the first sitting president in the modern age to have experienced combat up close—to have smelled burning flesh and seen his crewmates alive one minute and dead the next. He felt no detachment from the horrors of war. The stark memories of seamen Jackson Kirksey and Harold Marney and their families had always weighed heavily on

Kennedy's mind. Now he had the authority as commander in chief to send thousands of men onto the battlefield, to live or die for their country. No president took this responsibility lightly, but only a select few knew what being on the receiving end of such an order felt like. Kennedy, despite his youth and inexperience, understood this responsibility better than most. He had risked his life for his country and witnessed others losing theirs. If American servicemen were to die in this growing conflict, the burden would be his.

When the ExComm meeting convened at 11:45 a.m., Acting Director Carter sat in for McCone, and Arthur Lundahl and another intelligence expert, Sydney Graybeal, also attended to explain the photos. President Kennedy sat at the head of the oblong table underneath a painting of George Washington in the Cabinet Room. He appeared calm, the jitters gone for now. As soon as the discussions were under way, he pressed a button directly under the tabletop. In the basement of the White House, a reel-to-reel tape recorder clicked on and captured almost every word exchanged. Kennedy's voice is especially clear because the microphones were hidden directly behind the president in a wall.

Lundahl had center stage. He had brought three enlarged black-and-white photographs taken by Steve Heyser during his first flight over Cuba. Using a pointer, he explained what each photo showed, emphasizing the many canvas-covered missile trailers and the missile erector-launchers. The trailers were eighty feet in length, consistent with the size used to haul missiles, and the canvas-covered objects were approximately sixty-seven feet, the exact size of the Soviet MRBM (medium range ballistic missile).

Then the questions began, and the tape recorded exactly who said what, while providing a fascinating glimpse into Kennedy's decision-making. The most important questions were simple and direct, and asked by the president.

PRESIDENT KENNEDY—How do you know those are missiles?
LUNDAHL—By the length, sir.

Having Lundahl and Graybeal at the meeting was essential, because Bobby Kennedy, like the president and most of the others, could not clearly discern the missiles or the launchers. Bobby later said the photos looked like "no more than the clearing of a field for a farm or a basement of a house."[3] Bobby and all the nonmilitary experts simply had to take Lundahl's word for it.

The president then asked when the missiles would be operational— vital information that would give Kennedy his time frame for removing them, which in turn would dictate the different steps he might take.

Although Lundahl and Graybeal knew the missiles were not yet operational, they did not have a precise answer.

PRESIDENT KENNEDY—Is it ready to be fired?
GRAYBEAL—No, sir.
PRESIDENT KENNEDY—How long? : . . We can't tell that can we, how long before it can be fired?
GRAYBEAL—No, sir. [A later estimate projected that they would be operational in approximately ten to fourteen days, which turned out to be accurate.]

A couple minutes later the conversation shifted to Heyser's second flight and Rudy Anderson's first, both conducted on October 15.

LUNDAHL—May I report, sir, that two additional SAC [U-2] missions were executed yesterday. They [the films] were taken to Washington area last night. They're currently being chemically processed at the Naval Center in Suitland [Maryland] and they're due to reach us at the NPIC [National Photographic Interpretation Center] around 8 tonight. Both of these missions go from one end of Cuba to the other, one along the north coast and one along the south. So additional data on activities, or these storage sites [referring to potential storage sites for warheads] which we consider critical may be in our grasp if we can find them.

After Lundahl and Graybeal had answered more questions, Rusk and McNamara dominated much of the conversation as the group explored various responses to the missile threat. Options ranged from a quick surgical strike on the missile sites to a full-scale invasion of Cuba during a bombing of the missiles.

Explaining why the Soviets had put missiles in Cuba, Rusk was prescient about Khrushchev's future bargaining chip.

> RUSK—Mr. McCone suggested some weeks ago that one
>   thing Mr. Khrushchev may have in mind is that he knows
>   we have a substantial nuclear superiority, but he also
>   knows that we don't really live under fear of his nuclear
>   weapons to the extent that he has to live under fear of
>   ours. Also, we have nuclear weapons nearby in Turkey
>   and places like that.
> PRESIDENT KENNEDY—How many weapons do we have in
>   Turkey?
> TAYLOR—We have Jupiter missiles.
> BUNDY—How many?
> McNAMARA—About 15.

The conversation about the US missiles in Turkey called attention to a sensitive issue for Khrushchev, who later said the Americans "would learn just what it feels like to have enemy missiles pointed at you."[4]

The ExComm meeting of October 16 focused primarily on the various pros and cons of US responses in order to glean the Soviet Union's ultimate objective. One issue not seriously examined or debated was why the United States deemed it so important to remove the Soviet missiles in Cuba. After all, the Soviets had plenty of intercontinental missiles in the Soviet Union capable of reaching the United States. As advisor Ted Sorensen wrote in a summary of the first ExComm meeting, "It is generally agreed that these missiles, even when fully operational, do not significantly alter the balance of power—i.e. they do not significantly increase the potential mega-tonnage capable of being unleashed on the American soil."[5] The real danger they posed was political. Kennedy had publicly stated he would not allow missiles in Cuba, and now he was being tested. All eyes were on him to stand up to the Soviets. Bundy later hit the nail on the head, saying, "Our public would simply not tolerate them [nuclear missiles] being so close to us." And the president later told Bobby essentially the same thing, saying that if he hadn't gotten those missiles out, "I would have been impeached."[6]

A little later in the ExComm meeting President Kennedy asked General Taylor, "How effective can the takeout [bombing all the missile sites] be?"[7] Taylor responded, "It will never be 100%, Mr. President." The president had great respect for General Taylor and had just recently appointed him as chairman of the Joint Chiefs of Staff. The Kansas City–born general had seen combat as commander of the 82nd Airborne Division Artillery in Italy during World War II and later became the first Allied general to parachute into Normandy, France, on D-day. Both Kennedy and Taylor had served valiantly in World War II, and now both men were working tirelessly to prevent World War III. Taylor's frank assessment heightened Kennedy's need for the U-2s to uncover more information, particularly key clues as to how many days remained until the missiles would be operational and equipped with warheads.

> PRESIDENT KENNEDY—You've got two problems. One is how much time we've got on these particular missiles before they are ready to go. Do we have two weeks?
>
> [. . .]
>
> BUNDY—We've authorized, Mr. President, we have a decision for additional intelligence reconnaissance.
>
> PRESIDENT KENNEDY—We'll go ahead with this maxim, whatever is needed from these flights.

The president gave the go-ahead for unrestricted U-2 overflights and potential low-level reconnaissance flights at a later date. For the low-level flights, ExComm later decided that the navy's VFP-62 reconnaissance organization had the best aircraft and photo equipment. The jets used for these missions—flying just five hundred feet off the ground and traveling between 550 and 600 knots—differed quite a bit from the soaring U-2s. But preparation for these flights would take time, and the first low-level reconnaissance did not begin until October 23.

The majority of the men sitting in the Cabinet Room espoused quick and forceful action during that first meeting, even Bobby Kennedy: "Better to get it over with [war] and take our losses."

At that point, there was no doubt in President Kennedy's mind that the missiles had to go. The question was how. Kennedy went on record, saying, "We're certainly going to do [option] one [the surgical strike]. We're going to take out those missiles."

JFK had learned much from the Bay of Pigs disaster, for which much of the fault lay with him. He had not asked enough questions or pressed the generals to submit various alternatives, and he had relied too much on the decision-making of others. Then, in the final days—when he should have followed his gut instinct that the endeavor had a high degree of failure—he watered down the invasion by reducing American aircraft involvement and demanding an alternate landing site. Now, on October 16, he faced a far bigger decision and was determined that no one—no matter how expert—would unduly influence or pressure him. He would be deliberate in his planning; for now he had established the objective that the missiles must go and would keep all options for accomplishing that goal on the table. In this first meeting he was leaning toward, but he would not commit to, a military solution. Lundahl had said the missiles were not yet operational, so the president knew he had a little time, and he put the burden on Lundahl and the U-2 pilots to find out just how much by ascertaining the missiles' readiness for launch equipped with nuclear warheads.

While the morning meeting did not yield a final decision to bomb the missiles and invade the island, ExComm ordered preparations in anticipation of such decisions. Arrangements would begin for deploying troops, moving tactical aircraft to advance positions in Florida, and organizing naval vessels to head toward Cuba.

KENNEDY KEPT TO his announced schedule that afternoon. Fortunately for him, UN ambassador Adlai Stevenson happened to be in Washington, and after a public ceremony, the president invited him into his family quarters. There he informed Stevenson about the missile presence in Cuba and outlined the preparations under way to possibly remove them by air strikes. Stevenson cautioned that before taking any military action, they needed to examine all potential peaceful solutions thoroughly. Buying into Khrushchev's comparison of US missile bases in Turkey and Greece with Russian military involvement in Cuba, the UN ambassador the next day presented Kennedy with a handwritten note that asked, "If we attack Cuba, an ally of the U.S.S.R., isn't an attack on NATO bases equally justified?" Later

Kennedy shared the note with Ted Sorensen. "Tell me what side he's on," the president said regarding Stevenson.[8]

While the president and the UN ambassador huddled, the Joint Chiefs of Staff did the same at the Pentagon. They discussed preparations for air strikes but also readiness for nuclear war, should it come to that. The group decided to advise the president not to use low-level reconnaissance flights quite yet, so as not to tip off the Soviets that they had discovered the missiles.

Later, at 6:30 p.m., ExComm met again. The president got back to the question that had nagged him earlier regarding how much time he had until the missiles were operational and "ready to fire." The answer: two weeks.

The president now had his maximum time frame to remove the missiles, and it didn't give him much breathing room. However, the information allowed him just enough daylight to reconsider a possible planned air strike on Sunday.

Kennedy and Rusk turned the conversation to the flights that Rudy Anderson and Steve Heyser had conducted the previous day.

> RUSK—The total readout on the flights yesterday will be
>   ready tonight, you think?
> CARTER—It should be finished pretty well by midnight.
> PRESIDENT KENNEDY—Now wasn't that supposed to cover
>   the whole island? Was it?
> CARTER—Yes, sir. In two throws [flight paths].
> PRESIDENT KENNEDY—Except for . . .
> CARTER—But part of the central and in fact much of the
>   central and eastern [part of Cuba] was cloud covered. The
>   western half was in real good shape.
> PRESIDENT KENNEDY—I see. Now what have we got laying
>   on for tomorrow?
> CARTER—There are seven, six or seven . . .

The discussion then returned to the various responses, such as a limited, surgical strike on the missiles, a broader air attack on both the missiles and all Cuban and Soviet aircraft and surface-to-air missiles, and a full air attack followed by an invasion with a quarter million soldiers and marines. The president called these courses one, two, and three; yet, alarmingly, no one clearly labeled them as such, and there was confusion among ExComm members.

> PRESIDENT KENNEDY—It seems we're going to have the general, number two we would call it, course number two, which would be a general strike and that you ought to be in a position to do that, then, if you decide you'd like to do number one we have the option.
>
> BUNDY—I agree.
>
> ROBERT KENNEDY—Does that encompass an invasion?
>
> PRESIDENT KENNEDY—No, I'd say that's the third course.

Then the president, finally, clearly defined the three options. In future exchanges during this meeting he was cognizant that he must be especially clear that these were options and he had not yet decided on one. And he also made clear that while he would like options one and two ready for launch on the weekend, he had not yet given the go-ahead. Obviously afraid that the generals believed one of these options would eventually be exercised, McNamara said, "I don't believe we have considered the consequences of any of these actions satisfactorily. . . . I don't know what kind of world we will live in after we have struck Cuba."

Taylor quickly pushed aside McNamara's sobering inquiry and informed the president of the Joint Chiefs of Staff's opinion of a limited military strike.

> TAYLOR—Mr. President, I should say that the Chiefs and the commanders feel so strongly about the dangers inherent in the limited strike that they would prefer taking no military action rather than to take that limited first strike. They feel that it's opening up the United States to attacks which they can't prevent, if we don't take advantage of surprise.
>
> PRESIDENT KENNEDY—Yeah, but I think the only thing is, the chances of it becoming a much broader struggle are increased as you step up the [attacks].

The meeting ended shortly after this exchange, with President Kennedy keeping all his options open. He encouraged the State Department to give more thought to their consequences as well as when to notify allies and whether to warn Khrushchev.

While the objective of removing the missiles was set in stone and the methods for doing so remained fluid, Kennedy was clearly leaning toward either a limited or a more general air strike. But before he committed he wanted more information about what was happening on all of Cuban soil. Missiles had been located in the San Cristobal area, but were there more in other locations? And the judgment that the missiles would be ready to fire in two weeks was just an estimate. The president needed to know their precise state of readiness. Only the pilots who strapped themselves into a temperamental aircraft that cruised on the edge of outer space could get him this information within the next few days.

CHAPTER TWENTY-ONE

Brass Knob

AFTER THE PRESIDENT gave the go-ahead for unrestricted U-2 over-flights, Colonel E. A. Powell of Strategic Air Command (SAC) headquarters arrived at Laughlin Air Force Base and met with senior staff and pilots, informing them of the need for maximum effort to monitor missile activity on Cuba. This top-secret order, authorized by the president, was code-named BRASS KNOB.

The Soviet missiles were nearly ready for firing. The clock was ticking, so the cautious approach of only using the higher-flying CIA U-2C models was scrapped, and a larger group of both air force and CIA U-2s was scheduled for launch on the morning of October 17. Rudy Anderson and Steve Heyser would fly from McCoy Air Force Base, each in a CIA U-2. Four other pilots—Buddy Brown, James Qualls, George Bull, and Roger Herman—would take off from Laughlin Air Force Base in Texas in the air force's U-2s.

Buddy Brown, recently turned thirty-three, had already been flying the U-2 for six years. Before joining the air force, the California native studied chemical engineering at Bakersfield College. He had enrolled in graduate school at the University of Nebraska and then joined the air force at the outbreak of the Korean War. Brown flew the F-86 Sabre as a combat pilot before turning to reconnaissance flying. "Back then I had two brain cells, one to eat and one to fly," Buddy Brown would say later.[1]

Jim Qualls, the same age as Buddy Brown, had been a star athlete at Frederick High School in Oklahoma and attended college before enlisting in the air force in 1949. He flew one hundred combat missions in the skies over Korea. Bull was steady, competent, and completely at ease in the cramped cockpit of the U-2. He would eventually mark 1,000 flying hours in the Dragon Lady. Roger Herman was the youngest. At thirty-one years old, the Tucson, Arizona, native had discovered a love of flying as a boy. He had flown his first solo flight at sixteen and earned his pilot's license a year later.

The pilots in the air force planes might have faced marginally higher risk, but the weather in which they were about to launch posed an even greater threat to all of them. A severe thunderstorm with strong wind gusts had descended on Laughlin right at the takeoff time of 3:25 a.m. The crosswinds were powerful enough that on any other day the flights would have been aborted. But because of the gravity of the situation, SAC decided to execute the mission.

Buddy Brown could scarcely believe it when the go-ahead for his flight came down. He had awoken at 11 p.m. to the sound of thunder shattering the skies. For a brief second, he thought the base was getting shelled. Earlier in the day, both Brown and Qualls had taken special sleeping pills that helped them both fall asleep and wake up quickly. The flight surgeon gave each a quick physical to make sure their blood pressure and temperature were normal.

"The flight surgeon knew you better than anyone else," Brown recalled years later. "If your blood pressure was 125 and it was normally 120, if your temperature was a little high . . . you would be grounded. You wouldn't be able to fly and your backup would fly. If you gained a couple of pounds, you wouldn't fly because you couldn't get into your pressure suit so they watched you very closely."

All readings were normal, and the pilots got into their flight suits and prebreathed oxygen for two hours. During this interval, Brown and Qualls were briefed on their mission. Each man was supposed to photograph a thirty-mile swath over Cuba.

Brown later recounted that as the support team drove him to his aircraft, "the rain was so severe I could hardly see more than a couple feet in front of the van."[2] Strong winds rocked the vehicle.

Once at the spy plane, the mobile officer opened the canopy, and as Buddy climbed in, both he and the cockpit were drenched. After the preflight checks, Buddy closed the canopy, and as sheets of rain pounded the aircraft, he said to himself, *Say your prayers, Buddy Boy.* Then he gave the U-2 full throttle and barreled down the runway, violently jolted by buffeting winds. Lightning lit up the sky as his plane began its climb through severe turbulence. Not until he reached 50,000 feet did the "roller-coaster" ride stop as he broke into a clear night sky. With his heartbeat returning to normal, he settled in for the long flight, hoping the other pilots made it out of the storm without incident.

The trip was 1,065 miles to Cuba from the runway near Del Rio, Texas, and both Brown and Jim Qualls made it there in less than two hours. Quall's mission had almost ended back at Laughlin, as the wing-tip of his U-2 narrowly missed the runway due to heavy crosswinds.

Buddy Brown's initial coast-in point for Cuba was on the western end of the island at Pinar del Río, and he soon turned his cameras on and photographed targets across the west side of the island. Buddy knew a surface-to-air missile (SAM) could blow him out of the sky at any moment, but like Anderson and Heyser, he did not dwell on that fact and focused entirely on the operation, searching for the next landmark below to keep himself on track.

Jim Qualls also flew back and forth in parallel lines for hours while his cameras sucked in everything within a thirty-mile radius. Qualls looked down and could see the SAM sites, which were about the size of a fingernail. They reminded him of the Star of David, but he realized that each point of the star was in fact a Soviet missile.

There was very little cloud cover, and the mission was going as planned for both pilots. They had been in the air approximately six hours when they completed photographing all their targets. Qualls flew back to Laughlin while Brown began the short flight north to the safety of McCoy Air Force Base in Florida. Both George Bull and Roger Herman also flew missions over Cuba that day, and each man made it safely back to Laughlin.

Unlike the dangerous weather conditions that Buddy Brown launched into at Laughlin, the skies were clear with only light winds at McCoy, and he touched down smoothly. Once he brought the aircraft to a stop, mobile operations personnel inserted pogo sticks beneath the wings for support, and then Buddy steered the aircraft to its parking spot. Vehicles converged on the U-2, and attendants hurriedly removed the film from the aircraft and whisked it away to a waiting jet. Buddy was surprised to see that the first person up the ladder to the cockpit was the SAC director of operations, Major General Keith Compton, who welcomed him home with a smile. That's when the full importance of his flight registered with the pilot, and he knew the photos he shot would eventually be in the hands of the president of the United States.

All the pilots landed safely. Years later, thinking about the thunderstorm that day at Laughlin Air Force Base, Buddy thought it was just short of a miracle that all four of the flimsy, lightweight planes launched without mishap or aborting. "Our Guardian Angel," said Buddy, "was watching over the 4080 Wing that night."

The Soviets had tracked all of these flights on radar but held back from unleashing their SAMs. How much longer the pilots' luck would hold was anybody's guess, but the more missions flown over enemy airspace, the more opportunities for the Soviets to change their minds and try to bring one down.

Steve Heyser had now flown over Cuba three times and Rudy Anderson, twice. Their commander at McCoy talked about perhaps using CIA pilots to pitch in with flights on October 18. This would alleviate the need to put Heyser and Anderson right back in the air. The commander worried that fatigue would catch up with the two men, which might very well prove catastrophic as one wrong decision could bring the aircraft tumbling down. On notifying his superiors of his idea, he received an immediate response: "No." Air force general Curtis LeMay did not want to let the CIA get a foot in the door of the flying part of this all-important operation. Instead, CIA pilot Jim Barnes began a brief training of Buddy and some of the other pilots on the agency aircraft.

But until that training was completed, only Anderson and Heyser could fly the CIA planes, and the two men became unusually valuable assets. The two pilots were not privy to the deliberations held by President Kennedy and ExComm, but when told they would be launching yet again on the very next day, both understood that a crisis was at hand. SAC and the White House agreed that after six successful flights using a combination of spy planes on October 17, they should not push their luck the next day. On October 18 they would only use

the better-equipped CIA U-2s, and that meant the two most experience pilots, Rudy Anderson and Steve Heyser, would be at the controls. Normally, pilots did not fly on consecutive days, both to prevent
fatigue and to allow them to assist in charting their next flight. But
there was nothing normal about October 1962.

Like a coach who goes with his very best players at the most critical times, the leaders of SAC would clearly send these two men on as
many missions over enemy positions as possible.

In Washington, DC, October 17 was a day of meetings held by different working groups, including the Joint Chiefs of Staff and senior
officials at the State Department. They produced position papers and
set military-preparedness steps in motion. And of course the film analysts at the National Photographic Interpretation Center had been
working around the clock. The interpreters had completed their study
of the film from Anderson's and Heyser's October 15 flights over long
swaths of Cuba. As expected they found additional medium-range
ballistic missile (MRBM) locations, bringing the total to three, as
well as more SAM sites, for a grand total of twenty-three. But they
also discovered something unexpected and even more ominous—
indications of construction of a launch site for intercontinental-range
ballistic missiles (IRBMs). These long-range nuclear missiles could
travel 2,200 miles, far enough to knock out the United States' own
IRBM sites in the Midwest. This meant that from Cuba the Soviets
could potentially not only kill millions of Americans in every part of
the country except the Northwest but also diminish US nuclear retaliatory capabilities.

The new information solidified Joint Chiefs chairman General
Maxwell Taylor's opinion that an invasion should follow a full-scale
air attack on all military installations in Cuba. And it would need to
happen quickly, before placement of warheads on both the MRBMs
and IRBMs. The heads of each branch of the military supported him
unanimously.

President Kennedy maintained a normal schedule on this day as he
flew to Connecticut to campaign for Abraham Ribicoff, a longtime
supporter now running for the US Senate.

On October 18 ExComm reconvened in the Cabinet Room, and the president flipped the hidden switch to record the meeting. John McCone and Arthur Lundahl updated the group with analysis of the Heyser and Anderson flights flown on October 15 and the discovery of at least one IRBM site under construction.

Anxious for more information, Kennedy inquired about the six flights flown the day before.

> PRESIDENT KENNEDY—These missions, they don't know what coverage they got do they?
>
> LUNDAHL—The total picture has not yet emerged, sir.
>
> McCONE—We think we got the entire island. I think you should know that these six missions involve about 28,000 linear feet of film. When this is enlarged it means the center has to examine a strip of film 100 miles long and 20 feet wide. Quite a job.

As on the day before, the group brainstormed different options, laying out the pros and cons, with some calling for surprise air attacks and others advocating a naval blockade so that no additional military equipment would reach Cuba. The president had not made a decision and wondered if the blockade option would ever lead to removal of the missiles. "He [Nikita Khrushchev] could go on developing the things he has there," said the president. And Bobby Kennedy, who would later advocate for the blockade, was at this point clearly against it, calling it "a slow death." The group kept the door open for an invasion, if it should come to that, and also discussed the likelihood that any military action against the Soviets would probably result in Khrushchev's taking action in Berlin. President Kennedy especially believed a military strike would have this result.

The president next played devil's advocate to push the group to view the situation from every possible angle.

> PRESIDENT KENNEDY—Say the situation was reversed, and he [Khrushchev] had made the statement about these missiles in Turkey similar to the one I made [about Cuba]. And he made the statement that serious action could result if we put them in, and we went ahead and put them in?

Kennedy clearly understood the military advantages of a surprise attack but kept pressing the group about the ramifications. He didn't think the generals had given enough thought to consequences, especially the series of escalating steps that each side would prompt the other to take if it felt threatened. The lengthy meeting was freewheeling, with every member getting a chance to talk, speculate, and plan.

Speechwriter Ted Sorensen, who had been battling painful ulcers, began drafting a speech for the president to give should he authorize an air strike. Sorensen stared at the blank page affixed to his typewriter and began pressing the keys: "This morning, I reluctantly ordered the armed forces to attack and destroy the nuclear buildup in Cuba. . . . Americans should remain calm, go about your daily business, secure in the knowledge that our freedom loving country will not allow its security to be undermined." Sorensen finished the draft in the hope that President Kennedy would never read it aloud.[3]

That evening JFK kept his prearranged meeting in the Oval Office with Soviet foreign minister Andrey Gromyko and Soviet ambassador Anatoly Dobrynin. The president sat in the rocking chair he favored to help alleviate his back pain; Gromyko sat just to his right on a white couch, with Dobrynin next to him. The meeting was cordial, but Gromyko dominated the conversation, citing a long list of grievances regarding actions by the United States around the world. Kennedy wisely opted not to tip his hand on the missiles but did express concern over the Soviet military buildup on Cuba. Gromyko assured the president that the Soviets had placed only defensive weapons on the island and that the bulk of their effort related to helping Cubans grow enough food to feed themselves.

After the meeting with Gromyko and Dobrynin, the president met with Dean Rusk, Llewellyn Thompson, Mac Bundy, and Robert Lovett (Truman's secretary of defense and now an advisor to Kennedy), giving them an overview of this exchange. Kennedy described how Gromyko "had been in this very room not more than ten minutes earlier and told more barefaced lies than I have ever heard in so short a time. All during his denial that the Russians had any missiles or weapons or anything else in Cuba, I had the pictures in the center drawer of my desk, and it was an enormous temptation to show them to him."[4]

But the president was disciplined enough to hold back. There was no sense flouting his knowledge until he had decided on a course of action.

Later that night, at approximately 9 p.m., the president met with more advisors in the Executive Mansion. This group included McNamara, deputy defense secretary Roswell Gilpatric, Taylor, Bobby Kennedy, Bundy, George Ball, Alexis Johnson, Ed Martin, and Sorensen. These advisors (except Bundy) reached a consensus to begin the action with a blockade. The president favored this response but still wanted a bit more time before committing to it. Arthur Schlesinger Jr. later explained that JFK liked the idea of a blockade because "it would avoid the shock effect of a surprise attack, which would hurt us politically throughout the world and might provoke Moscow to an insensate response against Berlin or the United States itself. If it worked the Russians could retreat with dignity. If it did not work, the Americans retained the option of military action."[5]

Late that night the president finally got to bed. The day had been demanding but would be child's play compared to the upcoming few days. The crisis would of course be mentally taxing, but it would take a physical toll as well. Kennedy would have little time for his usual midday swim to stretch his back and relieve the pain, fewer opportunities to take his daily forty-five-minute nap after lunch, and many more late nights of phone calls and meetings. With each upcoming day the pressure would ratchet upward for a decision whose consequences no one could know for sure.

WHILE THE WHITE HOUSE buzzed with discussion about how to respond to the Soviets, Rudy Anderson and Steve Heyser completed their October 18 mission over Cuba. They were aloft for approximately six hours, longer than the day before, and covered a good portion of the island. Both landed safely back at McCoy. Flight planners knew the risks were increasing, because each mission discovered installation of more SAM sites. Mission planners did all they could to protect the unarmed pilots by having them enter and exit Cuban airspace from new directions and locations on each flight. They also instructed the pilots not to fly in a straight and level path over the island for more than thirty seconds. Making slight but frequent turns became the norm.

It was later determined that SAMs defended virtually the entire island: just one surface-to-air missile could travel over twenty-five miles to deadly effect. Rudy Anderson, Steve Heyser, and the others didn't know this on October 18, but they suspected as much and hoped that the Dragon Ladies, and a little luck, would keep them safe.

CHAPTER TWENTY-TWO

General Curtis LeMay and the President

AFTER RUDY ANDERSON and Steve Heyser's safe return, it was decided, after much deliberation, that the two men needed a day of rest and that the October 19 missions would use the air force's U-2s. Pilots Edwin Emerling and Bob Primrose, both originally from Iowa, and Jerry McIlmoyle all launched from Laughlin Air Force Base at ten-minute intervals beginning at 4:20 a.m.

This was Jerry McIlmoyle's first flight over Cuba, and he later said, "When I coasted out over Corpus Christi and later looked down and could see the Yucatán Peninsula over to the right, it was just as the sun was breaking. And when I saw Cuba I thought how beautiful it was. Then I thought how dangerous it was to me."[1] Every pilot who flew over Cuba understood the risks—that the Soviets had surface-to-air missiles (SAMs) pointed up at them—but without exception, each man did his job without so much as a word of protest. They had been trained for exactly this sort of surveillance mission; they just never dreamed the stakes would be so high.

PRESIDENT JOHN F. KENNEDY and Secretary of Defense Robert McNamara met with the Joint Chiefs at 9:45 a.m. on Friday, October 19. The Chiefs had previously met on their own and unanimously agreed to recommend a massive surprise air attack, hitting missiles, SAMs, and airfields where the MiGs were stationed. The group that met in the Cabinet Room with Kennedy and McNamara included General Maxwell Taylor, air force chief of staff Curtis LeMay, chief of naval operations George Anderson, army chief of staff Earle Wheeler, and Marine Corps commandant David Shoup.

LeMay was by far the most opinionated of the group. He'd distinguished himself in the air force in World War II, first by leading many bombing missions against the Germans and later by coordinating the incendiary bombing raids, some sixty in total, over Japan. This included the firebombing of Tokyo, called the most destructive bombing raid in history, killing an estimated 100,000 Japanese and leaving over 1 million homeless. However, both Franklin Roosevelt and Harry Truman supported LeMay, knowing that if the United States had to invade Japan, an estimated 1 million American casualties might result. Some viewed LeMay as a military genius; others thought him bloodthirsty.

LeMay was the youngest four-star general since Ulysses Grant, and like Grant, he conducted warfare in an all-out manner, justifying his means as shortening the duration of the war and possibly saving lives in the long run. Many of the pilots that he commanded knew the man as a no-nonsense warrior, but one they admired: no armchair general, he had risked his own life during World War II and knew what it was like to take fire.

When it came to the Russians, LeMay felt the United States had been too soft, letting them spread communism around the world without the proper response. In 1956, he even staged a mock nuclear raid on the Soviet Union, using hundreds of B-47 bombers that launched from Greenland and Alaska and headed over the Arctic and toward the Soviet Union, before turning back right at the border. This was classic LeMay, using intimidation and surprise to show the Soviets he could more than stand up to them.

Now, as head of the air force and Strategic Air Command, LeMay felt a showdown with the Soviets was imminent, and he was certain of a US win. If nuclear weapons had to be used, he knew the United States had far superior technology, particularly with its long-range bomber aircraft carrying nuclear bombs.

While many Americans had great respect for this warrior, President Kennedy loathed him. JFK thought LeMay simplistic and the worst kind of saber rattler.

GENERAL TAYLOR KICKED off the meeting between Kennedy and the Joint Chiefs by saying, "The benefit this morning, Mr. President, would be for you to hear from the other Chiefs' comments, either on our basic, what I call the military plan, or how they would see the blockade plan."

It wasn't long before LeMay chimed in: "I'd emphasize, a little strongly perhaps, that we don't have any choice except direct military action."

Then a few seconds later the cigar-chomping air force general moved on to his next point of contention, talking as a teacher would to a student who has fallen behind in his studies.

LeMay—Now, as for the Berlin situation, I don't share your view that if we knock off Cuba, they're going to knock off Berlin. We've got the Berlin problem staring us in the face anyway. If we don't do anything to Cuba, then they're going to push on Berlin and push real hard because they've got us on the run. If we take military action against Cuba, then I think that the—

PRESIDENT KENNEDY—What do you think their reply would be?

LeMay [raising his voice]—I don't think they're going to make any reply if we tell them that the Berlin situation is just like it's always been. If they make a move we're going to fight. I don't think it changes the Berlin situation at all except you've got to make one more statement on it.

So I see no other solution. This blockade and political action, I see leading into war. I don't see any other solution. It will lead right into war. This is almost as bad as the appeasement at Munich.

The comparison between the blockade and Neville Chamberlain's notorious appeasement of Adolf Hitler was a blatant shot across the bow, but Kennedy held his tongue. Some also saw LeMay's comment as a slight against the president's father, Joseph P. Kennedy, who had supported Chamberlain's appeasement policy. JFK had even written about the issue as the topic of his senior thesis at Harvard. While he had criticized Chamberlain for being too lenient with Hitler, he also agreed with his father's belief that the British had no appetite for war at the time. Kennedy knew that both students and historians would debate his own actions in the escalating crisis over Cuba for generations. Which side of history would he be on?

Chief of naval operations George Anderson then made his case for a prompt air strike, followed by army chief of staff Wheeler, who pushed even harder: "Mr. President, in my judgment, from a military point of view, the lowest-risk course of action if you're thinking of protecting the people of the United States against a possible strike on us is to go ahead with a surprise air strike, the blockade, and an invasion."

Kennedy heard him out, and then simply said, "Thank you, General."

None of the men in the room, not even the president, then knew that Nikita Khrushchev had authorized the use of tactical nuclear weapons against US invading forces should the Americans try to take Cuba by force. The Soviets had armed their ground forces with approximately one hundred of these short-range missiles. They were waiting and ready to fire, able to obliterate an invading army.

Next to speak in the Cabinet Room was Marine Corps commandant Shoup, who added his endorsement to an immediate surprise strike. In a rambling monologue, Shoup emphasized that the longer the United States waited to take action, the more difficult the job would be.

LeMay then tried to ratchet up the pressure on the president.

LeMay—I think that a blockade, and political talk, would
     be considered by a lot of our friends and neutrals as being
     a pretty weak response to this. And I'm sure a lot of our
     own citizens would feel that way too. You're in a pretty
     bad fix, Mr. President.
President Kennedy—Re-say it?
LeMay—You're in a pretty bad fix.
President Kennedy—You're in it with me.

Kennedy chuckled awkwardly, probably amazed at LeMay's impertinence and somewhat cavalier, simplistic attitude when nuclear war was a very real possibility. LeMay saw the solution only from a military perspective: a surprise attack would be the most effective approach. The president found himself fighting a mental battle on two fronts. While he tried to outthink Khrushchev and anticipate the Soviet leader's next move, he also had to manage his own generals, some of whom were trying to push him closer to war.

The conversation turned to the vulnerability of the US military base at Guantánamo and how to protect it. General Taylor predicted that if the United States launched an all-out air attack on Cuba, "Guantánamo [would] cease to be a useful naval base, become more of a fortress . . . in a permanent state of siege."

The generals continued to pressure Kennedy to take more forceful action than a blockade or an air strike limited to the nuclear missiles. LeMay, in particular, once again challenged the president, who still had not announced his decision. "So if you take out the missiles," said LeMay toward the end of the meeting, "I think you've got to take out their air with it, and their radar, communications, the whole works. It just doesn't make any sense to do anything but that."

Kennedy did not see the decision in such black-and-white terms and again pointed out that a full assault on Cuba could mean the loss of Berlin. LeMay countered, "If you lose in Cuba, you're going to get more and more pressure right on Berlin."

Before the exchange could get heated, General Taylor jumped in and assured the president, "The worldwide problem has certainly been before us, Mr. President. We haven't ignored it."

The meeting soon drew to a close. The president was running out of time until the missiles became operational.

DURING THIS PERIOD when the Joint Chiefs were advocating a massive military attack, both President Kennedy and his brother Bobby were evolving from their initial reaction—to just take the missiles out— toward a more measured approach. Bobby endorsed the idea of first trying the blockade.

For Bobby, a good part of that change of preference had to do with the consequences of a sneak air attack on the missile bases and other installations. He equated such a step with Japan's surprise attack on Pearl Harbor. When he first learned about the missiles and he and the president were leaning toward an air strike during the initial ExComm meeting, Bobby had passed a note to his brother. It read, "I now know how Tojo felt when planning Pearl Harbor."[2] In his fixation on the attack at Pearl Harbor, he progressed from feeling like he was about to wage it to arguing that a surprise attack was un-American. He later told the ExComm members that "for 175 years we had not been that kind of country. A sneak attack was not in our traditions. Thousands of Cubans would be killed without warning and a lot of Russians too."[3]

While Pearl Harbor influenced Bobby, his brother found inspiration in a book he had just read, Barbara Tuchman's *The Guns of August*, chronicling how World War I started. This Pulitzer Prize–winning work illuminated how nations can tumble into war not so much by strategy as by reaction to events. The president drew the parallel that if he launched surprise air strikes, the Soviets would have no option but to respond, and soon the dominoes would start falling on the way to all-out nuclear war, which neither side wanted. The two brothers even talked about the book, with the president emphasizing how simple miscalculations led to consequences few had foreseen. Bobby later recalled that his brother pointed out how "stupidity, individual idiosyncrasies, misunderstandings, and personal complexes of inferiority and grandeur"[4] all had led to escalating responses and counterresponses. In his book *Thirteen Days*, Bobby explained that the president did not want to "challenge the other side needlessly, or precipitously push our adversaries into a course of action that was not intended or anticipated."

At about noon on Friday, October 19, the president kept to his campaign schedule and flew to the Midwest, while his advisors continued to work on hammering out the specific actions and time frames of the different political and military options. For Kennedy, the charade of campaigning must have been a lonely endeavor. He sensed that before the weekend was finished he'd have to distill the many pieces of advice and his options down to a cohesive plan. Just one man, the president, had to make a decision that could mean life or death for millions of people across the globe.

CHAPTER TWENTY-THREE

SAMs Tracking U-2s

BY SATURDAY, OCTOBER 20, the sleep-deprived ExComm members began to show strain, with some expressing impatience and others indulging in fits of anger. John Kennedy's wise men were overworked and exhausted. Ted Sorensen had worked into the predawn hours of Saturday morning on the latest draft of JFK's televised speech to the nation. In an effort to get the tone just right, he had read and reread the speeches given by President Woodrow Wilson and Franklin Roosevelt to Congress before World War I and World War II.

Bobby Kennedy later wrote that the burden of making recommendations that could "affect the future of all mankind" was tremendous. "That kind of pressure does strange things to a human being, even to brilliant, self-confident, mature, experienced men. For some it brings out characteristics and strength that perhaps even they never knew they had, and for others the pressure is too overwhelming."[1]

Bobby also realized that sending the president on a campaign trip to Chicago to keep up the appearance of normality was likely a mistake, because he and Robert McNamara asked him to return to Washington, DC. They felt they had a good working plan to present to him about the merits of the blockade and how it would work.

The president used the flimsy excuse that he was suffering from a cold and needed to return to the White House. He called Press Secretary Pierre Salinger early that morning and ordered him up to his hotel suite. When Salinger entered the room, Kennedy was in his bathrobe, scribbling on a notepad.

"Here's something I'm writing for you," JFK said. "You're gonna have a press conference to announce it."

A short time later, Salinger gathered the press corps.

"The assistant White House physician Dr. George Berkley noticed that the President's voice was very husky," Salinger lied. "This morning when he examined the President, he found the President had developed a slight temperature and that he was suffering from a minor upper respiratory ailment."

Salinger then told reporters that Kennedy was cancelling his schedule for the next two days and heading back to the White House, which of course set off media speculation that something serious was brewing. On the flight back to Washington, Salinger found himself alone with JFK and noticed that he appeared healthy.

"Mr. President, you're not sick," Salinger said. "What the hell's going on?"

"You're gonna find out as soon as you land in Washington," Kennedy informed him. "And then, grab your balls."[2]

Military movements of troops, ships, and planes toward Florida and the Caribbean had also broken the secrecy of the crisis. Now, wild speculation centered on Cuba.

Back at the White House with the ExComm members at 1:30 p.m. on Saturday, Kennedy must have felt bone weary. But the demands on the young president were just beginning. He read Sorensen's draft and took a swim to help alleviate his back pain. Then he gathered his top advisors once again.

Because the meeting was held in the Executive Mansion of the White House and not the Cabinet Room, it was not taped, but National Security Council executive secretary Bromley Smith recorded the minutes. John McCone and then Ray Cline, CIA deputy director of intelligence, updated the president regarding the latest estimate of missile sites and military installations. Next Arthur Lundahl explained the details in the latest U-2 photos and proclaimed, "During the past week we were able to achieve coverage over 95% of the island." When Lundahl completed his presentation, the president surprised everyone by getting to his feet and walking over to Lundahl to say, "I want to extend to your organization my gratitude for a job very well done."

Although Kennedy was thanking the staff of the National Photographic Interpretation Center, he had not forgotten that without the
U-2 pilots, particularly Rudy Anderson and Steve Heyser, Lundahl's
group would have nothing to analyze. He was just biding his time to
thank those men for bringing him out of the dark and into the light of
the Soviets' duplicity.

The meeting lasted a grueling two hours and forty minutes, with
each person passionately explaining his particular recommendation,
ranging from opening negotiations with Soviets to the surprise attack
advocated by the Joint Chiefs of Staff. CIA director McCone expressed
his grave concern that if the Soviets learned what the Americans had
discovered from the U-2 photos, Nikita Khrushchev and his military
generals might try to beat them to the punch and order an immediate
nuclear attack.

Kennedy rejected both the negotiation option and the surprise attack and ultimately informed the group that he was "ready to go ahead
with the blockade and to take actions necessary to put us in a position
to undertake an air strike on the missile sites by Monday or Tuesday."[3]
Bromley's minutes went on to say, "It is possible that we may have
to make an early strike with or without warning next week. He [the
president] directed that air strike plans include only missiles and missile sites."

When the meeting adjourned, Kennedy worked on his draft
of the speech to inform the nation of the missiles and his response,
while General Maxwell Taylor went back to the Pentagon and told
the Chiefs, "This was not one of our better days."[4] Earle Wheeler
quipped, "I never thought I'd live to see the day when I would want
to go to war."

Later that evening, the president took a swim in the White House
pool with his close friend and advisor Dave Powers. "If we were only
thinking of ourselves, it would be easy," JFK said. "But I keep thinking about the children whose lives would be wiped out."[5]

US GOVERNMENT OFFICIALS, primarily in the State Department, used
Sunday and Monday to prepare summary papers for US allies to inform them of what was taking place. Meanwhile the Joint Chiefs prepared for the blockade and potential air strikes if the Russians ran it.

As a precaution, Strategic Air Command (SAC) scattered its most critical aircraft among civilian airfields around the country to reduce vulnerability should the Russians attack. B-52s equipped with nuclear bombs circled continuously—as soon as one came in for a landing, another launched to take its place. Preparations were made for all-out war.

The Joint Chiefs were not the only disappointed governmental officials. Sunday night McCone informed Lyndon Johnson of the president's decision, and Johnson replied, "We are telegraphing our punch." The vice president also thought the blockade would be ineffective because Cuba already had the missiles. He told McCone, "We are locking the barn after the horse is gone."[6] JFK had also ordered CIA director McCone to drive north from the nation's capital to Gettysburg, Pennsylvania, where the former president was living with his wife, Mamie, in retirement. For Kennedy, Ike and former president Harry Truman were the only other men living who had faced a similar challenge, and the young president needed sage advice.

After briefing Eisenhower on the Cuba crisis, McCone reported back to the president that his predecessor had found the situation "intolerable" and would support decisive military action to prevent any further military buildup on the island of Cuba.[7]

President Kennedy's televised speech to the country was scheduled for Monday evening, October 22, and details about the crisis began to leak. Kennedy requested that the major newspapers not publish specifics until after the broadcast. Some editors complied, but the press knew from the military buildup that there was a crisis tied to Cuba. The *Washington Post* ran a headline on Sunday reading, "Marine Moves in South Linked to Cuban Crisis."[8] The article gave few details, which only heightened the public's anxiety to know just what was happening. Kennedy's speech became more critical than ever. He didn't want to panic the American public, but he had to let them know about the gravity of the situation. The president needed to find the perfect balance in the most important speech of his life.

ON MONDAY, MOST of the ExComm members assembled in the Cabinet Room at 3 p.m. for one last meeting before the president announced his policy. The group discussed the fine points of disseminating the rationale for the blockade and tackled anticipated questions from both the media and US allies, as well as Soviet responses. The group also discussed the blockade and the series of steps to take if a ship did not stop at the quarantine line.

President Kennedy focused his efforts on getting consensus on action resulting from various scenarios. One very important issue brought up by the president but not fully answered was the following: "What are we going to do when one of our U-2s are shot down, which we have to anticipate maybe in the next few days, over a SAM site? What will be our response there? Number one. And secondly, what will we do if the work continues on these sites, which we assume it will. . . . If they shoot down one of our U-2s, do we attack that SAM site or all the SAM sites?"

Kennedy instructed the group to consider the issue of the U-2s and be prepared to offer detailed recommendations the next day. It seemed no matter how many meetings the ExComm group held, there was always unfinished business. Though pulled in different directions, the president at least appeared calm.

Kennedy also had two bargaining chips in dealing with the Soviets: the removal of Jupiter missiles from Italy and from Turkey. Eisenhower reinforced this during a morning phone call with JFK.

"If this thing is such a serious thing; here on our flank, you've got to use something," Ike told his successor.

Kennedy also voiced his concern about protecting the unarmed U-2 pilots as they continued their flights over Cuba. The United States would have to meet any Soviet military action against the airmen with a similar response. "We have to assume as surveillance continues with the U-2s, these SAM sites may shoot one down and at that point we were just discussing what action we would take in attacking the SAM sites. I assume this would only be the first in a rather increasing number of steps."[9]

Eisenhower went on to praise Kennedy's efforts thus far to eliminate the nuclear threat from Cuba. "You're making all the moves that you can. . . . You've made up your mind and you've got to get rid of it."

Monday, October 22, had already been grueling, but the president's work was far from done. Two critical tasks lay ahead of him: informing the leaders of Congress and then informing the nation and the world. Twenty members of Congress gathered in the Cabinet Room at 5 p.m. for a briefing by Kennedy, assisted by McCone and a few other members of ExComm. Some senators, such as Richard Russell of Georgia and J. William Fulbright of Arkansas, forcefully stated that the blockade was much too weak a response and that nothing short of military air strikes or an invasion could remove the missiles and keep America safe. Russell got under the president's skin by saying, "It seems to me we're at the crossroads. We're either a world-class power or we're not."[10]

Carl Vinson, a Democrat from Georgia, was a particular thorn in Kennedy's side. As chairman of the House Armed Services Committee, Vinson held great influence in Washington. He told Kennedy that he thought a blockade was a hopeless exercise and pushed for a full-scale landing of US marines on the beaches of Cuba. The president told Vinson that troops were being put into position to do just that and would be deployed if the blockade was unsuccessful.[11]

These members of the House and the Senate asked a barrage of questions, some quite specific in military matters. Senator Russell dominated the early stages of the meeting after the president's team gave the summary of what was happening in Cuba and the intended response. At one point Russell asked if the SAM sites also had complex electronics installed. McCone answered in the affirmative.

> McCONE—On the surface to air we have found that their radar have been latching onto our U-2s the last couple of days, and while they have not fired a missile at us, we think that they will within a short time.
>
> SENATOR THOMAS KUCHEL OF CALIFORNIA—My God. Are those pictures taken with a U-2?
>
> McCONE—They are taken with a U-2. And, Mr. President, I would just like to say for the advantage of . . . Everybody here knows we have briefed a number of people. We're just referring these to pictures taken from military reconnaissance planes. We're making no reference to the U-2s involved.

McCone and Kennedy clearly didn't want the word "U-2" used in any public statements. They all remembered the Gary Powers fiasco, and they didn't want to divert attention away from what the Soviets had done clandestinely toward the US capability to fly thirteen miles above the earth and enter the sovereign airspace of another country.

Once the congressional leaders left the meeting, President Kennedy shared his frustration with Ted Sorensen. "If they want this job, fuck 'em. They can have it. It's no great joy to me."[12]

Bobby Kennedy, who was not at the congressional meeting, saw the president just after the briefing ended. "He was upset by the time the meeting ended. When we discussed it later he was more philosophical, pointing out that the Congressional leaders' reaction to what we should do, although more militant than his, was much the same as our first reaction when we first heard about the missiles."[13]

Former secretary of state Dean Acheson flew to London and Paris to share the U-2 photos with leaders in both countries. When British prime minister Harold Macmillan examined the pictures taken by Rudy Anderson and Steve Heyser, he stated simply, "Now the Americans will realize what we here in England have lived through for this past many years." French president Charles de Gaulle said that he had no need to see the U-2 photos; in his mind, a great nation like the United States would not act if there were "any doubt about the evidence."[14]

Meanwhile, on that same day in Moscow, Soviet police arrested Colonel Oleg Penkovsky, who had smuggled photos of Soviet ballistic missiles to the West. CIA director McCone did not mention the arrest to fellow members of ExComm, viewing it strictly as an operational intelligence matter. The KGB's chief interrogator later said that Penkovsky was questioned nearly one hundred times before he was shot and cremated.[15]

THE U-2 PILOTS certainly would not get public credit for their extraordinary flights. Nor were they told that the CIA director thought it just a matter of time before they were fired on. The pilots, however, well understood that they might be playing Russian roulette, only with SAMs. They either knew Gary Powers personally or knew the precise details of his incident, and they knew the same thing could happen to them. But all of this remained unspoken among the pilots, because no SAMs had been fired to date.

At McCoy Air Force Base, additional crews, navigators, and personnel were arriving to guarantee the men and equipment necessary to continue flights over Cuba. All future U-2 reconnaissance missions would launch from McCoy rather than Laughlin simply because it was closer to the island. A total of nine sorties over Cuba were flown from October 20 to 22. Rudy Anderson flew two of them. He had made clear to planners that he wanted to fly as many missions as possible, and they granted him that wish. While the other pilots often had several days off between flights, Rudy spent less time on the ground, having flown on October 15, 17, 18, 20, and 22. Some of the pilots used their days off to golf or drink beer in the officers' club, but Anderson mostly kept to himself. He displayed his intense and serious personality not just before and during flights but most of the time on the ground as well. "Rudy was in high gear all the time," recalled operations officer Tony Martinez. "He was very competitive, patriotic, and very, very dedicated. He was an absolute perfectionist."[16]

Anderson's sense of duty, combined with his personal drive, motivated him to ask Steve Heyser if he could take one of his missions. Heyser, already having flown several missions over Cuba, was willing to oblige and told Anderson that was fine with him as long as operations officer Martinez agreed. Martinez obliged, resulting in Rudy's flight on October 22. (Steve Heyser had not flown since his flight on October 18.) There was no safety issue here, because Anderson was still getting at least the minimal amount of rest required between flights. The October 22 flight fulfilled his goal of conducting the most flights over Cuba of any of the U-2 pilots. This was mission number five for him; Heyser and Buddy Brown had four missions, and the other pilots had one or two flights each. The friendly competition was not as unusual as it seems: throughout history some military men have repeatedly volunteered for the most dangerous missions. In fact, it's quite possible that personal ambition aside, Anderson viewed each flight as a chance to help protect the people of the United States. Being a pacifist and not wishing to fly fighter jets or bombers, he might have decided that his unarmed flights in the U-2 would accomplish a twofold objective: serving his country during a time of crisis and maybe even saving lives.

CHAPTER TWENTY-FOUR

Taking a Stand

THE U-2 PILOTS at McCoy Air Force Base and their operations officer, Tony Martinez, gathered around the black-and-white TV. The group had been billeted in two large single-family homes on the base to limit their contact with other air force personnel so that no one outside the spy plane pilots knew they were flying over Cuba. Now, at 6:55 p.m. on the night of Monday, October 22, the men sat quietly waiting for the president to address the nation. They knew he was going to announce the United States' response to the missiles they had been photographing, but they didn't know just what that response would be. By now, Fidel Castro had mobilized 270,000 Cubans, insisting all would fight to the last man and were willing to die for the Revolution.[1]

Tension filled the air, maybe more so than in the homes of other American citizens—most of these air force men had received training with nuclear weapons during their prior stints as F-84 fighter-bomber pilots. They were aware that B-52s were now circling off the northernmost coast of the Soviet Union, loaded with nuclear bombs. Some, like Jerry McIlmoyle, had even seen a nuclear bomb detonation at Yucca Flats, Nevada. These pilots knew all too well the horrors that nuclear weapons could unleash, and they understood that President John F. Kennedy's upcoming speech would likely push the nation one step closer to war.

At Laughlin Air Force Base in Texas, the pilots' wives also gathered together to watch the speech. Many had not heard from their husbands in several days and hoped the president could provide some information as to their mission.

At precisely 7 p.m. President Kennedy appeared on the TV screen, seated at his desk in the Oval Office wearing a dark suit and blue shirt. He had been fitted into a tight corset and sat on two pillows. Two microphones were on his desk, and a horde of TV people stood off camera, their lights shining in his eyes and their film equipment running. Either President Kennedy was at peace with his decision and the thoroughness of his deliberations, or he was one hell of an actor. He addressed the nation calmly, clearly, and firmly, exuding determination. One would never suspect that he had just come out of a grueling meeting with the leaders of Congress. His words were measured, unhurried, and deliberate.

> Good evening, my fellow citizens. This Government, as promised, has maintained the closest surveillance of the Soviet military build-up on the island of Cuba. Within the past week unmistakable evidence has established the fact that a series of offensive missile sites is now in preparation on that imprisoned island. The purpose of these bases can be none other than to provide a nuclear strike capability against the Western Hemisphere.

The president described the missiles, the scope of the Soviet undertaking, and the Russians' false assurances that they would deliver no offensive weapons to Cuba. He then used a touch of history to justify the United States' response: "The 1930s taught us a clear lesson: Aggressive conduct, if allowed to grow unchecked and unchallenged, ultimately leads to war."

A minute later the president added a chilling statement, not just to brace Americans for what could follow but to warn Nikita Khrushchev: "We will not prematurely or unnecessarily risk the costs of worldwide nuclear war in which even the fruits of victory would be ashes in our mouth—but neither will we shrink from that risk at any time it must be faced."

The next part of his speech outlined the steps being implemented, emphasizing that the blockade was an initial step and that the US armed forces were preparing for any eventuality. And in a brilliant turn of phrase, Kennedy painted the conflict as one not just of the

Soviet Union against the United States but of the Soviets versus the entire Western Hemisphere: "It shall be the policy of this nation to regard any nuclear missile launched from Cuba against any nation in the Western Hemisphere as an attack by the Soviet Union against the United States, requiring a full retaliatory response against the Soviet Union."

He closed by appealing to the American people to show courage and patience during the ordeal:

> The path we have chosen for the present is full of hazards, as all paths are, but it is the one most consistent with our character and courage as a nation and our commitments around the world. The cost of freedom is always high—but Americans have always paid it. And one path we shall never choose, and that is the path of surrender or submission. Our goal is not the victory of might but the vindication of right—not peace at the expense of freedom, but both peace and freedom, here in this Hemisphere and, we hope, around the world. God willing that goal will be achieved.

The speech lasted seventeen minutes.

The U-2 pilots huddled around the TV set were not immune to fear and trepidation. Jerry McIlmoyle remembers letting out a sigh of relief when the president announced a blockade rather than immediate air strikes. But Kennedy's declaration that the launch of a nuclear weapon from Cuba against any country in the Western Hemisphere would result in "a full retaliatory response against the Soviet Union" ratcheted Jerry's concern up a notch. After the speech, he recalled, Steve Heyser—whom all the pilots looked up to—said he believed Kennedy would not lead the country to war except as a last resort. The pilots nodded, but they were one somber group after the speech. "All I could think to do at that moment," recalls Jerry, "was to pray and ask God not to let war break out. Then I picked up the phone, called my wife Patty and told her I loved her, and went to bed." Patty, Jane Anderson, and the other U-2 wives now knew the secret their husbands had so closely guarded.

There was a lot of praying in the United States that night, and despite earlier warnings in the press that a crisis was brewing, many people were shocked by the magnitude and ramifications of the confrontation. The news that Kennedy announced to the country's citizens was as alarming as anything that had come out of a president's mouth since Franklin Roosevelt announced the Pearl Harbor attack. Fortunately Kennedy's delivery was reassuring and showed that he was in control. His voice contained just a hint of anger when he spoke about how the Soviets had assured him they would send no offensive weapons to Cuba. Mostly, he balanced the need for both forceful-ness and calm in those seventeen minutes. The speech was brilliantly executed—galvanizing, confident, and wise.

Still, the administration knew that Khrushchev's response was unpredictable. He might tell his ships to run the blockade and test whether Kennedy would really sink them. He might put his own blockade on West Berlin. He might order immediate installation of the nuclear warheads on the missiles in Cuba. Or the Soviet premier might take a defensive approach—a deadly one for the U-2 pilots at McCoy—by giving authorization to shoot down any plane that flew over Cuban airspace.

Fidel Castro was sure to be defiant as a result of the president's speech, but Kennedy and his advisors felt certain that leaders in Mos-cow, not Havana, were calling the shots. To be on the safe side, how-ever, the Joint Chiefs of Staff kept twenty-two fighter jets in a holding pattern over Florida both during and after the speech. No one knew for sure if a response would come via a public statement, closed com-munication, or surprise military action.

WHILE AMERICANS WENT to bed that night filled with anxiety, out on the high seas at least twenty-five Soviet ships continued steaming toward Cuba. Getting ready to intercept them were ninety navy ships, eight aircraft carriers, and several squadrons of aircraft. To give the Soviets time to communicate with their ships, the blockade would go into effect at 10 a.m. on October 24. The quarantine line was orig-inally set for eight hundred miles outside Cuba, partly because the Soviets had shipped IL-28 bombers to the island. The bombers were still being assembled, but they had a range of just over seven hundred miles, and once operational they could reach the naval blockade line. Despite that risk, on Tuesday Kennedy moved the quarantine line to a five-hundred-mile radius around the island. The bomber threat took a backseat to the administration's hope that the Soviets might turn their ships back. Kennedy theorized that in the time it took the Soviet ships to travel that extra three hundred miles toward confrontation, cooler heads might prevail at the Kremlin.

All of the US military had gone into Defense Condition (DEF-CON) 3, an advanced state of readiness for war. Thousands of US marines were sent to Florida and placed on standby as the first wave of the invasion force. Nearly two hundred B-47 bombers carrying nuclear weapons were dispersed to thirty-two locations across the United States, as a group of Polaris nuclear submarines moved silently into position around the Caribbean. Preparations were made for an all-out invasion if the Russians failed to accept the quarantine line. Secretary of Defense Robert McNamara asked for 250,000 troops, 2,000 sorties over various targets in Cuba, and an additional 90,000 marines and army paratroopers for the invasion force. The United States was also prepared to pay a heavy toll. The Pentagon estimated that American casualties would exceed 25,000. The next terrifying step was DEF-CON 2, which the United States entered on October 24. It was one step away from war.

THE INTERPRETERS AT the National Photographic Interpretation Center worked through that Monday night, analyzing the latest batches of film from U-2 flights on October 20 and 21. More than just providing the proof of what the Soviets were doing on Cuba, the analyses were also instrumental in prioritizing targets for bombing missions. Meanwhile General Curtis LeMay updated Secretary of Defense Mc-Namara that Atlas and Titan missiles, aimed at the Soviet Union, were ready for firing.

On the other side of the world, Khrushchev was digesting Kennedy's speech. Almost immediately, he along with the Soviet Presidium decided to continue with the construction of the missile launch sites. As the United States had missiles in Turkey and Italy, they reasoned, the Soviets should have the same in Cuba. And like the United States they raised their military's war readiness not only in Cuba but around the world.

Khrushchev continued to publicly insist the weapons in Cuba were defensive. Knowing the US military would be on high alert, he reversed his earlier decision to allow his generals in Cuba to authorize the use of tactical nuclear weapons. Instead that authorization must come from Khrushchev if the United States launched an invasion. The premier, like Kennedy, worried that the situation could spin out of control. If there was to be nuclear war, he would make that decision. Besides the tactical nuclear weapons already in Cuba, many of the nuclear warheads for the missiles were there as well. As far as the blockade went, he ordered most vessels on the way to Cuba to return to the Soviet Union but let four submarines and a limited number of ships continue to the island to test Kennedy's resolve.

CHAPTER TWENTY-FIVE

Crusaders

THE AMERICAN PUBLIC'S response to John F. Kennedy's speech varied widely from person to person and even from city to city. There was pervasive tension but no widespread panic (although there were pockets). Most people woke up on Tuesday morning, October 23, and went about their business. But a cloud of fear forced them to keep an ear tuned to the radio or an eye on the TV to find out as much as they could and, more importantly, to glean news of what the Russians were doing. After all, Kennedy had squarely put the ball in the Soviet court, and Tuesday seemed to pass in slow motion as people anxiously waited for a Russian response.

Many people purchased extra water, food, gasoline, and flashlights—the same items one might stockpile in response to an oncoming hurricane. The US civil defense was woefully inadequate, and fallout shelters would hold only a fraction of the population. Fear made some people physically ill, knowing that of all the crises in the past, this one could really mean the end. Richard Neustadt had served as an advisor to President Kennedy at the beginning of his term and was now teaching at Columbia University in New York. After Kennedy's speech, Neustadt wrote to Ted Sorensen, "The reaction among students here was qualitatively quite different from anything I've ever witnessed. . . . These kids were literally scared for their lives."[1]

A grim-faced CBS news anchor Walter Cronkite summed up the stakes in a special report on October 24: "There is concern there might be shooting by ships at sea and the possibility that an invasion [of Cuba] might have to be undertaken to ensure that those bases are eliminated. And if an invasion is undertaken the Russians have said they would retaliate with rocket fire. We have said if there's a rocket fired from Cuba we would retaliate, and there goes the whole ballgame."[2] It's no wonder some people felt terror like never before.

At Laughlin Air Force Base, wives of the U-2 pilots recognized that their husbands' situation, at least for the time being, was even more perilous than that of ordinary Americans. Their men were on the front lines of the conflict, flying unarmed and unprotected. Jane Anderson and the other wives knew their husbands were involved in aerial reconnaissance of Cuba and that at some point tempers could flare and surface-to-air missiles be fired. Jane had been keeping a secret to share with her husband upon his return. She was pregnant with their third child and wanted to share the joyous news with him in person. She hoped this baby would be a girl, the little redhead they had always dreamed about.[3]

Jeanne Maultsby privately hoped her spouse, Chuck, would not be pulled from his current duty in Alaska for the far more dangerous mission in Cuba. The couple had recently welcomed a third child, another boy, they had named Kevin. Jeanne could not imagine the thought of raising her sons on her own. She wrote to her husband in Alaska regularly, and while the distance between them was difficult, the alternative would be excruciating. Her husband might be champing at the bit to join Rudy Anderson in the skies over Cuba, but Jeanne did not envy Rudy's distraught wife or the rest of the families caught between peace and nuclear war.[4]

A missile fired from Cuba could reach Washington, DC, in an estimated twelve minutes. Should there be enough time, the president and his family would be whisked into a bunker beneath the White House. The plan—in theory—called for a special group of rescuers from Olmstead Air Force Base in Pennsylvania to helicopter to the White House and dig the president out of the rubble. In truth, a nuclear bomb would probably kill him.

Another scenario, which called for more time, had a higher chance of success. If the military perceived a high likelihood of a nuclear attack on Washington, a helicopter would take the president and other key governmental officials to a bunker hidden in the mountains of

Virginia. Of course, if word got out that the president was evacuating, the very thing the government was trying to prevent—wholesale
panic—would ensue.

Early in the crisis, President Kennedy had discussed the situation
with his wife, Jackie, during a stroll in the Rose Garden and given her
the option to go to Virginia. The Army Corps of Engineers had built
a massive secret underground shelter at Mount Weather, near Blue-
mont, Virginia, about fifty miles west of Washington, DC, in 1949
after the Soviet Union detonated its first atomic bomb. Mrs. Kennedy
resisted the idea. And what if there was no warning—no time to flee?
The First Lady's secret service agent, Clint Hill, then briefed her on
her options should missiles fall on Washington.

"You know about the bomb shelter here, under the White House,"
Hill told Jackie with his hand gently touching her elbow. "In the event
a situation develops, where we don't have time to leave the area, we
would take you and the children into the shelter for your protection."[5]

Jackie Kennedy stared back at Hill and spoke to him defiantly.
"Mr. Hill, if the situation develops, I will take Caroline and John, and
we will walk hand-in-hand out onto the south grounds [of the White
House]. We will stand there like brave soldiers and face the fate of every other American."

"Well, Mrs. Kennedy, let's pray to God that we will never be in
that situation," Agent Hill replied.

The horrors of nuclear war were almost too much for people to
contemplate, and Kennedy himself said it best in his TV speech: "even
the fruits of victory would be ashes in our mouth."

Robert F. Kennedy Jr. was nine years old in October 1962. He
did not see his father much during those tension-filled days, but US
marshals stationed at their home kept close watch on the family. Shipments of canned food and fruit cocktail were brought in and stored
in the basement. Kennedy Jr. and his older brother Joe spoke to their
father by phone. Both wanted to go to the bunker at Mount Weather,
not because they were necessarily afraid but because they were boys
and wanted to see something cool.

"Can we go to Mount Weather?" they asked.

"No," the attorney general replied firmly. "You need to go to
school because if you don't go to school, then everybody's going to
panic and you need to be good soldiers."

Bobby Kennedy's voice began to crack. "Sons, I want you to know that if there is nuclear war, none of us will want to survive."

"Everyone was on red alert," Kennedy Jr. told the authors of this book. "We were doing duck and cover drills at our school, Our Lady of Victory in downtown Washington. We were all waiting for the day we would wake up dead."[6]

RFK Jr. remembers his Jesuit teachers discussing the religious and moral issues weighing on Americans.

"Who will you allow into your bomb shelters with you?" the priests asked the students. "Is it right to keep someone out of the shelter if it meant that your family would live?"

Young Kennedy and his classmates, children of nine and ten years old, were being asked to make impossible ethical choices. The conversations spilled over onto the playground.

"We decided that we wouldn't let anyone in if they had sores on them," he remembers.

Kennedy Jr. also recalls the moral questions running through his uncle's mind. "The mere thought about what could happen to his own children weighed heavily on President Kennedy," RFK Jr. said. "Caroline and John were quite young as were we. He spoke to my father about the need to do whatever they could to keep us alive."

The president was also concerned about the Cuban people.

"He knew that thousands of innocent people would be wiped out if US forces invaded the island of Cuba. In a way, they reminded him of the two islanders that saved his life and the lives of his crew in the South Pacific. They did so in such a humane way for a total stranger, a white man, while putting their own lives at risk. President Kennedy felt a great debt to people of color around the world because of what he had gone through during World War II."

In Russia the civilian response to the crisis was more muted. Sergei Khrushchev, son of Premier Nikita Khrushchev, told us, "There was no panic in Russia, no end-of-the-world talk. Russians had lived with adversaries close by and with enemy missiles near the border, whereas America was protected from enemies by two oceans. The missiles in Cuba were something entirely new for the American public to process, while nuclear threats or risk was something the Soviets had lived with for years."[7]

THE PRESIDENT'S SPEECH might have stripped the element of surprise from any forthcoming air attack, but it also liberated the military to authorize low-level reconnaissance flights, code-named BLUE MOON. Now that the Soviets knew about US knowledge of the missiles, the United States had no intelligence secret to keep under wraps, and low-level flights could provide more detailed pictures than the high-flying U-2s. Better photos would not only give analysts the means to ascertain the status of the missile sites but help the United States gain worldwide support. United Nations members, as well as the media, would soon be clamoring for Kennedy to show proof of the missiles. Laypeople needed to see the higher-quality, better-resolution photos of the missile sites provided by low-level flights.

The best aircraft to do the job was the navy's RF8 Crusader. This supersonic jet, which could reach speeds in excess of 1,100 mph, was normally equipped with four Sidewinder missiles and four 20mm cannons. But the jet had been converted for reconnaissance by removing the weapons and installing five cameras for high-speed photos. Instead of flying thirteen miles above Earth, as the U-2 did, it came in low over its target—sometimes just above treetop level. The cameras worked best between one hundred and five hundred feet above their target, and the aircraft had the advantage of flying beneath cloud cover.

While the Crusader's speed was impressive, navigation was basic: pilots followed a flight plan plotted on a map and used landmarks such as roads, rivers, and railroads to guide them to their targets.

Members of the navy's Light Photographic Squadron 62, known as VFP62, commanded by Captain William Ecker, flew these reconnaissance Crusaders. The commander, a former fighter pilot who had served in the Pacific during World War II, later switched to reconnaissance and said that jet photo reconnaissance was "a constant challenge and a much more rewarding type of job."[8] He reasoned in part that the country didn't have to be at war for the recon pilot to perform missions.

Ecker and eleven other pilots had been pre-positioned on October 19 at Naval Air Station Boca Chica in Key West, Florida. They had been following developments in the Cuban Missile Crisis and were anxious to do their part. But President Kennedy held them back until the morning after his speech, October 23.

These low-level flights entailed considerable risk, first and foremost because of their provocative nature. The Crusaders would be screaming through Cuban airspace toward a Soviet military installation at 400 mph and close enough to the ground that soldiers could see the pilots. The Soviets and Cubans would have no way of knowing if the planes were delivering bombs or taking photos. Zooming in at such low altitude rendered the Crusaders susceptible not only to anti-aircraft fire but even to bullets from machine guns.

The six pilots chosen for the first mission were Commander Ecker, Lieutenant Commander Tad Riley, Lieutenant Commander James Kauflin, Lieutenant Gerald Coffee, Lieutenant Christopher "Bruce" Whilhemy, and Lieutenant John Hewitt. They were told to remove everything from their wallets except their Geneva Convention cards and a small amount of cash. Each pilot had a .38-caliber pistol loaded only with tracer bullets to use as a signal if shot down.

Tad Riley was a career navy man, having earned an ensign's commission upon his graduation from the University of North Carolina in 1952. He had just returned from a six-month Mediterranean cruise aboard the carrier USS *Saratoga* when ordered to the Pentagon on October 17 and grilled by four navy captains about his ability to fly over locations marked on a map of Cuba. His answers instilled confidence in the higher-ups, who included General Curtis LeMay. Riley then joined the other pilots in Florida.

They would fly in teams of two. The senior pilot would take the lead, navigate to the target and shoot the photos. The junior pilot would position himself a quarter mile behind the veteran and move from side to side to photograph anything of interest that the lead pilot missed.[9]

Captain Gerald McIlmoyle
survived two SAMs fired at
him by the Soviets during
a U-2 flight over Cuba.
(Courtesy: US Air Force)

Chuck Maultsby preparing for flight with "The Thunderbirds," 1959. *(Courtesy: Chuck Maultsby Jr.)*

Chuck Maultsby with sons Chuckie and Shawn, 1959. *(Courtesy: Chuck Maultsby Jr.)*

Rudy and Jane Anderson cutting the cake at their wedding. *(Courtesy: Tripp Anderson)*

John F. Kennedy lost two members of his PT-109 crew when a Japanese destroyer collided with their vessel in the Solomon Islands on August 2, 1943. *(Courtesy: JFK Library)*

Robert F. Kennedy Jr. insists that JFK's experiences during World War II impacted his critical thinking during the Cuban Missile Crisis. *(Courtesy: JFK Library)*

The Soviet Union's installation of offensive nuclear weapons on the island of Cuba posed a clear and present danger to the United States, just 103 miles away. *(Courtesy: JFK Library)*

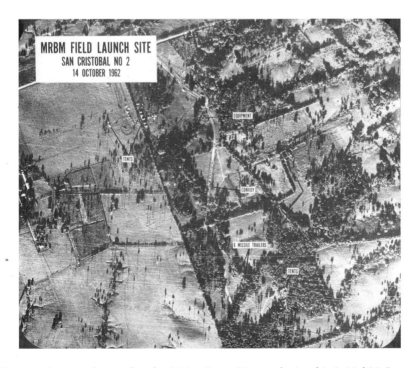

Reconnaissance photo taken by Major Steve Heyser during his initial U-2 flight over Cuba in October 1962. *(Courtesy: JFK Library)*

The first nuclear missiles were delivered to Cuba in the Soviet ships *Poltava* and *Omsk*, which arrived on the island in early September 1962. *(Courtesy: JFK Library)*

Soviet premier Nikita Khrushchev thought Kennedy was weak during their summit in Vienna, Austria, in 1961 and therefore felt emboldened to install nuclear missiles in Cuba. *(Courtesy: JFK Library)*

President Kennedy announces the quarantine against Soviet ships entering Cuba during a live televised news conference on October 22, 1962. *(Courtesy: JFK Library)*

General Maxwell Taylor and Secretary of Defense Robert McNamara strategize with the president in the Oval Office. *(Courtesy: JFK Library)*

The body of an American hero, Rudy Anderson, laid to rest. He was the first casualty of the Cuban Missile Crisis. *(Courtesy: Tripp Anderson)*

CHAPTER TWENTY-SIX

Close Encounters

AT ABOUT NOON the Crusader pilots received final approval to launch and ran out to the aircraft, climbed the three steps to the cockpit, and were strapped in by the support staff. Engines were started, and the whirling turbine blades first made a low growl that soon became a "deafening, high-pitched whine."[1] Heat blasted from the engines, which generated a thrust of 10,200 pounds, and ground crews stayed clear of the front of the planes, as the engines' intake could suck a man right inside and shred him to pieces.

The pilots went through their final checks, including the proper functioning of the five camera shutters. Then they gave the thumbs-up sign and blasted down the runway. There was no verbal communication with the control tower in the event the Soviets were eavesdropping. Once airborne, they rocketed toward Cuba, expecting to cover the ninety miles in just eleven minutes. To elude enemy radar, they stayed just a hundred feet above the ocean, glad for a light rain that washed off the salt spray that covered the windshields and camera lenses.

Captain William Ecker and Lieutenant Bruce Whilhemy, a 1958 graduate of the US Naval Academy at Annapolis, were teamed together and headed straight toward the San Cristobal site that Steve Heyser and Rudy Anderson had first photographed showing medium-range ballistic missiles. The other two teams of pilots would cover high-priority sites in central and eastern Cuba.

Ecker recalled that he emerged from the rain showers into sunshine just in time to see the Havana skyline and then headed toward San Cristobal, paralleling a range of small mountains on the right. "All of a sudden the San Cristobal missile complex appeared! I called to Bruce to move out farther to the right so that we would get maximum coverage of the target area, rather than flying close together or in tandem."[2]

Tad Riley flew low over the surface-to-air missile (SAM) sites, and a few surprised men on the ground actually waved at him. "The second day, they didn't wave anymore," he later said.[3]

The pilots got the photos they needed and steered for home. The antiaircraft guns below them remained silent, either ordered not to shoot or caught off guard, as the Crusaders appeared unexpectedly and briefly, perhaps for a second or two. The pilots put their afterburners on "to let them know we were there,"[4] an attempt to intimidate and harass the Cubans and Soviets with the Crusaders' screeching engines.

The mission was a success, but unfortunately a "granddaddy" of a thunderstorm lay between the pilots and Florida. Afraid of wind shear, Ecker elected to pass under it at a very low altitude but still feared being "torn to pieces by the storm."

WHILE THE CRUSADERS were attempting to get through the thunderstorm with their precious cargo of film, ExComm was meeting to determine what action the United States would take if the Soviets shot down a U-2. Robert McNamara began that part of the conversation, addressing President John F. Kennedy.

> MCNAMARA—Now, you asked me yesterday to consider
> reaction to a U-2 accident, and we would recommend
> this: That SAC [Strategic Air Command] be instructed to
> immediately inform the Joint Chiefs, as far as myself and
> yourself, upon any deviation from course of U-2 aircraft
> that is unexplained. They maintain a minute by minute
> check on the U-2s as they proceed through their flight
> pattern. They will be able to tell us when a U-2 moves off
> course and, we believe, why, particularly if it's shot down.

That information can be in here in a matter of minutes, literally 15 minutes after the incident.

We are maintaining aircraft on alert that have the capability, if you decide to instruct to do so, to go in and shoot the SAM site that shot down the U-2. It would be approximately 8 aircraft required to destroy the SAM site. We would recommend the information on the U-2 action to come in here so that we can present recommendations to you at the time that the action is required. I believe we would recommend that we send the 8 aircraft out to destroy the site, and have it destroyed within 2 hours of the time the U-2 itself was struck.

The president asked McNamara if they would be able to rescue a pilot downed in the ocean, and the defense secretary answered in the affirmative. Kennedy then began to add details to his strategy if a U-2 was shot down: "If we lose one of our officers in the planes, then the next fellow we send out . . . I suppose what we do is, when we take out that SAM site, we announce that if any U-2 is shot down, we'll take out every SAM site."

The Joint Chiefs must have felt some measure of satisfaction. The president had finally, and unequivocally, authorized bombing SAM sites if the Russians shot down a US plane. Though far less than the large-scale bombing raid that the Joint Chiefs had called for, this at least promised offensive action on the part of the United States. General Curtis LeMay, in particular, took heart when Kennedy went on record, clearing the way for a retaliatory attack that would show both the Soviets and the Cubans that the US Air Force was not afraid to strike back.

Bobby Kennedy worried about the critics of a quarantine—those who would point out the danger of turning away Soviet ships after the missiles were already in place in Cuba.

PRESIDENT KENNEDY—We recognize the missiles are already there. But we also recognize there's not a damn thing anybody can do about the missiles being there unless we had invaded Cuba at the Bay of Pigs or a previous Cuban invasion a year before.

A bit later in the conversation, Kennedy, trying to leave no detail unconsidered, worried that three airfields in Florida had become congested with U.S. military aircraft, making it easy for the Russians or Cubans to disable a number of them in a single bombing raid.

> PRESIDENT KENNEDY—We have to figure that if we do
> execute this plan we just agreed on this morning [the
> response against a SAM site if a U-2 was brought down]
> that they are going to strafe our fields, and we don't want
> them to shoot up 100 planes. We've just got to figure out
> some other device.
>
> TAYLOR—This is one of these rather humorous examples of
> the over-sophistication of our weapons. We have every-
> thing except to deal with a simple aircraft coming in low
> [and strafing].

The president suggested relieving some of the congestion by using the civilian airport at West Palm Beach.

Near the end of the meeting, the group voiced its impatience to see what the low-level photos provided by the Crusaders would reveal. The Crusaders, however, were still conducting their missions at the very moment that ExComm wondered what the jet pilots might uncover, and John McCone made clear that the photos would not be available until that night.

Dean Rusk then took a moment to remind everyone in the room just how lucky they were on this day. "I think it is very significant that we are here this morning. We've passed the one contingency [following Kennedy's speech], an immediate, sudden, irrational strike."

NOT LONG AFTER the meeting adjourned, the president received a short letter from Nikita Khrushchev. It contained nothing that would lead him to believe Soviet ships would turn back. Khrushchev flatly said the US quarantine was "in violation of international norms and freedom of navigation on the high seas"[5] and later added that Kennedy's actions "could lead to catastrophic consequences."

In his response Kennedy made the point he had been stressing with his own advisors: do not let the crisis spin out of control. He said he hoped the United States would not have to fire at any Soviet ships and closed by writing, "I am concerned that we both show prudence and do nothing to allow events to make the situation more difficult to control than it is."[6]

ECKER AND WHILHEMY made it through the storm and sped their way north. To expedite the processing of the film, the pilots flew straight to Florida's Naval Air Station Jacksonville, where the navy housed its photo lab. The two pilots looked each other's planes over en route to make sure there were no bullet holes or fuel leaks. They landed in Jacksonville and were pleased to learn that the other four pilots who flew over Cuba had already safely touched down. Nobody reported being fired at, but this was to change in future flights. As Ecker explained, "On later missions we would see popcorn flax [37mm AAA fire] which exploded in white puffs in our mirrors."[7]

After landing and shutting down the engine, Bill Ecker was extricating himself from the cockpit when the chief photo officer, Bob Koch, appeared at the side of the plane and said, "Stay put, you're going to Washington."

Ecker, who had thought his day's work was done, never even got to leave his aircraft. The Joint Chiefs wanted to hear every detail of his flight in person. So while the plane was being refueled, Ecker ate a ham sandwich and drank a small carton of milk, and then he was airborne again, arriving just outside the nation's capital at Andrews Air Force Base in less than an hour.

The meeting was considered so critically important that a waiting helicopter flew Commander Ecker to the Pentagon. The lieutenant had not been told whom he would meet with, and when he entered a small conference room he was greeted by Maxwell Taylor, chairman of the Joint Chiefs of Staff, and George Anderson, chief of naval operations. They ushered him over to a square table, where more of the top military brass were seated, along with some of the president's advisors. Taylor motioned Ecker to take a seat.

Ecker, who had been in the air for hours and was still in his flight suit, had to slide behind a general to get to the one empty seat. While doing so, he apologized, saying, "You'll have to pardon me, General, I'm kind of smelly and sweaty."[8]

The general removed the cigar from his mouth and barked, "You've been flying an airplane haven't you? You ought to sweat and smell. Now sit down!"

Curtis LeMay wanted to waste no time hearing Ecker's debriefing.

The lieutenant didn't have that much to say. He had only been over the missile site for a couple seconds, but he said he did see the complex, noted that some of it was camouflaged, and did not think he had been shot at. The urgent debriefing lasted all of ten minutes.

If Ecker was short on details, the photos he took were not. After viewing the high-altitude U-2 photos for a week, analysts at the National Photographic Interpretation Center found the low reconnaissance images, with their more exact detail, a welcome change. Adlai Stevenson would use these photos at the United Nations when he confronted the Russians. The ambassador now had the evidence to back up the US claim that the Russians had stationed offensive weapons on Cuba and were working around the clock to complete the missile sites.

ALSO ON TUESDAY, October 23, three U-2s performed a mission over Cuba. Steve Heyser was back in the air after four days' rest. Roger Herman and another U-2 pilot, Daniel Schmarr, also flew that day. Dan Schmarr was an elite pilot and a good family man. The Spokane, Washington, native had also discovered a love for flying at an early age. He told his sister that as a child, he would fall asleep and dream that he was a bird waving his arms and soaring past clouds. He was married to his childhood sweetheart, Kay, and together they had three kids. When asked later in life about the key to parenting, Schmarr said, "The best thing one can do for their children was to love their mother."[9]

The SAC termed all three U-2 missions "100 percent successful."[10] It was beginning to look like the Soviets would not attack American aircraft and perhaps instead test the US Navy on the high seas.

At 6 p.m. that night, President Kennedy met again with his advisors in the Cabinet Room. The topic at hand was whether the Soviets would allow the US Navy to board its ships if they passed the quarantine. It would mark the first time that armed American military personnel and armed Soviet troops would be in close proximity during the crisis.

> PRESIDENT KENNEDY—They're going to keep going. And we're going to shoot the rudder off, or the boiler. And then we're going to try to board it. And they're going to fire a gun and then machine guns. . . . So I would think that the taking of those ships is going to be a major operation. You may have to sink it rather than just take it.

Soon after, attention focused on the doomsday scenario and America's readiness to withstand a nuclear attack. Steuart Pittman, assistant secretary of defense for civil defense, walked the president through the numbers. Pittman said that a nuclear strike around 1,100 nautical miles from Cuba would potentially kill 92 million Americans in fifty-eight cities. When asked by Kennedy about evacuating people from likely target cities a week before a potential strike, Pittman said the cities were actually the safest places, as buildings might serve as adequate protection from the initial nuclear blast, subsequent heat, and exposure to radiation.

At the president's request, Bobby Kennedy met privately with Ambassador Anatoly Dobrynin at the Soviet embassy that evening. RFK had been using back channels to continue a dialogue with the Russians and had learned from journalist Charles Bartlett, serving as an intermediary, that the Soviet ships planned on plowing through the American quarantine. RFK met with Dobrynin in a sitting room on the third floor of the Soviet embassy located near DuPont Circle. The agitated attorney general accused the Russian diplomat of betrayal. Coyly, Dobrynin said that he was only working with information that his government had shared with him. RFK then asked what the Soviet ship captains had been instructed to do if and when confronted by US warships. Dobrynin said that the captains "would not bow to any illegal demands for a search on the high seas." RFK got up to leave. He reached the doorway of the sitting room and addressed Dobrynin once more.

"I do not know how this will end, but we intend to stop your ships."[11]

The attorney general returned to the White House after 10 p.m. and briefed his brother. JFK tossed out the idea of arranging an immediate summit with Khrushchev, then thought better of it. There would be no meeting until Khrushchev accepted Kennedy's resolve in the matter.

Also on Tuesday night, the world caught its first glimpse of Soviet premier Nikita Khrushchev since the onset of the missile crisis. Ironically, the Russian leader attended the American performance of *Boris Godunov*, starring New York opera singer Jerome Hines, at the Bolshoi Theater. As Khrushchev participated in a champagne toast to the American performers backstage after the show, Radio Moscow issued a statement assuring that "not a single nuclear bomb would hit the U.S. unless aggression is committed."[12]

Still, the Soviets had not clearly defined "aggression." President Kennedy and his top advisors could only guess what they planned to do next.

CHAPTER TWENTY-SEVEN

The Quarantine

THE QUARANTINE WENT into effect at 10 a.m. Washington time—1400 hours Greenwich Mean Time—on Wednesday, October 24. It would initially comprise twelve destroyers from the Second Fleet's Task Force 136, the attack carriers *Enterprise* and *Independence*, the anti–submarine carrier USS *Essex*, aerial anti–submarine warfare squadrons based in Puerto Rico and Bermuda, nine escorting destroyers, and six utility ships. The armada would have air support from as many as 448 fighter planes and 67 reconnaissance aircraft. The ships spread out in an arc five hundred miles from Cape Maisí, Cuba. Among the ships called for this historic duty was the *Joseph P. Kennedy, Jr.*

President John F. Kennedy met with members of ExComm at 10 a.m. As the quarantine became effective, the Strategic Air Command (SAC) upped the general defense condition to DEFCON 2, the level just below full-scale war. If US troops invaded Cuba, the Pentagon estimated that 18,500 American soldiers would perish in the first ten days. The nation's 1,400 nuclear bombers were put on twenty-four-hour alert. Bomber pilots took to the skies immediately with pre-assigned targets in the Soviet Union and remained in the air, refueled every nine hours by aerial tankers. Military bases across America prepared intercontinental ballistic missiles for launch. Navy submarines, loaded with ballistic missiles, sat submerged off the Atlantic coast. More than two hundred high-priority targets in the Soviet Union were selected for immediate destruction, including the Kremlin. The United States was preparing for thermonuclear war.

Meetings about the strategy for Cuba dominated the president's schedule that day. He signed the official proclamation for quarantine on Soviet ships entering Cuba at just after 7 p.m. in the Oval Office. The night before, Kennedy had signed the formal instrument of quarantine and had to ask the date. The ordeal was weighing heavily on him. Members of the media noticed that the normally impeccably dressed JFK's collar stuck out over his lapel, and his handkerchief was not folded to keep his initials from showing. Also on Tuesday night, the Soviet vessel *Poltava*, carrying twenty nuclear warheads, had retreated before reaching the quarantine line. This was good news. But two other Russian ships, the *Kimovsk* and *Yuri Gagarin*, showed no sign that they would respect the quarantine as each continued to sail for Cuba.

On Wednesday morning, October 24, the ships were edging close to the five-hundred-mile quarantine line. The moment of reckoning would soon arrive for the world's two superpowers. "This is the moment we had prepared for, which we hoped would never come," Bobby Kennedy later wrote. "The danger and concern that we all felt hung like a cloud over us all and particularly over the President."[1]

As the ExComm meeting commenced, CIA director John McCone updated JFK on Soviet action on the ground in Cuba. Surveillance indicated rapid progress in completion of the intercontinental- and medium-range ballistic missile sites. "No new sites have been discovered."

McCone told Kennedy that the previous day's U-2 flights had photographed buildings being assembled for nuclear storage and that Cuban naval vessels had formed blocking positions in the bays of Banes and Santiago. Rudy Anderson, Steve Heyser, and other U-2 pilots had gathered massive photographic evidence. The film alone was twenty-five miles long.[2]

"The launching pads, the missiles, the concrete boxes, the nuclear storage bunkers, all the components were there, by now clearly defined and obvious," Bobby Kennedy wrote in his crisis memoir *Thirteen Days*. The consensus around the room was that several of the launching pads would be ready for war in just a matter of days.

Defense Secretary Robert McNamara then explained that the *Yuri Gagarin* and *Kimovsk* were expected to reach the quarantine line by noontime. The *Kimovsk* was about fifty miles ahead of the *Gagarin*, and a Soviet submarine escorted each ship.

"It's a very dangerous situation," McNamara told the president.[3]

When Kennedy asked what type of warship the Americans would use to intercept the Soviet vessels, McNamara said the plan was to use a destroyer accompanied by the aircraft carrier *Essex*, which was equipped with antisubmarine helicopters.

"It's believed that it would be less dangerous to our forces to use a destroyer," McNamara added.

McCone was then handed a note saying that all ships currently identified near the quarantine line had either stopped or reversed course. It was not clear at that moment whether they had been outbound to the Soviet Union or headed from Russia to Cuba.

"Makes some difference," Dean Rusk said dryly.

While McCone left the meeting to seek clarification, the group learned that a Soviet submarine had taken position between the oncoming Russian ships and the *Essex*. The president's secret tape recorder captured the conversation.

> PRESIDENT KENNEDY—If this submarine should sink our destroyer, then what is our proposed reply?

General Maxwell Taylor answered that American anti–submarine warfare patrols would cover the Red Navy sub, and a signaling arrangement, delivered to the Soviet Foreign Office the night before, had been put into place to order the vessel to surface.

> McNAMARA—Here is the exact situation. We have [practice] depth charges that have such a small charge that they can be dropped and they can actually hit the submarine, without damaging the submarine. . . . We propose using those as warning depth charges.

The defense secretary went on to explain that when US forces came upon the submarine, they would ask the captain to surface using sonar signals and then depth charges. No one in the room believed the Soviets would respond to the sonar signals, so the depth charges would be necessary.

PRESIDENT KENNEDY—If he doesn't surface or if he takes
some action . . . to assist the merchant ship, are we just
going to attack him anyway? At what point are we going
to attack him?

McNAMARA—I think it would be extremely dangerous, Mr.
President, to try to defer attack on the submarine in the
situation we're in. We could easily lose any American ship
by that means.

The president put his hand to his face and covered his mouth. He
opened and closed his fist as he looked to his brother Bobby.

"His face seemed drawn, his eyes pained, almost gray," Bobby observed. "We stared at each other across the table. For a few fleeting
seconds, it was almost as if no one else was there and he was no longer
the President."[4]

Bobby had seen that look in his brother's eyes before. He'd seen
it when Jack was ill and almost died after back surgery, and he'd seen
it when both learned that their older brother, Joe, had been killed in
World War II. He had seen it at times of great stress, none greater than
this very moment, when the fate of the world was at stake.

One mistake or misinterpretation on either side could lead to nuclear war. As a navy veteran himself, JFK knew that every man, despite his training, was capable of miscalculation, of simple human error
that could have catastrophic consequences. If the Soviets mistook the
depth charges for an attack, there would be blood in the water, with
the possible firing of missiles to follow.

To avert potential disaster at the critical point of interception, Secretary McNamara said they would send in helicopters to harass the
submarine in hopes of moving it out of the area. "This is only a plan,"
he cautioned. "There are many, many uncertainties."

President Kennedy turned his focus to Berlin. For every action in
the waters off Cuba, there would be a reaction in Western Europe and
elsewhere around the globe. He expected Nikita Khrushchev to "close
down" Berlin, allowing no movement in or out of the divided city.
The only option then would be to take to the air. JFK was told that
American airmen were flying fighter planes at that very moment in
the corridor between West Germany and Berlin, ready to shoot down

Soviet MiGs if necessary. Should that happen, World War III would be imminent.

"I felt we were on the edge of a precipice with no way off," Bobby Kennedy later wrote. The theoretical discussions were over. Each decision made in the room could spell the difference between life and death for millions. "The moment was now—not next week—not tomorrow [no time for another meeting or another message to Khrushchev], none of that was possible."[5]

John McCone reentered the Cabinet Room with welcome news: the Soviet ships that had stopped and reversed course had all been inbound for Cuba. There was a collective sigh of relief.

"We're eyeball to eyeball," Dean Rusk told Mac Bundy. "And I think the other fellow just blinked."[6]

But the president knew that neither side was out of troubled waters just yet.

PRESIDENT KENNEDY—Now is this all the Russian ships, or would this just be selected ones?

McCONE—This is apparently a selected bunch, because there's 24 of them.

General Taylor then confirmed that three ships were turning back from the quarantine line, including the *Poltava*. Taylor said that Admiral George Anderson, chief of naval operations, was scrambling planes to the area. The concern now was that the US Navy would fire upon a Soviet ship as it was turning back to Moscow.

The Americans had been planning to intercept the *Kimovsk*, a wide freighter with seven-foot hatches and loaded with R-14 missiles, before 11 a.m.

PRESIDENT KENNEDY—I would think that we ought to be in touch with the *Essex*, and just tell them to wait an hour and see whether that ship continues on its course.

The president gave the order that no Russian ships were to be stopped or intercepted. US planes were also authorized to photograph and trail Russian ships as they turned around.

AFTER WAKING UP in his underground bunker in Havana, Fidel Castro spent the day conferring with Soviet military commanders and meeting with his own troops on alert at strategic positions around the island. Castro was frustrated by Russia's apparent unwillingness to engage the Crusader pilots that were performing low-level overflights of Cuba. The Crusaders had been buzzing Soviet missile sites at three hundred feet, and Castro felt that his forces had every right to shoot them down, or "fry them." He inspected a surface-to-air missile (SAM) site overlooking a potential landing beach for US forces in the resort area of Tarara. He was confident that the SAMs could reach the U-2 planes flying over the island, as the Soviets had used the same weapons system to shoot down Francis Gary Powers in 1960. On the beach below, Castro's forces worked day and night digging trenches in the sand and fortifying concrete bunkers. The scene was reminiscent of German preparations for the Allied landings along the coast of France just before D-day. Later that day, Soviet forces intensified their drills as they practiced procedures for aiming and firing their missiles. It was a dress rehearsal for a nuclear strike, and all knew that the real thing could happen at any moment.

As day became night in Washington, DC, President Kennedy met with congressional leaders to update them on the unfolding situation. Dean Rusk then read aloud a cable that suggested Khrushchev was ready to negotiate. British peace activist and Nobel laureate Lord Bertrand Russell had passed Khrushchev's statement along to US Intelligence. The Soviet premier was also using back channels to communicate with the American president.

"The Soviet government will not take any decisions which will be reckless," Khrushchev wrote. "We will do everything in our power to prevent war from breaking out. We would consider a top-level meeting useful. . . . As long as the rocket nuclear weapons have not been used, there is a possibility of averting war."[7]

Since Khrushchev extended no direct invitation to speak, Kennedy found it pointless to respond. The president later had dinner with journalist Charles Bartlett, who had been serving as an intermediary with the Russians. Earlier in the day, Bartlett had lunched with his Soviet contact, Georgi Bolshakov. The Kennedys were angry with Bolshakov because he had kept feeding them lies that the weapons being installed in Cuba were for defensive purposes only. Bobby Kennedy had slipped Bartlett two black-and-white U-2 photos of medium-range ballistic missiles in Cuba to show Bolshakov at lunch. The Russian was shocked. He pulled out his blue notebook and read back his notes from his conversations with Khrushchev, who had stated the weapons were SAMs to defend Cuba from attack. The Soviet told Bartlett that it appeared that he too had been duped. Bartlett reported back to the White House and delivered this news to the president during a small dinner gathering with the First Lady, her sister Lee Radziwill, Bobby and Ethel Kennedy, and fashion designer Oleg Cassini.

JFK respected and trusted Bartlett. They had been friends since 1946, and Bartlett and his wife, Martha, had introduced Kennedy to Jackie at a small dinner party at their Georgetown home in 1951. On the night of Wednesday, October 24, 1962, Bartlett understood better than most what stress Kennedy was under and yet felt comforted by the president's calm demeanor.

"The President's coolness and temper were never more evident than they were that week," Bartlett later recalled. "He kept very balanced."[8]

Once JFK had informed Bartlett that several Soviet ships had turned back that morning, the newspaperman was elated.

"Why I should think you'd really feel like celebrating," Bartlett told the president.

"Well, you don't want to celebrate in this game too early," JFK replied. "Because anything can happen."[9]

Charles Bartlett and the other guests went home wondering what the next day would bring. Just before 11 p.m., President Kennedy received a new message from Premier Khrushchev, which read in part:

You, Mr. President, are not declaring quarantines, but advancing an ultimatum and threatening that unless we subordinate ourselves to your demands, you will use force. . . . You are no longer appealing to reason, but wish to intimidate us. . . . [T]he Soviet Government cannot give instructions to the captains of Soviet vessels bound for Cuba to observe the instructions of the American naval forces blockading the island. . . . [W]e shall not be simple observers of piratical actions of American ships on the high seas. We will then be forced for our part to take the measures which we deem necessary and adequate to protect our rights. For this we have all that is necessary. Respectfully yours, N. Khrushchev[10]

President Kennedy studied the letter very closely. His advisors pointed to the last paragraph, which read like a thinly veiled threat. The Soviets planned to challenge the quarantine. JFK took out a small White House notepad and penned his response, which was sent to Moscow at 2 a.m. He informed Khrushchev that he had learned "beyond doubt" that the Soviet military had set out to establish a set of missile bases in Cuba. President Kennedy ended the message by urging his Soviet rival to repair "the deterioration of our relations."[11]

The president then picked up the phone and, through a secure line, called his friend Bartlett at home.

"You'd be interested to know I got a cable from our friend," JFK said. "And he said those ships are coming through, they're coming through tomorrow."[12]

CHAPTER TWENTY-EIGHT

Until Hell Freezes Over

As DAWN BROKE on Thursday, October 25, the Soviet tanker *Bucha-rest* edged the quarantine line. The time was 7:15 a.m. The tanker, traveling at seventeen knots, was roughly five hundred miles from Cuba. Expected to arrive in Havana the next day, the *Bucharest* was intercepted by several American ships, including the destroyer *Gearing*, which signaled the tanker's captain to provide the ship's name, desti-nation, point of origin, and the type of cargo on board. The *Bucharest*'s captain explained that his ship had come from the Black Sea, bound for Havana, and carried nothing but petroleum products. There was no visible suspicious cargo on deck and little room belowdecks to hide nuclear materials. The destroyer was instructed to let the ship pass but maintain close surveillance. The blockade had exempted tankers like the *Bucharest*, but some members of ExComm insisted that the large vessel be inspected.

> TED SORENSEN: If it's important to board a Russian ship, and it seems to me it is, this may be the best chance you'll have with them. They'll never let you board a ship that really has something serious on it.

President John F. Kennedy pondered the thought. Boarding a So-viet tanker that had no military use might put the United States at odds with other countries. The United States had already won the first round in this test of wills as fourteen Soviet ships had turned around the previous day. By allowing the *Bucharest* to pass through, he would be giving Nikita Khrushchev "sufficient grace" and more time to negotiate a way out. JFK decided to let the *Bucharest* pass for now.

> PRESIDENT KENNEDY—This is not the appropriate time to
> blow up a ship. . . . If I wrote back to Khrushchev, we
> could justify withholding the action until about five this af-
> ternoon, if that's the way. Let's think a little more about it.

The *Bucharest* would arrive in Cuba the next day with no intervention from the US Navy. Upon learning that the Soviet tanker had made it through the quarantine line unmolested, the Cuban people took to Havana's streets in celebration.[1]

But President Kennedy knew that to show resolve the United States would have to make good on its promise to board a Soviet vessel. The most likely candidate for that action was the tanker *Grozny*. Secretary Robert McNamara told the president that the *Grozny* had behaved "rather peculiarly" over the past twenty-four to thirty-six hours as it deviated from its established course to Cuba. Instead of moving directly east, the tanker had moved northwest for a period before resuming its course.

> McNAMARA—It's of great interest to us because it's not only a
> tanker, but it has a deck load. And it declared a deck load
> of, as I recall, of ammonia tanks. But these could very
> well be, and as a matter of fact probably are, missile fuel
> tanks on deck.

The *Grozny* was expected to reach the quarantine line by 8 p.m. on Friday night, and the US Navy planned to intercept it. Members of ExComm were also very concerned with the latest developments on the island of Cuba, where Soviet and Cuban troops were going to great lengths to conceal missile sites from view. Low-level surveillance photos from the Crusader flights over the island had spotted large camouflage nets drying on the ground after a heavy rain.

"As soon as it [the camouflage netting] dries, they put it on everything in sight," McNamara explained. "They're camouflaging trucks;

they're camouflaging erectors; they're camouflaging missiles. It's really a fantastic sequence of action."[2]

But by camouflaging the missile sites, the Soviets had reduced their readiness to initiate or respond to attack. Pulling the large nets off would use up critical time. Defense Secretary McNamara told President Kennedy that he believed the Americans could conduct more low-level surveillance with "little risk of an incident."

A couple hours later, a Crusader piloted by Lieutenant Gerald "Jerry" Coffee flew over Cuba. This was Coffee's second reconnaissance mission over the island. He was a UCLA graduate from Modesto, California, and happily married to his high school sweetheart, Bea. Together they had four children. Coffee earned his navy wings in 1959 and had been flying Crusaders out of Cecil Field in Florida with two deployments on the USS *Saratoga*, where he made two hundred landings.

Now the former Eagle Scout was photographing medium-range missile sites near Sagua la Grande, along Cuba's northern coast. Flying at a speed of 460 mph, Coffee was en route to an intermediate-range missile site at Remedios when he spotted a military encampment and motor pool just north of his intended target. The camp was unlike anything he'd seen so far, so he took a strip of photographs before heading back to his base in Florida. The decision to grab the pictures proved significant. After close inspection, analysts determined for the first time that the Soviets had deployed mobile, nuclear-tipped SAMs, or FROGs (Free Rockets over Ground), on the island.[3] These missiles could have annihilated an invasion force of US marines and forced Pentagon strategists to reconfigure plans for an all-out assault on the island. The commandant of the Marine Corps later wrote a letter of appreciation to Coffee, praising him for providing "the most important and most timely information for the amphibious forces which has ever been acquired in the history of this famous Navy-Marines fighting team."[4]

Thick cloud cover forced the U-2 pilots to wait for better weather to return to the skies over Cuba. Some of the airmen, like Charlie Kern, tried to keep loose during nonflying hours. Kern, an Arizona State University graduate, had flown a high-altitude reconnaissance mission over the island on October 20. A skilled pilot with nearly a decade of flying time, Kern checked out in the U-2 in 1961 and was now among a group of elite US airmen tasked with gathering evidence of the Soviets' nuclear buildup on Cuba. Still an affable fellow who enjoyed hunting and fishing in his free time, he socialized frequently with his fellow pilots while each man waited for his name to be called for the next mission. While Kern and others "hoisted a few" at the officers' club at McCoy Air Force Base, Rudy Anderson spent most of his time alone in his quarters.

"Rudy Anderson was a very serious guy and didn't participate in much of the partying like the rest of us," Kern later recalled.[5]

Instead, Anderson focused vigilantly on the opportunities and even the dangers that lay ahead.

PRESIDENT KENNEDY DID not like Adlai Stevenson, and the feeling was mutual. The two politicians had been at odds since 1956, when Stevenson had spurned JFK's attempt to join the Democratic ticket as the nominee for vice president. Four years later, Stevenson drew Kennedy's ire again with his reluctance to endorse him before the Democratic National Convention. JFK had referred to Stevenson as an "old woman."[6]

Still, Stevenson maintained great influence over the Democratic Party base, so Kennedy could not shut him out of his administration altogether. Stevenson thought he deserved the post of secretary of state, but in Kennedy's view that was out of the question—Stevenson would have to pay for his perceived mistreatment of Kennedy in the past. Instead, the president sent him to the United Nations, where as US ambassador he would handle diplomatic disputes and international bickering of no great consequence.

But the events and circumstances of October 1962 had elevated Stevenson's importance to the Kennedy administration. A battle was raging inside the United Nations. UN secretary-general U Thant of Burma had proposed a suspension of up to three weeks of both the US quarantine and the Soviet arms shipments to Cuba. Khrushchev approved U Thant's plan unconditionally as he had nothing to lose. President Kennedy knew the plan would put him at a huge disadvantage with his Soviet counterpart because it did not address the fact that nuclear weapons had already arrived on the island and that work would continue to make them operational and therefore a clear and present danger to the United States. The time had come to show the world evidence of the Soviet Union's great deception.

The UN Security Council was set to meet at 4 p.m. on October 25. Customarily, these meetings were attended by reporters working the diplomatic beat, their stories often buried in the back pages of newspapers. On this day, the meeting would be broadcast live. American citizens gathered around their television sets and radios. The wives of the U-2 airmen huddled in groups in tiny living rooms at Laughlin Air Force Base in Del Rio, Texas. Jane Anderson had not heard from her husband in several days. She had hoped the broadcast might provide her with some more information as to what he was doing and maybe when he would be coming home to her, their boys, and the baby now growing inside her.

Earlier that afternoon, U Thant had appealed to both sides once again. He urged Khrushchev to ensure that Soviet ships sailing toward Cuba would keep away from the quarantine line. The secretary-general also pleaded with President Kennedy to order all US ships to avoid confrontation with Russian vessels over the next few days to allow all parties to work toward a peaceful resolution.

Adlai Stevenson entered the Security Council chamber as cameras rolled. He sat down, took off his eyeglasses, fidgeted with his earpiece, and moved his microphone closer so that everyone could hear him clearly. President Kennedy, his brother Bobby, and the other members of ExComm watched the meeting on a television screen in the White House Situation Room. Few, including JFK, had confidence that Stevenson would deliver a forceful message on behalf of the United States. But it was Stevenson's show now, and all had to watch and wait. Unlike a meeting of the UN General Assembly, the gathering of members of the Security Council was an intimate affair. The twenty council members took their seats around a semicircular dais; more diplomats and interpreters sat behind the council members or at a table in the middle of the room. An overflow of diplomats, UN staffers, and reporters fought for position and a better view at the chamber entrances.

Soviet ambassador Valerian Zorin chaired the meeting. Time had not treated the aging Russian statesman well. Zorin had experienced bouts of forgetfulness and had even stopped meetings to ask what year it was.[7]

Ambassador Stevenson asked for the floor. He put his glasses on again and began to read his statement aloud.

"Today we must address our attention to the realities of the situation posed by the build-up of nuclear striking power in Cuba," Stevenson told the council and the world.

Stevenson took a moment to praise the Soviets for turning their ships around the previous day and avoiding direct confrontations at the quarantine line. He then thanked Khrushchev himself for his assurance that the Soviets would not make any "reckless decisions" with regard to the crisis. Following these brief pleasantries, Stevenson then went on the attack, pressing Ambassador Zorin about whether he would deny that the USSR had placed offensive weapons in Cuba.

"Yes or no?" Stevenson demanded. "Don't wait for the translation. Yes or no?"

Zorin smiled nervously as uneasy laughter filled the chamber. He then reminded Stevenson that he was not in an American courtroom and that the American diplomat was not a prosecutor. In reality, Khrushchev and others may not have told Zorin the truth, or he may have simply forgotten it due to his declining mental state.

"In due course, sir, you'll have your reply," Zorin added.

"You are in the court of world opinion right now," Stevenson countered. "I'm prepared to wait for my answer until hell freezes over if that's your decision. I'm also prepared to present the evidence in this room."

Adlai Stevenson then brought in the aerial photos captured by the American reconnaissance pilots and set them up on easels for the UN Security Council and the world to see. He had initially objected to such a display, thinking it circus-like. But in this moment, he sought to make a show of strength with the whole world watching. In the vein of a courtroom prosecutor, Stevenson pointed out each of the missile sites and described them in great detail.

The first series of black-and-white photographs showed the rapid transformation of an area north of the village of Candelaria, near San Cristobal. The first photo, taken by a U-2 in late August, showed nothing but a peaceful Cuban countryside. The next photo of the same area, taken in October, showed tents and trucks. The third photo, captured twenty-four hours later, showed several tents large enough to house up to five hundred troops and, more importantly, seven mobile nuclear missile trailers and four erector-launcher mechanisms in fir-ing position. The next display included three successive photographic enlargements of a missile base in the area of San Cristobal. The diplo-mats all stood for a closer look.

"These enlarged photographs clearly show six of these missiles on trailers and three erect," the ambassador explained. The trailers were designed for intermediate-range missiles that could travel 2,200 miles—far enough to reach Washington, DC, and New York City.

Stevenson displayed and described more photos taken by the U-2s and the Crusaders that showed concrete launch sites, bunkers, buildings to store the missiles, and trucks to move the missiles to the launchpad.

"These weapons . . . these launching pads . . . are a part of a much larger weapons system," Stevenson warned. "To support this build-up, to operate these advanced weapons systems, the Soviet Union has sent a large number of military personnel to Cuba, a force now amounting to several thousand men."

The evidence was irrefutable. The photographs clearly illustrated that the Soviets were lying. "We know the facts here and so do you," Stevenson told Zorin. "Our job here is not to score debating points. Our job, Mr. Zorin, is to save the peace. And if you are ready to try, we are."

The American surveillance pilots were glued to the television as they saw, for the first time, the images they had captured during both high- and low-level flights over Cuba. The men understood fully for the first time that their president, their government, and the people of the United States were all counting on them. They also knew that they would soon be called upon to return to the skies over Cuba.

CHAPTER TWENTY-NINE

Pressure Points

ADLAI STEVENSON'S STRONG and theatrical performance at the United Nations surprised President John F. Kennedy and the members of ExComm.

"I never knew Adlai had it in him," the president commented. "Too bad he didn't show a little more of this in the 1956 election."[1]

But the United States could not afford to wait until hell froze over for a Soviet response. President Kennedy needed Nikita Khrushchev to act swiftly before events spiraled out of control and out of their hands. Just after 5 p.m. on Thursday evening, CIA director John Mc-Cone informed fellow members of ExComm that fifteen Soviet ships, including the *Grozny*, were still inbound for Cuba. The group was still looking for a Russian vessel to board to demonstrate America's intent and resolve, and Defense Secretary Robert McNamara identified the *Marucla*, a Lebanese dry cargo ship sailing under Soviet charter, as a likely candidate. But just as the US Navy received orders to intercept the vessel, it had turned around. The destroyer USS *Pierce* was now shadowing another vessel, a passenger ship from East Germany believed to be carrying Soviet missile technicians. McNamara asked the group whether the navy ship should force the vessel to halt, which could mean firing on the East German ship with 1,500 passengers on board. UN Secretary-General U Thant had pleaded with the United States to avoid confrontation with Soviet ships while a diplomatic accord was sought. Mac Bundy argued that movement against the ship was justified because technically it was an East German ship, not a Soviet vessel.

> McNAMARA—I hate to start with a passenger ship, Mr. President. I think there's great problems.
> PRESIDENT KENNEDY—It might be sunk, you mean?
> McNAMARA—Yes, or seriously disabled and loss of life.[2]

McNamara urged the president to consider boarding the *Grozny* instead. The Soviet ship was now roughly 1,000 miles from Cuba. The president wanted to wait on deciding a course of action until Khrushchev issued a response to U Thant's latest proposal requesting that he halt all ships headed to Cuba. The president's brother Bobby didn't like this idea. He believed the Russians would think the United States was backing off and that the president was weak. It would only reinforce the opinion Khrushchev had formed of Kennedy during the summit in Vienna in 1961. Discussion then shifted to the idea of adding petroleum, jet fuel, and missile fuel to the quarantine's contraband list and cutting off Cuba's petroleum supply, which would bring the island's economy and the Soviets' freedom of movement to a grinding halt. The idea intrigued the president, as he sought a way to apply pressure to the situation. RFK agreed. "We've got to show people we mean it," he stressed.[3]

John McCone then provided the president with sobering news. The CIA had just learned that some of the medium-range ballistic missiles (MRBMs) deployed to Cuba were dangerously close to becoming operational.

OVERNIGHT, ATTENTION TURNED back to the *Marucla*, which surveillance aircraft had spotted during a flight over the Atlantic Ocean. Two destroyers, the USS *Pierce* and USS *Joseph P. Kennedy, Jr.* then trailed the 7,268-ton ship. On the morning of Friday, October 26, the US Navy performed its first inspection and boarding of a Soviet ship. The crew, all from Greece, put up no resistance. Members of the boarding party—six officers and men from the *Kennedy* and the executive officer of the *Pierce*, all unarmed and wearing their dress whites—studied the ship's manifest and inspected the hatch. The *Marucla* was sailing with a declared cargo of truck parts, sulfur, and paper. Nothing appeared out of the ordinary, so the vessel was allowed to proceed. President Kennedy monitored the events from his private quarters. When he learned that a destroyer named for his brother Joe had participated in the interception, he recognized the irony immediately.

"The press will never believe that we didn't stick the *Kennedy* in the way of the *Marucla* just to give the family publicity," he joked to his press secretary, Pierre Salinger.

In reality, the navy made considerable effort to get the *Kennedy* into position to make the intercept, as the destroyer had to sail at a high speed of thirty knots to reach the *Marucla* in time for boarding.

A few hours later, Adlai Stevenson returned from New York. Despite the hard line he had drawn during his confrontation with Valerian Zorin the night before, Kennedy's advisors still believed the ambassador was not strong enough to negotiate with the Soviets and U Thant on his own. The president brought in John J. McCloy—a hard-nosed Wall Street lawyer who had served as assistant secretary of war during World War II—to give Stevenson's bark some bite. Stevenson was ordered to include McCloy in all further talks at the United Nations. U Thant's proposal focused on the Soviets' suspending inbound ships to Cuba but said nothing about the nuclear weapons already delivered to the island. If the United States were to continue down a diplomatic route, the Soviets would have to agree to halt any further buildup of missile sites or long-range bomber facilities, and UN inspectors would have to take over the sites to ensure that all were inoperable. This didn't mean simply flipping a switch—President Kennedy and his team wanted the sites dismantled.

Meanwhile the Soviets showed no sign of slowing down. McCone informed the group of "rapid construction activity"[4] on the island and the Russians' continued use of camouflage tents to conceal nuclear equipment. Surveillance photos from overflights taken the previous day revealed no new missile sites, but road construction in Remedios indicated plans to locate a second intermediate-range ballistic missile site there. McCone was referring to the photos taken by Crusader pilot Jerry Coffee. Most alarming was Coffee's photo of a FROG missile launcher, also referred to as a battlefield "Luna" missile, which meant Russian troops could use tactical nuclear weapons against an invasion force of US marines. A Luna missile could carry a nuclear warhead sixteen to twenty miles and easily take out the US military base at Guantánamo. If the Crusaders' cameras had captured one Luna missile, most military experts believed there must be more.

The CIA estimated that the Soviets were spending between $750 million and $1 billion on their arms buildup in Cuba. Such a high price tag led some ExComm members to believe that Russia had no intentions of dismantling the sites and losing its investment. But if all the missile sites became operational, a greater cost would be exacted—thousands if not millions of human lives.

FIDEL CASTRO FEARED the worst. The Cuban leader had heard from his journalists in America that the United States was calling for a liquidation of Soviet missiles in Cuba.

"War appeared imminent. A first strike might take place at any time," Castro said years later. "I said to myself, 'If Cuba is in such an unfortunate war, we will disappear from the map.'"[5]

Castro penned a letter to Khrushchev warning the Soviet premier that the Americans were poised to attack within seventy-two hours. He believed that they would first attack by air with the goal of destroying certain objectives, most likely the nuclear sites, and that a second wave might entail a full-scale ground invasion of the island.

"You can be sure that we will resist with determination, whatever the case," Castro wrote. "The Cuban people's morale is extremely high and the people will confront aggression heroically."[6]

In the letter, Castro shared his feelings with Khrushchev that "the imperialists' aggressiveness" made them extremely dangerous, and if the United States managed to invade Cuba, he urged the Soviet leader to eliminate this threat forever. Castro was asking Khrushchev to bomb the United States with nuclear weapons.

"However harsh and terrible the solution, there would be no other. . . . We will maintain our hopes for saving the peace until the last moment. . . . But, at the same time, we are serene and ready to confront a situation which we see as very real and imminent," he wrote.

CASTRO WAS NOT crying wolf. The threat posed by the United States was all too real. The US Air Force was preparing for war. More fighter jets were stationed throughout Florida in readiness to attack Cuba, while bombers, loaded with nuclear missiles, stayed aloft over European, American, and international skies awaiting word to retaliate if the Soviets struck first. Many of the nuclear bombers had taken off from civilian airports. Minnesota's Duluth Municipal Airport hosted eight nuclear-armed aircraft, while at Memphis Airport, massive B-47s dominated the flight line surrounded by armed guards. Some airports were ill equipped to handle the situation. At Boston's Logan International Airport, a lieutenant colonel had to purchase fuel for his B-47 at a local station using his personal credit card.[7] But now those bombers were in the air, and all branches of the military were putting the finishing touches on their readiness for war or assisting with the quarantine. The US military was poised for its biggest land invasion since D-day. The plan, code-named Operation Scabbards, called for an initial bombing campaign involving three major air strikes per day until the air defenses and, most importantly, the missile sites were destroyed. More than 1,000 air strikes were planned for the first day alone. The bombing campaign would soften the target for 23,000 paratroopers from the 82nd and 101st Airborne Divisions to drop into Cuba and seize the island's major airports. US marines would then secure the city of Havana and cut off communication and travel to the missile sites. Finally, a massive force of 120,000 troops, a total of eight divisions, would invade the island to engage in an intense ground campaign against Soviet and Cuban troops.

But the U-2s and navy Crusaders still acted as President Kennedy's eyes on Cuba, keeping him informed of Soviet activity. The results from the initial Crusader flights on October 23 were so successful—clearly revealing launching pads, missiles, and even people—that more flights followed, beginning on October 25. Each daily batch of photos showed that work on the missile sites had not stopped but rather accelerated. Photo analysts even projected that the San Cristobal MRBMs were almost fully operational, and Kennedy might have only hours to make his decision.

Crusader pilots not only gathered intelligence but intimidated as well. Secretary of Defense McNamara ordered them to fly over Cuba in force to resemble an air strike to project American power. McNamara also knew that Soviet and Cuban troops on the ground might become accustomed to these kinds of flights, so when the planes came with real bombs, should it come to that, the enemy would be lulled into thinking they were just there to take pictures.

The low-level Crusader flights were indeed terrifying to those on the ground, but the end result might be equally terrifying if troops manning the surface-to-air missile (SAM) sites felt the need to lash out and developed an itchy trigger finger, regardless of orders. Imagine those Cuban artillerymen during hours of boredom scanning the skies, and then suddenly, seemingly out of nowhere, a Crusader comes roaring toward them at 400 to 500 mph, just barely above the treetops. The jets were so close that one technician later said, "We could see the pilot in his helmet."[8] The artillerymen had no way of knowing if the Crusaders were going to drop a bomb and blow them to smithereens or merely shoot their cameras. The Cubans tasked with protecting the SAM sites pleaded for permission to fire at the predatory birds streaking by.

On October 26, no less than fourteen Crusader sorties were launched. Castro had had enough. He may not have had command of the SAMs or the more advanced MiGs, but he did control the more traditional antiaircraft guns and would allow his men to open fire on October 27. None of the batteries that fired scored a hit. Castro stated, "The inexperience of our artillerymen, that had recently learned to operate these pieces, probably made them miss as they fired on the low-flying aircraft."[9] But the unarmed Crusader pilots attributed their safe passage to their speed and evasive maneuvers. Whatever the reason, flights were becoming more hazardous, and pilots wondered when an aircraft might be hit. Pilot Tad Riley explained a close call as follows: "Once I saw a gun position pointing in the opposite direction from my approach. The gunner was looking over his shoulder and frantically cranking his gun around to track me."[10] Cubans at the missile sites even fired rifles and pistols at the Crusaders.

The risks were growing, and the Crusader pilots didn't feel safe until they cleared the Cuban shoreline, where armed fighter jets waited to protect them should a MiG be on their tail. The MiGs never seriously challenged the Crusaders, much to the chagrin of the Soviet and Cuban pilots who hungered for a chance to take down an American air force jet.

The Kremlin must have calculated that while the Crusaders and U-2s continued their picture taking, time favored the Soviets. Each day more and more launch sites neared completion. Khrushchev didn't want to risk a US invasion or massive military strike by engaging the enemy with MiGs until the nuclear missiles were on the launching pads. (Once the sites were completed, installation of the warheads would take only a few hours. US surveillance never did locate the various storage bunkers with any degree of certainty.)[11] Khrushchev figured that when the missiles were ready to launch, the United States would not dare attack or invade.

The MiGs certainly had the ability to bring down an unarmed Crusader, especially by sneaking up on it from the rear. And the Soviets could easily bring down larger reconnaissance planes (other than U-2s), such as the US RB-47s that flew the periphery of Cuba using electronics to monitor Soviet air defense radar. As recently as 1960 a MiG had blasted a US RB-47 out of the sky during its surveillance mission off the Soviet Kola Peninsula. Of the six-man crew only two survived when they bailed out after the MiG opened fire and the RB-47 went into a tailspin. They were captured, interrogated, and held in a Soviet prison. Khrushchev later decided to release the men but not while President Dwight Eisenhower and Vice President Richard Nixon were in the White House. Thinking of the upcoming election, the premier did not want Nixon to beat Kennedy and decided not to assist the incumbents with good news. Instead he waited and released the two pilots four days after the new president was sworn in. Even in 1961 the Russians were trying to influence US elections.

Even without the Soviet or Cuban threat, intelligence-gathering missions had their hazards. During the height of the Cuban Missile Crisis on October 27, an RB-47, tasked with pinpointing the location of the Soviet ship *Grozny*, crashed during its launch from Kindley Air Force Base in Bermuda. The aircraft could not gain the proper thrust due to an incorrect fuel mixture loaded by the maintenance crew, and within seconds of becoming airborne, it slammed into the ground, killing the entire four-man crew: Major William Britton, aircraft commander; First Lieutenant Holt Rasmussen, copilot; Captain Robert Constable, navigator; and Captain Robert Dennis, observer.[12]

SAMs never posed a threat to the Crusaders due to the low flying altitude (five hundred feet and below) they adhered to over Cuba. Designed to hit high-altitude planes, a launched surface-to-air missile didn't start locking in on its target until it had traveled 1,500 feet.

Ironically, the Crusaders' bigger danger was much lower-tech: a bird strike. William Ecker joked, "If the Cubans wanted to improve their defenses they should have placed dead goats along the hillsides and let the vultures circle over them."[13] Humor aside, a bird sucked into an engine could bring down a low-flying, high-speed Crusader.

The Crusaders' speed and low altitude spared them as casualties when the enemy started firing. But could the high-flying U-2s also escape unscathed? CIA director McCone had said on October 23 that he expected the Soviets to fire SAMs at U-2s "in a short time." Mc-Cone likely didn't know that SAMs had been fired at Jerry McIlmoyle and that Jerry had been lucky to escape unharmed.

Back in Washington, the decision-makers at the Pentagon were now on a war footing. General Maxwell Taylor told the president that the Joint Chiefs were eager to begin limited air strikes against the missile sites, with a much larger air strike to follow against the SAM sites in Cuba. The president continued to explore his options. The United States needed to immobilize the nuclear weapons through a physical separation of the missile and the launcher.

> PRESIDENT KENNEDY—There are two ways to do this. . . .
> One is the diplomatic way. Which I doubt, I don't think
> it will be successful. The other way is, I would think, a
> combination of an air strike and probably invasion, which
> means that we could have to carry out both of those with
> the prospect that they [the missiles] might be fired.[14]

CIA director McCone told the president that he too was leaning toward an air strike to eliminate the threat. At 1:00 p.m., a weary JFK left the ExComm meeting and took a swim in the White House pool. At about the same time, John Scali, a journalist from ABC News, was having lunch with a Soviet KGB officer named Alexander Fomin at the Occidental Grill a few blocks away.

"War seems about to break out," Fomin stated somberly. "Something must be done to save the situation."[15]

Fomin passed papers to Scali indicating that Khrushchev was ready to make a deal. If the United States pledged not to invade Cuba, the Soviets would remove the nuclear missiles under the watchful eye of UN inspectors. Scali rushed over to the State Department with the proposal. Dean Rusk discussed the back-channel proposal with other members of ExComm and then ordered Scali to reengage with Fomin. The ABC News reporter told the Russian that the United States was interested in negotiating but that time was running out and a deal must be struck within forty-eight hours. At the United Nations, Secretary-General Thant issued his own proposal outlining a similar deal.

Just after nightfall, President Kennedy finally heard from Nikita Khrushchev himself in a lengthy letter that arrived by cable in four parts. The US ambassador in Moscow had received the original letter earlier that day. Embassy analysts believed the Soviet premier had written it himself because it was jumbled and edited on the fly, with words crossed out and replaced by other words in violet ink. Khrushchev wrote,

> I think you will understand me correctly if you are really concerned about the welfare of the world. Everyone needs peace: both capitalists, if they have not lost their reason, and, still more, Communists, people who know how to value not only their own lives but, more than anything, the lives of the peoples. . . . We have always regarded war as a calamity, and not as a game nor as a means for the attainment of definite goals. . . . War is our enemy and a calamity for all the peoples. . . . We must not succumb to intoxication and petty passions. . . . I have participated in two wars and I know that war ends only when it has rolled through cities and villages, sowing death and destruction everywhere.[16]

Premier Khrushchev then returned to the debate about whether the nuclear missiles in Cuba should be considered "offensive" or "defensive" weapons.

> Let us take, for example, a simple cannon. . . . A cannon is a defensive weapon if it is set up to defend boundaries or a fortified area. But if one gathers artillery and adds to it the necessary number of troops, then the same cannons become offensive weapons, because they prepare the way for artillery to attack. . . . These missiles are a means of extermination and destruction. But one cannot attack with these missiles—even nuclear missiles of a power of a hundred

mega-tons, because only people, troops can attack. Without people, any weapons however powerful, cannot be offensive. . . . Only
lunatics or suicides, who themselves want to perish and destroy the
whole world before they die, could do this. We, however, want to
live and do not at all want to destroy your country.

Khrushchev then reminded Kennedy of their summit in Austria
and, more importantly, the Bay of Pigs invasion—the black mark on
his presidency.

We were grieved by the fact—I spoke about it in Vienna—that a
landing took place, that an attack on Cuba was committed, as a
result of which many Cubans perished. You yourself told me then
that this had been a mistake. . . . We know how difficult it is to accomplish a revolution and how difficult it is to reconstruct a country
on new foundations. We sincerely sympathize with Cuba and the
Cuban people.

Finally, the Soviet leader extended the olive branch.

If assurances were given by the President and the Government of
the United States that the USA itself would not participate in an
attack on Cuba, and would restrain others from actions of this sort,
if you would recall your fleet, this would immediately change everything. . . . I spoke in the name of the Soviet Government in
the United Nations and introduced a proposal for the disbandment
of all armies and for the destruction of all armaments. . . . Armaments only bring disaster. . . . Let us therefore show statesmanlike
wisdom. I propose: We, for our part, will declare that our ships,
bound for Cuba, will not carry any kind of armaments. You would
declare that the United States will not invade Cuba with its forces
and will not support any sort of forces which might intend to carry
out an invasion of Cuba. Then the necessity for the presence of our
military specialists in Cuba would disappear. . . . There, Mr. President, are my thoughts, which, if you agreed with them, could put
an end to that tense situation which is disturbing all peoples. These
thoughts are dictated by a sincere desire to relieve the situation, to
remove the threat of war. Respectfully yours, N. Khrushchev.

Members of ExComm dissected the letter. Secretary of State Dean Rusk thought it revealed desperation. JFK advisor Dean Acheson found the text confusing and believed that Khrushchev must have been "either tight or scared."[17] Whereas others saw fear and opportunity, the president's brother and closest advisor saw hope.

"I had a slight feeling of optimism as I drove home from the State Department that night," Bobby Kennedy later wrote. "The letter, with all its rhetoric, had the beginnings of perhaps some accommodation, some agreement."[18]

The president shared his optimism. JFK told his brother that for the first time, he was hopeful that both sides just might pull back from the brink of war.

CHAPTER THIRTY

Lost!

CHUCK MAULTSBY WAS 4,000 miles away from his fellow U-2 pilots flying the Cuban missions from McCoy Air Force Base in Florida, and he wished he could be in on the action. Instead he was in Alaska's frozen tundra.

Maultsby's work in Alaska began in July 1962. The Defense Atomic Support Agency needed a replacement pilot for its High Altitude Sampling Program over the Arctic, and he was sent to Eielson Air Force Base just south of Fairbanks. U-2 planes were the perfect aircraft for collecting radioactive particles from nuclear bomb tests, and the Alaska location was closest to the Soviet Union. The samples could yield information on Soviet atomic weapons. Because the radioactive particles from the USSR's tests drifted over international airspace, the air force could gather samples and monitor the United States' adversary without flying the spy planes over Soviet soil.

The U-2 pilots did their duty, choosing—or at least trying—to ignore the health risks from flying into the stratosphere where plutonium and uranium isotopes drifted after a Soviet nuclear test. It was just one more inherent hazard of their ultrasecret profession.

Specially equipped U-2s had an intake door in the nose of the plane that the pilot would open to trap samples in a filter. The lack of visual landmarks made flights in the Arctic especially dangerous—frozen earth blended with frozen ocean into, from the pilot's perspective, a white wasteland. Complex celestial navigation was the rule in such conditions. Close proximity to magnetic North would throw a normal compass off kilter, and the aircraft's gyrocompass was prone to error. More than one pilot had found himself a few degrees off course when he finally sighted an identifiable landmass.

Whenever the nuclear-sampling U-2s flew over inhospitable terrain, efforts were made to have a search-and-rescue (SAR) team as close as possible, should the pilot have to make an emergency landing. An air force Douglas DC4, carrying SAR paramedical personnel (nicknamed "Duck Butt"), would depart about three hours before the U-2, following the planned sampling flight path. The U-2, the faster of the two aircraft, would later pass the SAR plane. When the SAR aircraft reached Barter Island, at the northeastern tip of Alaska, it would orbit there until the spy plane returned. This method would at least put the DC4 in the general vicinity of the U-2 for a portion of its flight and potentially offer aid if the spy plane went down. However, with subzero temperatures, an injured U-2 pilot had only a brief window for rescue before he froze to death. And if the spy plane went down to the north of Barter Island, the chances of the rescue plane finding it were just about nil.

Although Maultsby flew eleven Arctic missions during the summer months, he never became fully acclimated to the almost twenty-four-hour sunshine and lack of visual landmarks. He was relieved when transferred back to Laughlin in September 1962, thankful to dodge the Arctic winters. Back in Texas, Chuck got to spend time with his three boys, including five-month-old Kevin. He was also happy to enjoy quiet time with Jeanne, who was proud that she could again fit into the favorite dress she had worn before getting pregnant. But the air force had other ideas for Maultsby beyond domestic bliss and sent him back to Eielson Air Force Base in late September for a second tour in Alaska.

The upcoming missions differed from the ones he had flown there in the summer in one major respect. The U-2 pilots would now fly all the way to the North Pole and back, some 3,000 miles. The radio beacon at Barter Island could assist them only during the first third of the trip. From that point northward, the pilot would rely solely on celestial navigation. Maultsby later said, "From there [Barter Island] to the North Pole was nothing but ice, stars and polar bears."[1] Nor were there any safe landing zones should an emergency arise.

Isolated in remote Alaska, Maultsby did not know much about the drama unfolding in Washington, DC, and Cuba.

"We heard that some of the U-2 drivers in our squadron were flying over Cuba to ascertain whether or not the Russians were off loading missiles onto Cuban soil," he wrote years later. "If they were, things could get dicey in a hurry."[2]

Maultsby's assessment was a grand understatement.

On October 26, the day before his next mission, he went through preflight planning with his team and then tried to get some sleep. The noisy shuffle of airmen through the barracks in heavy snow boots made that impossible. Frustrated, he went down to the operations building and grabbed a cot. After a few hours, Maultsby awoke at 8 p.m. and ate a breakfast of steak and eggs. He was concerned that he'd only managed a few hours' sleep with a long mission ahead.

At midnight on October 27 (4 a.m. in Washington, DC), Chuck began his first flight to the North Pole. He wasn't flying over Cuba, but the mission was still dangerous. Only two other U-2 pilots had previously made the trip, and flying only by celestial navigation for approximately two-thirds of the 3,000-mile trip was anything but routine for even the most experienced pilot.

The flight progressed smoothly en route to Barter Island. The SAR crew, or "Duck Butt," called Maultsby on a prebriefed frequency to say that they'd be arriving over Barter Island at about the same time.

"Good luck," the Duck Butt crew told him. "We'll keep a light on in the window for you."[3]

As he continued to push on toward the Pole, Maultsby used a series of charts that showed exactly where certain stars should be in relation to his view from the cockpit. The flight was a strange mix of old and new: the pilots navigated like explorers from the time of Christopher Columbus but were searching for evidence of atomic bomb detonations rather than a new continent.

Celestial navigation was nothing new for Maultsby, but what would happen if he couldn't clearly see the stars? He was about to find out.

An aurora borealis, also known as the northern lights, suddenly appeared in the dark sky. Its shimmering streaks of color, primarily shades of green and pink, obscured the stars. These strange and vibrant lights are a result of solar activity whereby particles from the sun's atmosphere reach Earth's atmosphere, creating a phenomenon of shifting colors in the night sky.

Bands of color that danced in the frozen air now covered the formerly dark sky and tiny stars above Maultsby and his U-2. The display would be beautiful for anyone on the ground lucky enough to see it; but not for Maultsby. The pilot was trying to get a fix on a star with his sextant, but the aurora borealis made it difficult to discern one star from another. This was his first experience with the northern lights, and it could not have come at a worse time—or on a worse day.

He continued toward the Pole, hoping the aurora would fade out. It did not. In fact the glowing lights became more powerful. Maultsby didn't consider turning back; instead, calculating that the lights would soon abate, the pilot held his heading and continued on, reaching what he thought was the North Pole at the predetermined time. There he executed his turn to put him on a course for home, trying to follow the same track as before.

Rather than feeling relieved that he had reached his objective and was on the return leg to the familiar tarmac of Eielson Air Force Base, Maultsby sensed uneasily that something was amiss. The northern lights were still obscuring his view, and he began to suspect he might be slightly off course. He put out a call to the Duck Butt rescue plane, hoping its crew could help nail down his position, but he got no answer. Maultsby was about as far away from mankind as one could be without a spaceship.

Further into the flight south, the shimmering northern lights finally faded, and Chuck could clearly see the stars. None of the alignments matched his chart. He now knew for certain that he had strayed off course but had no way of knowing in which direction.

He had no landmarks to guide him, and this was his first night flight; he couldn't see a "single light from horizon to horizon." He felt as if he had left planet Earth and entered an entirely different galaxy.

Maultsby estimated he was four hundred miles from Barter Island when he made radio contact with the rescue plane. That reassured him that he wasn't too far off course. But a bit later, when he should have been directly over the island, he could not pick up the radio beacon's signal. Someone from Eielson Air Force Base briefly called him over the single-side band radio but could not hear his return call.

Next he radioed the Duck Butt rescue crew, who said they were orbiting the island and receiving the Barter Island radio beacon loud and clear. Concerned, the rescue plane announced it would start shooting flares every five minutes.

Maultsby never saw the flares, and for the first time in this long, grueling trip he felt a twinge of panic. He was either far to the east or far to the west of Barter Island. If he was far to the west, he knew he was in serious trouble—he could be flying close to or over the USSR, and the Soviets would surely be tracking him by radar. All sorts of dire thoughts must have raced through the pilot's mind on that realization—first and foremost perhaps that if the Soviets were as on edge as the Americans, being so close to confrontation, they would use every means to blast his plane out of the sky. Survival would be a long shot, but he had managed it once before over Korea and maybe could do it again. But this wasn't wartime Korea. This was the unforgiving Arctic, and even if he somehow managed to bail out, by the time the enemy located him, he'd be as frozen as a block of ice or digesting in the belly of a polar bear. And if, in a true long shot, he was taken prisoner, what good was that? He had spent more than two years as a POW of the Chinese, and no man should have to endure captivity more than once. His mind raced, and he had to fight down his fear. If he had strayed west, his options were bleak. Chuck Maultsby knew that he'd be captured or killed.

CHAPTER THIRTY-ONE

A Single Mission

RUDY ANDERSON WAS not originally scheduled to fly on Saturday, October 27. Strategic Air Command (SAC) had initially planned to launch three flights but scrubbed all three at the last minute because Crusaders were going to cover the same areas of Cuba. There was no need for redundancy, and it was best to keep the men fresh should they be needed on Sunday. It looked like all the U-2 pilots would have a day of rest that Saturday.

Then SAC flight planners decided to send a U-2 to cover the eastern part of the island where Crusaders would not be flying.[1] Rudy was ready. The night before, he had asked operations manager Tony Martinez to put him on standby in case another pilot was needed. Tony granted his wish.[2] And now the opportunity had come up, and Rudy was prepared. His one concern was that he had not spoken to his wife, Jane, in several days. Normally, they talked by phone, and although he could not reveal details about his mission or its duration, he always gave her clues about when to expect him home. Rudy would ask nonchalantly about whether she'd picked up his uniform from the cleaners and drop other subtle hints that he was coming home soon. But the secrecy surrounding the flights over Cuba made any contact with the outside world verboten. Plus he had no idea when or if he'd be returning to her.

Rudy Anderson ate his usual breakfast of steak and eggs with the other pilots originally scheduled to fly, and once told his was the sole mission launching that morning, he had a physical exam and flight briefing.³ Then he conducted his hourlong preflight breathing of 100 percent oxygen, followed by a study of his target folder. His physiological support team (PST) helped him squeeze into his pressure suit, and together they boarded the air-conditioned van that carried him to his plane.

Once in the cockpit of his U-2, Anderson and a PST tech went through several checks followed by more checks from Captain Roger Herman, who had the job of clearing Rudy to launch.⁴ Herman conducted a "press to set" procedure that sent a burst of oxygen into Anderson's suit, briefly inflating it to make sure it was functioning correctly.

Everything was in order. Herman slapped the pilot on the shoulder and said, "Okay, Rudy, here we go, have a good trip. See you when you get back."

Anderson responded with a thumbs-up, and Herman closed the canopy. Rudy had taped two photos above his control panel: one of his beautiful, smiling wife; the other of his two boys. Staring at the photos, he must have truly believed that his mission could save their lives and those of millions more around the world. He could not bear to think of the bloodshed on the invasion beaches or the vaporization of large cities and small towns in the United States and the Soviet Union. He prayed to God that his aerial photographs would lead to the de-escalation of the conflict. Both sides simply had too much to lose.

LEAVING MCCOY AIR Force Base at 9:10 a.m. eastern standard time, Anderson had relatively clear skies. While he had performed five earlier spy missions over Cuba during the crisis, none of the pilots who did multiple missions viewed such flights as routine, and Major Anderson was no exception. Jerry McIlmoyle's October 25 flight also lurked in the back of his mind. McIlmoyle's close encounter with an exploding surface-to-air missile (SAM), combined with the escalation of the crisis, put Rudy Anderson at full alert as he entered Cuban airspace.

His mission would take him over the easternmost third of the island, coasting in from the north, initially in a straight line heading south-southeast. He would be passing within range of no less than eight SAM sites.[5]

At about 11 a.m., Jerry McIlmoyle, Steve Heyser, and Buddy Brown were just beginning a round of golf on McCoy's golf course when they heard the distinct roar of Anderson's U-2 taking off. Not scheduled to fly that day, Heyser and McIlmoyle had decided to grab their golf clubs and relieve some stress. Brown was a late addition as he had been scheduled to follow Anderson into the skies over Cuba, but his mission had been scratched. The pilots turned to see the aircraft climbing out at a steep angle. Suddenly, the Dragon Lady came into view for a brief moment before it soared high above the cloud cover. Jerry nudged Heyser and said, "There he goes, he's passing you." Steve Heyser only smiled; it didn't matter to him if Rudy flew the most missions over Cuba. He knew the goal was important to Anderson, and that was fine with him.

Jerry, Steve, and Buddy knew that with each additional flight, the risks to the pilots increased exponentially. The Soviets had fired on Jerry two days earlier and would likely do so again.

Steve certainly believed Jerry's account of what had happened. Both men closely followed the news that the Soviets were testing the blockade and that their medium-range ballistic missiles in Cuba were becoming operational. The crisis was escalating, and the U-2s were in the forefront of the peril. Yet both Heyser and McIlmoyle—just like Anderson—were willing to fly over the island again.

All the U-2 pilots at McCoy were pragmatic as well as patriotic. Earlier that month *Air Force Association Magazine* contained an advertisement for $10,000 in life insurance for combat crews, and all eleven pilots immediately applied for it.[6] They knew that they might not come back from any given mission and wanted to provide for their families in whatever way possible.

Anderson flew at the usual 72,000 feet, first crossing over Cuba at the northern coastal area of Cayo Coco, then continuing his trajectory over Esmeralda and next over Camagüey. So far so good. The weather was a mix of sun and clouds, the cameras were working fine, and

Rudy knew the extreme importance of the mission. His photos might reveal that warheads had been put on the missiles, indicating that they were ready for firing. In twenty-four hours the Joint Chiefs of Staff and President John F. Kennedy himself would likely be examining some of his film to guide them in planning their next steps. Anderson was serving his country, helping to keep it safe. The fact that his plane was unarmed suited his conviction that he could be a top-notch air force pilot without dropping bombs or blowing enemy pilots out of the sky.

ON THE GROUND in Cuba, Soviet radar was tracking Major Anderson's flight, and the technicians labeled this intruding aircraft "target 33."[7] Nerves were frayed: both the Soviets and the Cubans expected the United States to launch an all-out attack at any moment. And there was anger too, particularly among the Cubans. Why let the Americans invade their airspace in the high-flying U-2s and gather intelligence that would help make the inevitable attack that much more deadly and effective? Since October 14, when Steve Heyser first discovered the missiles, radar had painted the U-2s crisscrossing the island nation, and more recently—and even more egregiously—the low-flying reconnaissance jets were roaring by at treetop level, flaunting their superiority. The Cubans felt they had the right to defend their country from enemy aircraft. The Russians, they believed, should use the damn SAMs that they had so painstakingly shipped and assembled here.

Many of the Russians on the island agreed with their Cuban counterparts.[8] After all, the Cubans and Russians toiling in Cuba—not those in Moscow—would pay the ultimate price when the United States attacked. They could not understand Moscow's reluctance to let them defend themselves. But their orders were to withhold fire unless under attack. Some Soviets on the ground thought this gave them a bit of leeway to use their judgment to shoot down the offending US planes if they sensed an attack coming during the overflights. In a 2004 interview, Soviet colonel Grigory Danilevich, head of the political section of the antiaircraft division on the island, claimed that commands from Moscow changed constantly and were unclear. "There was a command [on October 26] to 'open fire in case of manifest attack.'"[9]

The nonstop intrusion of American aircraft over Cuban airspace and Moscow's reluctance to allow the SAMs to take them down angered and frustrated no one more than Fidel Castro. The American military continued to mobilize with the US troop and technician buildup in Guantánamo, the ever-increasing numbers of US Navy vessels patrolling just off the Cuban coast, and informers disclosing a massive increase in military activity in Florida.[10]

Castro's letter from the previous day calling for Moscow to launch a first strike against the United States had led Nikita Khrushchev to think he was becoming unhinged, and like Kennedy the premier worried that the situation would spiral out of control. On the morning of October 27, that is just what was happening.

SOVIET FORCES DEPUTY commander General Leonid Garbuz and deputy commander of air defenses General Stepan Grechko were monitoring the incursion of target 33 from a command center in Havana. "Our guest," said Grechko, "has been circling above us for more than an hour. I think we should give the order for downing the plane."[11] They thought a US attack was imminent, so why allow this U-2 to return more valuable data to their adversaries in Washington? The time had come to propose taking action to General Issa Pliyev, who commanded all Soviets in Cuba.

A phone call to Pliyev's headquarters proved futile as his aide-de-camp said he was not available. General Pliyev, known to be ill with kidney disease, was possibly too sick to take the call.[12]

Had Pliyev known what Garbuz and Grechko were planning, he would have taken the call even from his deathbed.

THE RADAR ACTIVATED by the Soviets included missile guidance radar (MGR), which they had not used since October 19, perhaps to keep the Americans guessing or to lull them into thinking the Soviets would not launch the missiles.[13] Activation of the MGR signaled that the SAMs were being prepared for firing and to lock in on their targets.

(The missiles that missed McIlmoyle might have been launched without full radar capacity so as not to alert him that they had been fired. A device in Jerry's plane that would have warned him that a missile had locked on to him never turned red as it should have. Either the device malfunctioned or the Soviets intentionally kept the guidance system off.)

On Saturday, October 27, however, SAC's RB-47s, gathering electronic intelligence just off Cuba, detected that the Soviets had activated their MGR systems. The pilots of those RB-47s alerted the Pentagon, but neither had the means to warn Rudy Anderson.[14]

CHAPTER THIRTY-TWO

MAYDAY! MAYDAY!

WHEN CHUCK MAULTSBY radioed to the Duck Butt rescue crew that he couldn't see their flares over the Arctic, the pilot of the DC4 asked him what stars he could see. Chuck responded that Orion's Belt was about fifteen degrees off his nose. The DC4 pilot immediately asked him to change course and steer ten degrees left.

Maultsby let out a sigh of relief. Yes, he was lost, and yes, he might be over the Soviet Union, but now he had the means to get back to safe sky. His reprieve was short-lived. A new voice came over the radio and told him to turn thirty degrees right. He flew in silence for a moment and then radioed the rescue plane pilot, asking if he had heard the latest instruction over the radio. He had not, and Maultsby's anxiety grew tenfold. If that pilot hadn't heard the unknown radio call, Chuck knew for sure he had strayed far west of Barter Island and was near Soviet territory. He didn't know, however, that he was now directly over the Soviet Chukotka Peninsula, and the Russians had pinpointed the trespasser.

From the Soviets' perspective, the sudden appearance of an intruder on their radar could mean a multitude of things, all of them cause for alarm. Was the United States conducting a probing mission in advance of an attack? Was a spy plane trying to enter their airspace in the least populated region? Or did the blip on the radar represent something far worse—an advance bomber carrying nuclear bombs?

Whatever was invading their airspace, they had to shoot it down before it got any closer to their eastern military installations.

The unknown caller reached out to Maultsby again, this time instructing him to make a thirty-five-degree right turn. The Western-sounding voice bore no hint of a Russian accent, but whom could it belong to? Was the speaker an accomplished Soviet linguistic expert steering him to the precise location where he could be eliminated—or perhaps directing him to a Soviet airstrip where he could land, putting the undamaged U-2, with all its secrets, in the hands of the Russians?

There was only one way to find out if the voice on the radio was friendly or hostile. If the caller was one of Maultsby's own people, he would know the secret code. "I challenged him," Chuck later said, "using a code that only a legit operator would know, but there was no response."

That moment or two of silence was terrifying. The unknown voice had been louder and clearer than that of the rescue plane pilot. Maultsby knew he must be hundreds of miles off course, to the west.

The Duck Butt pilot broke the silence with a weak transmission, asking Chuck if he could see the glow of the sunrise on the eastern horizon. Maultsby could not—he was too far west. Time was running out. The transmissions from the rescue plane were getting weaker and weaker, and the last one Chuck heard had told him to turn left by fifteen degrees.

He made the turn and at the same time flipped to the emergency channel and shouted, "MAYDAY! MAYDAY! MAYDAY!"

He knew he only had thirty minutes of fuel left. But what he didn't know was even more terrifying. A US radar installation at the western extremity of Alaska had picked up six Soviet aircraft flying upward toward Maultsby. He had penetrated three hundred miles deep into enemy airspace, and MiG fighter jets had launched from Pevek and Chukotka airfields. Their supersonic speed would bring them to the intruder in a few short minutes.

WHILE MAULTSBY'S MAYDAY call did not receive a confirmation from the rescue plane or Eielson Air Force Base, the Strategic Air Command (SAC) at Offutt Air Force Base in Omaha, Nebraska, was well aware of what was happening. At approximately 12:30 p.m. on

Saturday, October 27 (8:30 a.m. in Alaska), General Thomas Power, head of SAC, learned that a U-2 had gotten lost during its sampling mission to the North Pole. Powers, off base when informed, immediately drove to Offutt and joined the on-duty staff at SAC headquarters. A large screen showed the track of Maultsby's plane over Soviet airspace, followed by the flight paths of six MiGs. The data were courtesy of a successful covert operation whereby the United States had breached the Soviet air defense system. In effect, the air force could now see exactly what the Soviets saw, and the MiGs were closing the gap on the lost U-2. The situation was alarming to say the least, but SAC had to handle it carefully—the American military commanders didn't want to tip off the Soviets that they had penetrated their air defense system. They decided to share and compare information about the MiGs and the U-2 with the commander at Eielson Air Force Base, but they made clear that no communications must indicate how this information was known, lest the Soviets learn the SAC intelligence secret.

The US military was already at DEFCON 2, the highest state of readiness short of war, and the Soviets were in a similar heightened status. One miscalculation, and nuclear exchanges were terrifyingly possible. Adding to the apprehension from the Soviet perspective was a recent message to the Ministry of Defense from General Issa Pliyev in Cuba, warning that his sources thought an air attack on the island would likely occur on October 27 or 28.

To counter the MiGs closing in on Chuck, the air force scrambled two F-102 fighter jets from Galena Air Force Base in Alaska. If Maultsby was still flying and had not been shot down, these jets would protect him—or, God forbid, shoot him down themselves if need be to prevent the Soviets from striking first. A Soviet attack on an American plane could trigger an armed US response. Might SAC, or even the president himself, sacrifice an American pilot in hopes of preventing World War III? The pilots prayed they would never find out.

ON OCTOBER 27, 1962, the danger went far beyond Maultsby, the MiGs, and the F-102s. The outcome of this potential engagement threatened the entire world. The F-102s were carrying tactical nuclear missiles.

Because the United States had entered DEFCON 2, nuclear-tipped GAR-11 air-to-air missiles had recently replaced the F-102s' conventional missiles. The F-102s could now bring down multiple enemy aircraft with just one shot—the explosion would destroy any aircraft within a half mile. Incredibly, the decision to use these missiles was up to the pilots—no one could stop them from firing if they deemed it necessary. And the two pilots flying to Maultsby's aid might very well think it necessary to respond if attacked by a MiG. They had no other weapons except these nuclear-tipped ones, so their options were limited.

One can imagine the tension at SAC headquarters in Nebraska. Only the people manning the Soviet air bases might have been more anxious, still not knowing if the intruding aircraft was the vanguard of a wave of US bombers loaded with nuclear missiles or something else. President John F. Kennedy's fear from the start—of a miscalculation by individuals outside his control—was playing out over the skies of the easternmost section of the Soviet empire.

THE UNKNOWN VOICE spoke to Maultsby again, and this time the U-2 pilot did the only thing he could do: try to ignore it. Then he heard what sounded like Russian music.

Chuck was exhausted and frightened—he had been in the air for an astounding nine hours—but every neuron in his body was screaming for escape. His suppressed panic reared its head for the first time and affected him physically, his breath quickening and his pulse pounding in his head.[1] He now knew for certain that he had penetrated Soviet airspace, and he'd been around long enough to know both enemy surface-to-air missiles and aircraft would be targeting him for a kill.

At that moment, he made a critical decision. *I will not be a prisoner of war for a second time.* Maultsby turned the plane so that the Russian radio signal was behind him and tried to put as much space between himself and the Soviets as possible with what little fuel he had left.

Chuck figured that the Soviets had likely tracked him on radar, and maybe at this very moment a MiG was trying to intercept him, but in the night sky he had no way of spotting an enemy closing in on him. He continued to call Mayday, but no one answered.

While Maultsby dearly wished the U-2 could fly faster, the plane did have one thing going for it. It was at an elevation of 75,000 feet, while the MiGs could climb only to 60,000 feet.

Chuck calculated that his remaining fuel would power him for only twelve more minutes, so he had to think quickly. He would shut down the engine and glide as far as he could, then use the tiny amount of fuel left to help with a landing or in any new emergency. He made one last radio call saying he was going off the air; maybe the rescue crew would hear what he thought might be his final words.

As soon as he turned off the engine, Maultsby's pressure suit inflated to keep his blood from boiling. The suit pushed upward on his helmet, and because he had forgotten to fasten the lanyards that kept the helmet from rising, the lost pilot could no longer see the plane's instrument panel. As he wrestled his helmet into place, he thought, *What a fine mess I've gotten myself into.* And the mess kept getting worse. His windshield fogged up, and then his faceplate did the same.

The exhausted pilot dared not use his battery power to fix the windshield situation. He needed to save his batteries should he have to make one last radio call. If he had to bail out, he wanted to broadcast that decision in hopes the rescue plane could hear it.

Chuck Maultsby felt more alone now than ever, with only the sound of his breath to break the silence.

MAULTSBY NOW EFFECTIVELY sat in a glider coasting thirteen miles above the USSR. Amazingly, even with no engine power, the U-2 continued to cruise at that level. Chuck began to wonder if his altimeter was stuck. With his helmet fogged, he craned his head forward as far as possible and, using his tongue, licked the condensation off the faceplate. He had flown seven or eight minutes without power, but still the spy plane maintained its altitude of 75,000 feet.

Not until roughly ten minutes into the glide did the altimeter show the slightest change, indicating the beginning of a slow descent. Chuck couldn't do much except keep the wings level and pray that he'd make it to the border before he was blown out of the sky.

WHILE MAULTSBY WAS in mortal danger, members of ExComm began a morning meeting at the White House. The Soviet ship *Grozny*, which US surveillance had temporarily lost track of, was still steaming toward the quarantine line and was less than one hundred miles away. During the early part of the meeting, Defense Secretary Robert McNamara proposed launching night reconnaissance missions involving flares "to keep the heat on." The president asked him to hold off implementing that idea until they discussed it again in the evening, when they would make the decision based on what transpired during the day.

Most of the morning meeting revolved around discussion of a new proposal and letter from Moscow, announced publicly on Radio Moscow, stating that the United States had to withdraw its missiles from Turkey in order for the Soviets to do the same in Cuba. The ExComm members were astounded that they had not had time to respond to Nikita Khrushchev's late Friday proposal, and already the Soviets had upped the ante. During the meeting the president voiced his frustration but also his keen understanding of worldwide public perception.

> President Kennedy—He's [Khrushchev] got us in a pretty good spot here. Because most people would regard this as not an unreasonable proposal.

The group then discussed the many issues with the new proposal, including North Atlantic Treaty Organization coordination and the fact that officials in Turkey had not been consulted.

Even though it was a morning meeting, ExComm members were already showing signs of strain and fatigue from strategizing a response regarding the new Russian demands. They would soon have lots more to worry about.

CHAPTER THIRTY-THREE

"Some Son-of-a-Bitch Never Gets the Word"

SECRETARY OF DEFENSE Robert McNamara was at the Pentagon conferring with the Joint Chiefs of Staff when alerted in the early afternoon that a U-2 collecting radioactive samples near the North Pole had gone off course and might be somewhere over the Soviet Union. That message, alarming enough in and of itself, ended with the frightening news that "Russian fighters scrambled, ours too."[1]

McNamara reportedly shouted, "This means war with the Soviet Union!"[2]

Strategic Air Command (SAC) then told the secretary of defense that another U-2 had launched to continue the air samplings over the North Pole. McNamara immediately ordered that the plane return to base—he didn't need any other incidents occurring with Chuck Maultsby's flight still in question. Next, he called the State Department to tell Dean Rusk, fearing the Soviets might interpret the trespassing aircraft as the vanguard of an all-out attack. But there was no hotline to Russia to explain what was happening, and at that moment only the US authorities knew the incursion was an accident. The Soviets could only guess.

Rusk immediately called Roger Hilsman, head of the State Department's Intelligence and Research Office. Hilsman had just arrived at the White House to deliver a draft response to Nikita Khrushchev's most recent letter. Hilsman raced to the Oval Office.

President John F. Kennedy had just completed a light swim in the White House pool and was in his living quarters when the phone rang at 1:45 p.m. McNamara was on the other end of the line and alerted Kennedy to the Maultsby situation. Hilsman then knocked on the door and, after being let in, delivered the same message. He expected Kennedy to erupt in anger. Instead, the president gave a weary and sarcastic laugh, saying, "Some son-of-a-bitch never gets the word."[3] He had issued clear orders for all the military to be extra careful and make no moves that Moscow could view as provocative unless the orders came directly from the president.

Maybe the president didn't lose his temper because a couple days earlier another incident could have complicated the crisis. JFK's mother, Rose Kennedy, had written to Khrushchev to ask him to autograph some of his books and send them to her. When the president found out, he called his mother and demanded, "What in the world are you doing?!" Mrs. Kennedy answered that she was performing her customary Christmas shopping whereby she would give her children books signed by heads of state, and this year it was the Soviet premier's turn. JFK responded, "The Russians won't assume this is innocent. They'll give it some interpretation. Now I have to get my CIA people speculating on what the interpretation might be! The strengths, the weaknesses, the contingencies!"[4]

MCNAMARA AND THE Joint Chiefs got more bad news later that afternoon: the Soviet ship *Grozny* was still steaming toward the blockade and showed no signs of slowing down. From McNamara's perspective it looked like things were spinning out of control. There was more bad news to come.

CHUCK MAULTSBY, STILL lost somewhere near the Soviet border, continued gliding rather than using his engine. His activated pressure suit was uncomfortable, but now he felt an additional distress—this one from his bladder. He couldn't unzip his pressure suit without boiling his own blood. He would simply have to hold it or relieve himself inside the suit. About this time he started to see a faint red glow in the distance: the sun was coming up ahead of him. His first bit of good fortune—he knew he was heading east, away from the Soviet Union.

The altitude of the U–2 was steadily dropping, and when it reached 25,000 feet, Chuck pondered a new problem: clouds. They would obstruct his view, and he'd soon be low enough that he could slam into a mountain. He made another snap decision: he'd eject shortly after descending lower than 20,000 feet if he couldn't see what was ahead of him. He hoped that if and when the time came to bail out, he'd have emerged from Soviet airspace and might have a slim chance of survival. Beneath his seat was a survival pack containing flares, a compass, matches, chemicals (for starting a fire with damp wood), extra clothes, a first aid kit, water, and food. The pack also contained a single-shot short-barreled rifle: a Henry AR-7 that was collapsible, impact-resistant, water-resistant, and, most importantly for a U–2 survival pack, lightweight at 3.5 pounds. However, the rifle was small caliber, and while it might bag Chuck a seagull, it wasn't going to stop a polar bear, and it was no match for Soviet military weapons. The survival pack did not contain a cyanide pill or the poison needle. Both had been phased out for U–2 pilots after the Gary Powers incident.

When he descended below 25,000 feet, his suit started deflating, and he felt gratitude for small favors. The clouds broke and it was light enough to see the snow-covered terrain below, but there were no landmarks to steer by, just endless frozen tundra. He thought that if he had to bail out here, he stood little chance of being found before he froze to death.

Suddenly the sight of two fighter jets jolted Maultsby out of contemplation about parachuting into the frozen wasteland. The US Air Force F-102s had come up behind him, each on a different side of his aircraft, flying right off his wing. (The MiGs must have peeled off when Maultsby left Soviet airspace, frustrated that they could not climb the additional 15,000 feet to take out the spy plane.)

Finally found by friendly aircraft and now presumably over US airspace, Chuck still had a big problem. Where could he land? His plane was slowly going down.

He turned on his battery power and, using the emergency channel on his radio, called out to the pilots flying alongside him. One of the fighter jet pilots answered, "Welcome home. We've been following you for the past fifteen minutes."

To stay with Chuck, the F-102s had to cut back on their airspeed to a level so slow they risked stalling out. One of the pilots explained to Maultsby that they had passed a tiny airfield about twenty miles back.

Chuck responded that he'd make a left turn and that the pilot on that side should move out of the way. The fighter pilot did so and said, "I'll look for that airstrip." He didn't tell Maultsby the strip was simply packed gravel, but even so, it was vastly better than the ice chunks and frozen humps covering the tundra.

The jet led Chuck to the airstrip. The U-2 was now just below 15,000 feet and gliding at 160 knots. He scanned the earth below and could make out a few shacks and a radar station but no airstrip.

Fortunately, via his radio, he was able to contact the radar station. The radar operator explained that the runway paralleled the patch of land bordering the sea.

The U-2 had now glided down to 12,000 feet, and Maultsby banked the plane so that it circled above the tiny airstrip. Then he asked the radar operator where the south threshold of the landing strip was, knowing he'd need all the space possible. The man replied that he would go outside and park a truck on it. Chuck tried to tell him to park fifty feet off to the side, not on the runway, but the man had already left the building and was moving the truck. He then saw the man park, jump out, and wave his arms. The U-2 pilot felt like screaming, "Good . . . now I see where the threshold is, now move the damn truck!"

When he dipped below 10,000 feet, Maultsby restarted the aircraft's lone engine, the Pratt and Whitney J-57, which allowed him to lower the landing gear. Now he needed to know wind direction, but there was no wind sock, and the man on the ground was still in the truck with no radio. He simply had to hope there was no significant crosswind.

At 5,000 feet, Maultsby put potential buffeting by crosswinds and the possibility of hitting the truck at the beginning of the tiny strip out of his mind. He had no control over these factors, and he had to focus all his attention on making the best landing of his life. He'd made it this far—he had evaded Soviet fighter planes over enemy territory and managed to stay in the air despite major fuel problems—and now his freedom and survival were finally in sight.

When he descended below 1,000 feet, he started a gentle left turn out to sea and continued to align himself with the narrow airstrip. The accompanying F-102 pilot became nervous that Chuck was going so slow he was about to crash and shouted, "Bail out! Bail out!"

There was no time to explain to the fighter pilot how unusual the U-2 was, so Maultsby, nervous but now in complete control, simply snapped, "Hush," over the radio.

Even after lowering the aircraft's flaps, he was coming in too fast and made an instinctive decision. He shut the engine down. He would try to land "deadstick."

Now he was coming up on the truck but still going much too rapidly. He had to do something, or he could be killed on impact. Just fifteen feet above the truck, Chuck decided he had little choice but to activate his drag chute while furiously manipulating the rudder back and forth—anything to slow the plane. If not, he would career right off the end of the short runway, and the lightweight aircraft might flip or break apart.

He barely felt the wheels touch down as they gathered snow in front of them. Whether the snow helped or not, Chuck nailed his landing and later said it was his best touchdown ever. After rolling just two hundred feet, the aircraft came to a stop.

Maultsby sat stock-still, letting his heart rate return to normal as he stared straight ahead into the white void. Waves of weariness washed over him. Then a knock on the outside of the aircraft prompted Chuck to unfasten his seat belt and shoulder harness, open the canopy, and remove his faceplate. He sucked in bitter-cold air, but it was fresh—fresh Alaskan, not Russian, air.

Smiling in at him was a large bearded man who said, "Welcome to Kotzebue."[5] Maultsby responded, "You don't know how glad I am to be here!"

Chuck tried to climb out of the aircraft, but his legs wouldn't move—numb from sitting for an astounding ten hours and twenty-five minutes while airborne, the longest flight ever made by a pilot in a U-2. The bearded giant, whom he called "Grizzly," placed his hands under Chuck's armpits, hoisted him out of his seat, and helped him down to the frozen ground.

Above him, the two F-102s buzzed low, rocking their wings before departing toward the east. Maultsby knew that if they hadn't pointed him to the airfield, he probably wouldn't be alive.

By now a small crowd had gathered around the weary U-2 pilot. The group comprised of Eskimos who lived in the shacks by the airfield and personnel from the radar station. Grizzly helped the pilot take off his helmet, and before anyone could start asking questions, Chuck struggled to his feet and shuffled to the other side of the aircraft, where he finally relieved his bladder.

About twenty people were now waiting for Maultsby to finish so they could learn what had happened, but an urgent message came over the radio of Grizzly's truck saying that a C-54 needed to make an emergency landing on this very airstrip. The bearded man quickly took a rope out of his truck, tied it around the tail of the U-2, and towed it off the landing strip, just in time for the C-54 to come barreling down the runway. It turned out to be the very rescue plane and Duck Butt crew that had tried so valiantly to stay with the lost U-2 and direct Chuck back to the United States.

Grizzly drove Maultsby over to the C-54 so the pilot could thank the rescue team. However, the reunion was short-lived. Over the radio came an order for Chuck to call the commander of Eielson Air Force Base immediately. From a secure phone in the radar building, Chuck briefly told the commander what had happened, then asked if anyone had told Jeanne, his wife, that he had been overdue and lost. Maultsby learned that no one had, and he was relieved that she was spared the worry. Then the commander informed Chuck that while his wife might have been oblivious to his predicament, SAC and the White House were not. It was not hard for him to guess how they must have been feeling.

The commander ended the call by saying he was flying to the radar station in a C-47. He explained that he was bringing extra fuel so that he could fly the U-2 back to Eielson, and Chuck should plan on returning to Eielson with the crew of the C-47.

While Maultsby waited at the radar station, the radar commander showed him his flight path on a huge plotting screen. He had traced the entire flight on the map. Chuck wondered why, if the radar had clearly tracked his directional mistake, someone hadn't radioed him immediately and got him back on the correct path. But then his attention shifted to six small "curly Q" marks on the map. They appeared during the portion of his flight when he abruptly changed direction after hearing the Russian radio station. "What are those?" Chuck asked.

"Those little curly Q's," said the radar commander, "represent the six MiGs that were nipping up trying to shoot you down."

Maultsby realized just how close he had come to being blown to pieces. Had his fuel petered out earlier, he would have started the slow descent over Russian airspace, and the MiGs would have had an easy target.

The U-2 pilot felt his legs go weak and stumbled over to a chair. The radar commander followed him and said he knew Chuck was wondering why no one had radioed him when his flight was on the wrong path. "There is a good reason," said the commander, "why we couldn't help you. I can't tell you, but maybe the higher-ups will."

When Khrushchev learned that a US aircraft had entered Soviet airspace, he wondered, quite logically, what the hell was going on. Why would the United States, at the height of the crisis, send a spy plane over Soviet airspace? In a cable to President Kennedy, he asked, "How should we regard this? What is this: a provocation? One of your planes violates our frontier during this anxious time we are both experiencing, when everything has been put into combat readiness. Is it not a fact than an intruding American plane could easily be taken for a nuclear bomber, which might put us to a fateful step and all the more so since the U.S. Government and Pentagon long ago declared that you are maintaining a continuous nuclear bomber patrol?"[6]

CHAPTER THIRTY-FOUR

Target 33

OVER THE TOWN of Camagüey, Cuba, Rudy Anderson made a slight adjustment, altering course a bit more toward the southeast until he reached Manzanillo, where he made a hard turn to the east. He flew over the town of Guantánamo, just north of the US naval base there, his cameras recording Soviet military on the ground. This was an especially sensitive area as it housed the troops and weapons to attack the US naval base if the Americans launched the invasion. Among the weapons were tactical nuclear missiles that could reach the US troops at Guantánamo.

Once past Guantánamo, Anderson made a slight adjustment to the east-northeast and continued to Jamal (just south of Baracoa). He was now close to the easternmost tip of Cuba. Over Jamal he made a wide U-turn (now heading west-northwest). Anderson had covered approximately 70 percent of his prearranged miles over Cuba. While he could be thankful that he was now flying in the direction of home, he would also be hyperalert because he was in the region where Jerry McIlmoyle reported the near miss by two surface-to-air missiles (SAMs). Clouds were building below Rudy, but not enough to make him abort the rest of his mission.

GENERALS LEONID GARBUZ and Stepan Grechko agreed they had the authority to decide whether to fire the SAMs. They felt an invasion was imminent, and the reports of large numbers of Crusaders buzzing the island, with the Cubans responding with antiaircraft fire only, added to their apprehension. They were in communication with Colonel Grigory Danilevich at a command outpost in Camagüey, which also had target 33 on its radar screen. The two generals wanted to be sure the Camagüey men were tracking the same target on their monitor. Danilevich later said the anxiety was enormous, as was the uncertainty of action: "It [authorization for use of SAMs] was not a clear one. Where there is such great tension between two superpowers, why should there also not be confusion at the Division level?"[1]

The generals had watched target 33 come down from the north, turn toward the east, and now make yet another turn that would take the spy plane over additional military installations before heading to safety over the ocean. The spy plane appeared as a light dot on a huge screen, five meters high by ten meters wide, called a firing chart.[2] The dot moved across the screen, and the two generals worried the plane would escape back to the United States with its intelligence. The men made another call to General Issa Pliyev, but again he could not be located.[3]

If the two lower-ranking generals were to act, they must do so immediately. Time was running out. The men felt Pliyev would agree with them; the general had repeatedly asked Moscow for permission to shoot down spy planes but had not received the go-ahead. This time Garbuz and Grechko believed invasion was imminent, and they had the authority. Grechko announced, "Well, let's take responsibility ourselves."[4]

They gave the order to destroy target 33.

AT THE SOVIET air defense installation at Banes, the on-site officers received their instructions and readied their surface-to-air missiles. They had been training for this moment since the day they began assembling the SAMs in a secret spot beyond the prying eyes of the civilians of Banes. Now, thirteen days since the Americans had discovered them, they would have the chance to shoot down one of these spy planes flying at the edge of space. They had failed in their first attempt two days earlier, with the near miss of McIlmoyle, and this time they planned on getting it right. On a radar screen inside a van, they watched target 33 approach.[5]

At approximately the same time the Russians were painting Anderson's flight path, the Cubans were continuing to fire on the Crusaders. Antiaircraft artillerymen were spraying the sky with flak, hoping to send at least one of the invading aircraft cartwheeling to Earth.

NEAR MAYARI, ANDERSON made a slight turn to the north-northeast for one last group of photos over the Banes area. Knowing he would be heading for his home base in a matter of moments, he might have let his thoughts briefly turn to his family. His wife, Jane, had been in the dark as to his latest deployment to McCoy, but after John F. Kennedy's TV speech, she knew Rudy was making daring overflights of Cuba. Being the wife of a U-2 pilot was stressful in a number of ways, but earlier that year Jane had experienced being falsely informed of her husband's death when the air force bungled the next-of-kin notification. Every mission Rudy flew after that snafu was just a little harder for Jane to endure. And his thoughts might have turned to his young boys, Tripp and James, and the hope that, now that the crisis was public, they might soon be able to visit him at McCoy with Jane. They were the major reason he volunteered for as many missions as possible. He was keeping them safe, keeping them free.

Rudy Anderson had risked it all on six different flights over Cuba. He was proud of his and his fellow U-2 pilots' contribution to keeping the United States safe from nuclear attack.

THE RUSSIANS AT the Banes SAM site had their missiles trained on target 33. They were ready to fire, worried that if the orders did not come soon, the spy plane would "be out of the hitting zone."[6] Then over the radio came the command: "Target 33 is to be destroyed."

Two missiles were launched, at least one of them by Lieutenant Alexy Raypenko, a member of the Soviet Antiaircraft Rocket Unit.[7] He later said, "A task is a task, and you have to do it well. I just happened to be at the end of the chain."[8]

AT 11:19 A.M. eastern standard time Rudy Anderson must have felt a terrible jolt, much the same way Gary Powers had.

One of the two SAMs exploded close to Rudy's aircraft, but it was not a direct hit, which would have blown the plane into a hundred pieces. Instead, shrapnel from the SAM killed the Dragon Lady—and Rudy. We will never know for sure what happened in his final seconds. Did his plane's missile-detection device turn red? Did he have time to make a series of turns to try to elude the oncoming missile? Did he feel the thump of shrapnel hitting the plane and see the orange glow of the bursting SAM, as Gary Powers had, or did he black out as the second shrapnel came through the plane and into his body?

When small pieces of shrapnel pierced the upper part of his flight suit, decompression would have followed. He might have remained conscious for a few seconds until he passed out from loss of oxygen or as his blood boiled as the pressure suit deflated. If he was conscious for a few seconds, he apparently had no time or was simply unable to activate the destruct switch and then eject from the aircraft. If he did have three or four seconds before blacking out, Anderson probably struggled to control the crippled plane, and the last thing he saw before dying was likely blue sky spinning above him.

The plane started to plunge, not stopping until crashing just outside the village of Veguitas, near Banes. Rudy had been just thirty kilometers from reaching international waters and safety.

WHEN THE STRICKEN plane hit the ground, both villagers and military personnel ran to the crash site. They found the smoldering ruins of the strange-looking aircraft, and inside the cockpit, still strapped to his seat, was the pilot Rudy Anderson. Dead.

At some point in the plane's spinning descent, its tail and wings were torn off. But considering that Anderson's flimsy U-2 fell to Earth from thirteen miles up, it is odd that the plane's body was mostly intact after impact. In fact, the fuselage was barely crumpled, the words "US Air Force" still clearly legible on its side.[9] It looked more like a plane after a crash landing than after an out-of-control free fall. But because of the U-2's configuration and light weight, it usually did not plunge to Earth when shot but came spinning down slowly, like a leaf falling from a tree.

Word spread from the crash site that an American plane had been brought down, and soon Cuban radio was "boasting of a great victory over the Yankee Imperialists."[10]

BACK IN THE United States, Strategic Air Command knew almost immediately that something was amiss with Rudy's mission. SAC technicians could monitor the flight paths of their U-2s mile by mile, and when Anderson's flight dropped from the screen, and Rudy didn't send the secret radio signal that all U-2 pilots routinely transmitted when leaving Cuban airspace, they most definitely knew that an accident or missile strike had forced the U-2 down.

STEVE HEYSER AND Jerry McIlmoyle didn't need a tracking system to alert them that something terrible had happened. The two pilots had just finished playing a round of golf with fellow airman Buddy Brown and were sitting in the clubhouse. They could always tell when a U-2 was landing by the unique whine it made, and now, in the early afternoon, when Rudy was scheduled to return, that sound was missing. Minutes went by, and the men knew for sure their friend and fellow pilot was overdue. They left the clubhouse in silence and soon found operations officer Tony Martinez, who confirmed Anderson was overdue but had no additional information.

Jerry's mind started racing through scenarios. If forced to make an emergency landing, Rudy would have announced it over the radio and ditched into the ocean, where other aircraft or navy ships would find him. And if he had ejected over Cuba, the beacon in his seat pack would have activated, and SAC would know exactly where he was.

There had been no Mayday and no beacon signal, and Jerry had to face the reality of what he feared from the moment Rudy was overdue. SAMs, just like the two that had almost killed him two days earlier, had found their mark this time.

Jerry couldn't help but wonder about the photos he had shot of the exploding SAMs behind his plane. Why did the SAC commanders say there was nothing on the film when Jerry was certain he had captured the starbursts? If the true results of Jerry's images had been made known, would Rudy have flown? Would this Saturday flight have even been scheduled?

Jerry would never know, nor did he speculate. Two plausible reasons for quashing Jerry's report and film evidence, however, had nothing to do with pilot safety. Perhaps SAC and the Pentagon feared that if they shared them, President Kennedy or the secretary of defense would ground the U-2s at this most crucial juncture. SAC might logically have determined that the U-2 missions took priority over the pilots' lives—particularly because the massive air strikes were tentatively scheduled for Monday and the spy planes gathered intelligence about where to focus them. Or, perhaps SAC commander Curtis LeMay wanted the Soviets to take down one of his planes to open the door for retaliatory strikes and possibly a full air attack on all of Cuba. No hard evidence supports this theory, but LeMay's call for military action and frustration over the lack of it are well documented. And the question of why McIlmoyle's brush with the SAMs was hushed up has never been answered.

RECONNAISSANCE PLANES PATROLLING just off the island's shore reported that they did not spot Major Anderson's U-2 on their radar, nor did they see it crash. They searched the ocean but found no debris. Pilots in Crusaders risked their own lives flying directly over Banes in hopes of finding the downed aircraft. Some hoped that Anderson might have bailed out and was hiding in the jungle, ready to shoot off a flare if friendly aircraft appeared. These pilots located neither the pilot nor the wreckage. SAC labeled Rudy missing in action, but almost no one held out hope that he had somehow parachuted safely to the ground. Robert McNamara was informed but for some unknown reason held off telling the president, perhaps hoping for a miracle.

General LeMay immediately ordered his F-100 fighter jet pilots at Homestead Air Force Base to be briefed and prepare for attack flights to Cuba. They carried air-to-surface rockets, called Zunis, which would obliterate the SAM sites, killing both Soviet and Cuban defenders.[11] Launch awaited only the president's final approval.

CHAPTER THIRTY-FIVE

Kennedy and Khrushchev on the Brink

ON LEARNING OF the shoot-down Moscow immediately responded to the Soviet command in Cuba: "You were hasty. Ways of the settlement have been outlined."[1] In one key respect Nikita Khrushchev was no different from John F. Kennedy: from the start of the crisis both feared that a single incident might cause them to lose their grip on the situation. In an interview, Sergei Khrushchev, son of the premier, emphasized a similar view that his father worried something unexpected could lead to disaster. "Once a first shot is fired the two leaders [Kennedy and Khrushchev] lose control and different people, with different logic, take over."[2]

Premier Khrushchev now realized this very thing was starting to happen and that he and Kennedy had to come to an agreement. And that agreement could not wait for a day or two—at the very brink of nuclear war, if there was not an agreement in hours, the chances for a peaceful resolution would in all likelihood be gone. Sergei Khrushchev later wrote that the death of Rudy Anderson jolted his father into thinking the whole conflict could now explode. "It was at that very moment—not before or after—that father felt the situation was slipping out of his control."[3]

AT THE WHITE House, JFK was in the midst of the most stressful day of his presidency and even his life. And it was only early afternoon. He may have allowed his mind to wander briefly back to the desperate moments of his past—the loss of his brother Joe and his beloved sister Kathleen (or "Kick," as the family called her). He might have thought about his many brushes with death on the operating table and in the dark waters of the South Pacific. The images of lost seamen Harold Marney and Andrew Jackson Kirksey may have flashed before his eyes. President Kennedy was no stranger to death, which is why he had fought so hard to preserve life. He understood that the decisions he made in the next few minutes and hours would decide the course of human history. Would anyone be alive to record them?

Discussion of the new proposal/letter from Khrushchev to Kennedy, which added the additional demand that the United States remove its missiles from Turkey, dominated the morning ExComm meeting. That upsetting news was exacerbated when the president next learned of Chuck Maultsby's foray into enemy airspace, followed by the CIA summary of the situation in Cuba. The CIA update painted a bleak picture: "Detailed analysis of October 25 low-altitude photography confirms rapid pace of construction on the MRBM and IRBM sites. San Cristobal MRBM Sites 1, 2 and 3 and Sagua La Grande Sites 1 and 2 are considered fully operational."[4]

The president was now almost out of time to take action. Way back when he first learned about the missiles, he had asked when they would be operational and ready to fire and calculated that he would have to remove them before that time. Now the time had come. Yet the most recent letters from Khrushchev held out some hope of a settlement, and he extended his own self-prescribed deadline for attacking the missiles. The Joint Chiefs felt differently. They crafted a written recommendation to the president that he order massive air strikes on either Sunday, October 28, or at the latest Monday, October 29. President Kennedy held his ground and did not give the final approval. But the 4 p.m. ExComm meeting would throw a new emergency at him, one that would again call for a decision that could result in war.

The meeting started with a discussion of the firing on the Crusaders and possible scheduling of nighttime reconnaissance. At three different times in a two-minute period, the president said, "I think we better wait" with regard to the night flights. He was making his orders crystal clear—he didn't want anyone implementing a new tactic and later claiming he hadn't heard the president say, "Wait." One person going rogue could lead to disaster, and Kennedy wanted everyone on the same page, with clear instructions.

Across the world, inside his offices at the Kremlin, Nikita Khrushchev had similar fears. The night before, he asked his fellow Presidium members to join him for a night at the theater. There was a concert of Cuban musicians in Moscow, and Khrushchev thought a public outing would help dispel the growing worry and concern of the Russian people.

"Let's show both our own people and the entire world, that as far as we are concerned, the situation is still calm," Khrushchev told his advisors.[5]

Now, a few hours later, the situation was anything but calm. In fact, it was close to exploding. Khrushchev's generals urged him to hold fast—not to give in to the escalating situation or yield an inch to America's demands. The Soviet premier asked his military men if such a strategy would result in the deaths of 500 million human beings. The generals, according to Khrushchev, had little interest in discussing the apocalyptic body count. Instead, they worried that the Chinese or other Communist nations might accuse the Soviets of appeasement or weakness. "What good would it have done me in the last hour of my life to know that though our great nation and the United States were in complete ruin, the national honor of the Soviet Union was intact?"[6]

Back in Washington, the president and some members of Ex-Comm were discussing a potential compromise. Llewellyn Thompson, former ambassador to the Soviet Union, talked about the pitfalls of removing US missiles from Turkey in exchange for the Soviets doing the same in Cuba, but JFK was thinking two steps ahead.

THOMPSON—Mr. President, if we go on the basis of a trade, which I gather is somewhat in your mind, we end up it seems to me, with the Soviets still in Cuba with planes and technicians and so on, even though the missiles are out. And that would surely be unacceptable and put you in a worse position.

PRESIDENT KENNEDY—Yeah but our technicians and planes and guarantees would still exist for Turkey. I'm just

> thinking about what we're going to have to do in a day
> or so, which is 500 sorties, and 7 days, and possibly an
> invasion, all because we wouldn't take the missiles out of
> Turkey.
>
> We all know how quickly everybody's courage goes
> when the blood starts to flow, and that's what's going to
> happen to NATO. When we start these things and they
> grab Berlin, everybody's going to say: "Well, that was a
> pretty good proposition."

The president did not oppose removing the missiles from Turkey because he could move a Polaris-firing submarine into position off the Turkish coast to replace the land-based missiles. Importantly, President Kennedy used the word "blood" or "bloody" more than once during the meeting, trying to remind the group what the loss of life really meant. He had seen the blood flow firsthand in his PT-109 days, while some others in the group had never experienced the horrors of war up close and personal.

The meeting went on for a considerable period, with most every member offering an opinion and suggesting the response wording to Khrushchev's two proposals. Bobby Kennedy and Mac Bundy recommended only responding to the first proposal (that the Americans promise not to attack or invade Cuba and the Soviets remove the missiles) rather than the second proposal that also demanded the United States remove its missiles from Turkey. The president conceded that approach was worth a try but doubted it would work on its own. And he feared that if it didn't work, more time would have been wasted, and all the nuclear missiles in Cuba would be operational.

> PRESIDENT KENNEDY—The point of the matter is that
> Khrushchev is going to come back and refer to his thing
> this morning on Turkey. And then we're going to be
> screwing around for another 48 hours. I think we've got
> to make the key of this letter the cessation of work [on the
> missiles].

For this reason the president felt their response had to somehow include consideration of removing missiles from Turkey. At this point he was beginning to formulate his plan to extend a private offer to Khrushchev. He thought that without the private offer, Khrushchev would balk, and he would have to launch an attack on Cuba without having had the chance to make his very best proposal. He wanted to lead with a strong offer, and if the premier rejected it, he was not going to stand by for two more days "screwing around" while the work on the missiles was finalized. He wanted an answer by tomorrow, or he was going to attack.

A few minutes later the president drove the point home about work being halted on the missiles:

PRESIDENT KENNEDY—That's why we've got to end [the letter to Khrushchev] with saying, whatever we're going to do, that we've got to get a cessation of work.

BUNDY—That's right, Mr. President. But I think Bobby's notion of a concrete acceptance on our part of how we read last night's telegram [Khrushchev's first proposal] is very important.

A few moments later, General Maxwell Taylor broke into the discussion.

TAYLOR—Mr. President, the Chiefs have been in session during the afternoon on probably the same issues as we have over here. The recommendation they give is as follows: That the big [air] strike Oplan [Operation Plan] 312 be executed no later than Monday morning, the 29th unless there is irrefutable evidence in the meantime that offensive weapons are being dismantled and rendered inoperable. That the execution of the strike plan be followed by execution of 316, the invasion plan, 7 days later.

The words were no sooner out of Taylor's mouth than Bobby quipped, "Well, that was a surprise." There was weary laughter rather than an argument. The Kennedy's didn't always agree with Taylor's hawkish views, but they respected the man, and Taylor was always professional, unlike General LeMay.

Secretary of the Treasury C. Douglas Dillon backed up Taylor by reminding everyone that US low-level reconnaissance planes had taken antiaircraft fire.

> DILLON—Well, also, we're getting shot at as we go in for our surveillance. The Cubans are not just talking about it.

A minute later Robert McNamara asked if they were going to stop low-level surveillance flights because of "intense ground fire."

Taylor jumped in and said, "I wouldn't worry. I wouldn't pay any attention."

Then, seconds later, Taylor drove the point home again: "And we must not fail on surveillance. We can't give up 24 hours at this stage."

Whether reading the transcripts or listening to the tapes, one can't help but wonder if Taylor hadn't ordered that Jerry McIlmoyle's close call with two SAMs remain a secret. He might have felt that nothing should interrupt the intelligence gathering, based on which targets would be selected for the massive air strikes he advocated initiating within the next forty-eight hours.

Incredibly, neither McNamara nor Taylor had yet mentioned that a SAM had most likely shot down Major Rudy Anderson's U-2. The meeting droned on for several more minutes until that tragedy—a potential game changer—was announced.

> McNAMARA—I think the rush is what we do. A U-2 was shot down. They fired against our low altitude surveillance.

Bobby was stunned. He and the president were hearing this for the first time, whereas the Pentagon had found out several hours earlier.

> ROBERT KENNEDY—A U-2 was shot down?
> McNAMARA—Yes. [unclear] said it got shot down.
> ROBERT KENNEDY—Was the pilot killed?
> TAYLOR—It was shot down over Banes, which is right near a SAM-2 site in eastern Cuba. [unclear] saying the pilot's body is in the plane. Apparently this was a SAM site that actually had the Fruitcake radar [missile guidance radar]. It all ties in a very plausible way.

The president's response to this news was somewhat subdued.

PRESIDENT KENNEDY—Well now, this is much of an escalation by them isn't it?

Paul Nitze, assistant secretary of defense, said stridently, "They
fired the first shot!"

McNamara suggested continuing surveillance but firing back if
the other side shot first. But the president brought the discussion back
to the downed U-2, wondering why Moscow would shoot one down
at this particular time, especially with the Soviets offering to make a
deal.

The president, as poised as he'd been for almost two full weeks,
struggled to grasp this new information.

General Taylor took the opportunity to remind everyone that Ex-
Comm had agreed, just a couple days earlier, to respond to a U-2
shoot-down by eliminating the SAM site that fired on it.

TAYLOR—They [the Soviets] feel they must respond now. The
   whole world knows where we're flying. That raises the
   question of retaliation against the SAM sites. We think
   we—we have various other reasons to believe that we
   know the SAM sites [that fired on Anderson]. Two days
   ago—

Taylor never completed this last sentence. We can't help but wonder if he knew about the firing on McIlmoyle and was about to mention it. We will never know for sure.

PRESIDENT KENNEDY—How can we send a U-2 fellow over
   there tomorrow unless we take out all the SAM sites?
TAYLOR—This is exactly the effect.
McNAMARA—I don't think we can.
UNIDENTIFIED—It's on the ground?
TAYLOR—It's on the ground. The wreckage is on the ground
   and the pilot's dead.

As the group discussed their options, McNamara grew more and
more hawkish and proposed taking out several SAM sites using the

low-altitude flights while continuing the Crusader surveillance missions but grounding the U-2s. Backing up this call for action, Taylor chimed in, "They started the shooting."

Was the intel reporting solid? Had the shooting been a deliberate escalation? Were the Cubans involved or just the Soviets? Uncertainty reigned. It seemed the Soviet Union was prepared to go to war. The ExComm members had no way of knowing that the Russians on the ground in Cuba had fired the SAM without consulting their superiors in Moscow, and once again the incident was leading exactly to the outcome Kennedy had warned about: miscalculations, incorrect interpretations, and breakdowns in command and control that could lead to war. Bobby Kennedy later explained the despair and tension that filled the Cabinet Room that afternoon. "There was the feeling that the noose was tightening on all of us, on Americans, on mankind, and that the bridges to escape were crumbling."[7]

The more hawkish members were obviously looking for the president to authorize some type of retaliatory strike, but instead Kennedy held his cards close and did not give the go-ahead. In effect, the president reversed his earlier stance and deliberately held back on unleashing the might of the US Air Force. At perhaps the most critical moment in the crisis, Kennedy refused to succumb to pressure. Instead he would use every last minute to avoid more bloodshed and keep his options open.

WORD OF JFK's reversal reached General LeMay at the Pentagon. His air force fighter jets were fueled and ready to launch in retaliation for Rudy Anderson's death. Upon learning the president's decision, he immediately turned to an aide and said in disgust, "He's chickened out again. How in the hell do you get men to risk their lives when the SAMs are not attacked!"[8]

Instead the Pentagon issued a statement that a reconnaissance plane was missing and presumed lost over Cuba and that a search by air and sea was under way. They did not specify that the missing plane was a U-2, nor did they mention retaliation.[9]

THE TAPES AND transcripts of the ExComm meeting on October 27 (which would become known as "Black Saturday") clearly reveal that the group members were exhausted, oftentimes speaking over or snapping at each other. The exchanges included a healthy dose of confusion and frustration. A wide range of human emotions was on display. ExComm members even speculated that maybe Anderson wasn't shot down but instead had a mechanical failure. To this point, Treasury Secretary Dillon sarcastically responded, "If the plane is on the ground there, it was shot down. It didn't just come down and land."

President Kennedy left the room during the latter half of the meeting, but the tape recorder continued to run. With the president gone, Vice President Lyndon Johnson became more vocal. He voiced strong disagreement with nighttime reconnaissance flights.

> JOHNSON—I've been afraid of these damned flares ever since they mentioned them. Just an ordinary plane going in there at 2 or 300 feet without arms or an announcement. There was four of them [Crusaders in the morning] that had to turn back because of fire. Imagine some crazy Russian captain doing it. The damn thing [the flare] goes blooey and lights up the skies. He might just pull a trigger.

While McNamara then talked about the likelihood of reconnaissance flights being fired on the next day and US air strikes in response, followed "almost certainly [by] an invasion," Johnson seemed to back up President Kennedy's thoughts about a deal. "If you're willing to give up your missiles in Turkey why don't you . . . make the trade there and save all the invasion, lives and everything else?"

The group was split about removing the missiles from Turkey. Some felt they might be able to arrange a deal with Khrushchev without committing to such a withdrawal (in keeping with Khrushchev's Friday letter), while others, including the president, determined that addressing the Saturday letter (demanding removal of the Turkish missiles) was the key to a peaceful resolution. The conflicting letters had all members of the group wondering just who was in charge in Moscow. Their differing tone and even style led to speculation that the military had overthrown Khrushchev and taken over.

The president ultimately found a compromise between the two opinions (although he did not announce this specifically to the ExComm group). He would publicly answer in the affirmative

Khrushchev's Friday letter proposing to remove the Cuban missiles in exchange for a pledge from the United States not to invade or threaten Fidel Castro. But because President Kennedy felt the Kremlin would reject this solution (and that he could not afford to defer military action much longer with work on the missile sites going on around the clock), he would make a private promise to Khrushchev that he would guarantee the eventual dismantling of the missiles in Turkey, perhaps months from then. He would also insist that Moscow keep this verbal assurance secret to give him time to work it out with the Turkish government and the North Atlantic Treaty Organization. This also helped the president on the political front: keeping Turkey out of the public arrangement would lead the American voters to believe he had secured a better deal with Moscow and a clear win for the president.

WHILE THE EXCOMM meeting continued, the president and Bobby Kennedy managed a private discussion, apparently in the Oval Office. The president approved the letter to Khrushchev crafted by Bobby and speechwriter Ted Sorensen agreeing to promise no invasion of Cuba in exchange for removal of the Soviet missiles, with no promise regarding Turkey. The president instructed Bobby to meet with Soviet ambassador Anatoly Dobrynin that evening and privately convey US willingness to eventually remove the missiles in Turkey as well as the need to reach an agreement within hours, or the president might take military action.

The brothers discussed the death of Major Anderson, and the president commented on how it's "always the brave and the best who die."[10] JFK had seen this firsthand in the Solomon Islands years before. He went on to say that while politicians and officials pontificate and dine with their wives and families, young men on the front lines perish. And once again, JFK mentioned how war was rarely intentional but rather the result of miscalculations and that neither the Americans nor the Soviets wanted a conflict that would "accomplish nothing [and would] engulf and destroy all mankind."[11]

When the president and Bobby returned to ExComm at 7:20 p.m., the marathon meeting was still going strong, albeit disjointedly. President Kennedy still had not authorized retaliation for Anderson's death, and Treasury Secretary Dillon, angered that the Soviets were getting the upper hand, pressured him for action.

> DILLON—It would probably be more effective, and make
> more impression on him [Khrushchev] if we did do what
> we said we were going to do before, and just go in and
> knock out just one SAM site.

The president showed his exhaustion by asking a question posed and answered earlier.

> PRESIDENT KENNEDY—But we don't know where it [the U-2]
> was shot down yet, do we?

Four seconds of tape are excised as classified, but Kennedy was clearly given the location of the wreckage again. Then the president wondered if they could be certain that Anderson hadn't crashed due to mechanical failure. An unidentified voice said, "Havana has announced it, that he was shot down by anti-aircraft fire."

A tired Kennedy replied, "Oh they have, I didn't know that."

Still, the president refused to authorize a morning strike. Just a couple minutes later, he explained why he worried about escalating the crisis just now.

> PRESIDENT KENNEDY—We can't very well invade Cuba with
> all the toil and blood it's going to be, when we could have
> gotten them [the Soviet missiles] out by making a deal
> on the same missiles in Turkey. If that's part of the record
> then I don't see how we'll have a very good war.

The president then suggested the group "meet at 9 pm and everybody can get a bite to eat, and then come back and see whether we send this message."

Next, President Kennedy asked a few of the members to stay behind and join him in the Oval Office. There, he explained that Bobby had set up a secret meeting with Dobrynin, and the group deliberated one last time on exactly what the attorney general should say to the ambassador. Bundy, one of those attending this informal meeting, later said they agreed that the message should be simple: "No Soviet missiles in Cuba, and no U.S. invasion." Otherwise American military action was unavoidable. Dean Rusk proposed the exact wording for the other part of the oral message: "We should tell Khrushchev that while there could be no deal over the Turkish missiles, the President was determined to get them out and would do so once the Cuban crisis was resolved."[12]

Bobby then left for his meeting with the Soviet ambassador, which would take place in the attorney general's office at the Justice Department. The small group gathered in the president's office knew the thinly veiled ultimatum that Bobby was to deliver would be the president's last offer. If Khrushchev didn't accept it, the bombs would likely start falling within the next day or two.

CHAPTER THIRTY-SIX

Two Secret Meetings

CHUCK MAULTSBY SAT at the tiny radar station in Alaska totally exhausted from his ten-hour-and-twenty-five-minute odyssey over the Arctic and part of the Soviet Union. He was glad to board a C-47 for the flight back to Eielson Air Force Base, where he looked forward to some much-needed rest. Instead, when he finally arrived at Eielson, he got two pieces of bad news. The first was that he had thirty minutes to pack all his gear, because another plane was waiting to fly him out of Alaska and all the way to Omaha, Nebraska. He was being summoned to Strategic Air Command headquarters by SAC commander General Thomas Power. The next surprise was even worse. He learned that his friend and neighbor back at Laughlin Air Force Base, Rudy Anderson, had been shot down over Cuba and was most likely dead. "That bad news," wrote Maultsby, "really knocked the wind out of my sails."

Chuck had been through a terrifying ordeal, but he had survived. He would be going home to Jeanne and his boys. He could not imagine the pain that Rudy's family would endure.

Maultsby, now depressed, was the only passenger on the massive jet-powered KC-135 aerial refueling aircraft that launched for the long flight back to the lower forty-eight. This only added to his dread at meeting with General Power.

When the jet finally touched down at Offutt, Chuck was driven straight to the underground SAC command post and escorted into a meeting room. An easel holding an aeronautical chart of his flight stood at the front of the room. Within minutes General Power arrived, followed by several other high-ranking SAC officers, all of whom looked "like they had slept in their uniforms for days. . . . [T]heir eyes were bloodshot and they hadn't seen a razor for at least 24 hours."[1]

"Captain Maultsby," said Power, "how about briefing us on your flight?"

Chuck walked up to the easel and began retracing his trip. When he reached the point where his U-2 was at the North Pole, Power said, "Captain Maultsby, do you know where you went after leaving the Pole?"

At that moment, according to Chuck, the other men in the room squirmed in their seats "as if they were sitting on tacks." The pilot then explained that he knew he had mistakenly flown into Russian airspace. He soon found out that he had been over the Soviet Union for more than three hundred miles.

Power then said, "Too bad you weren't configured with a system to gather electromagnetic radiation. The Russians probably had every radar and ICBM [intercontinental ballistic missile] site on maximum alert."

Power ordered Maultsby to not tell a soul about his flight, then left the room, followed by the others. A brigadier general, the last to leave, turned to Chuck and said, "You are a lucky sonofabitch. I've seen General Power chew up and spit out people for doing a hellova lot less."

Incredibly, Maultsby's marathon day of close calls wasn't over. He boarded a U-3A for a flight to Laughlin Air Force Base, where he could finally get some rest and see his wife. The U-3A, a twin-engine Cessna, six-seat utility aircraft, is quite reliable but on this night ran into icy conditions. Chuck listened to the pilot request an unscheduled landing at an airport near Enid, Oklahoma. Then conditions caused one of the engines to lose partial power, and the pilot, Captain Ed Perdue, declared an emergency. As they approached the airport, ground control screamed at them to level off. Chuck could only think, *What a way to go after all that's happened.* "I could see the ground now," he recalled, "and was certain we wouldn't make it to the runway that was barely visible through light fog. I swear Ed was trying to hold the airplane up by pulling on the yoke."

Once again, Maultsby somehow landed safely. When he finally made it to Laughlin, he staggered into his home, where his wife, Jeanne, was shocked to see him. After a big hug and kiss, she asked what had happened, and Chuck said he needed a shower and then would tell her. Later she asked, "Does all this have anything to do with Rudolf Anderson being shot down?"

He said that it did not and recounted what happened. Then, finally, Chuck could lie down and get some sleep.[2]

When later told by his colonel that President John F. Kennedy had called him a "son of a bitch" on learning about Chuck's ordeal, Maultsby bit his tongue. He wanted to say, "I wish that sonofabitch [Kennedy] had been sitting on my lap! If I'd gotten the word, like simply a steer [direction], I wouldn't be sitting here. Just one steer would have prevented all this commotion."

THE STRAIN ON President Kennedy must have been tremendous, particularly during his wait to hear about his brother's meeting with Ambassador Anatoly Dobrynin. The message was nothing less than an ultimatum, and should Nikita Khrushchev turn it down, JFK might find himself forced to take action that could escalate into a thermonuclear holocaust. "This is the week I earn my salary,"[3] the president quipped to one of his advisors. That was quite the understatement. Considering the pressure he was under and the magnitude of the decisions he had to make, we are all lucky that someone as levelheaded as John Fitzgerald Kennedy occupied the White House on October 27, 1962. A lesser person would surely have cracked under the strain; nuclear war might well have followed. Instead, the president displayed an equanimity and resolve that allowed him to think his way through the crisis. He constantly put himself in his adversary's shoes and gave Khrushchev time to reflect on where the crisis was heading and to relay messages to the Soviets in Cuba that a resolution was still possible.

It's chilling to think that just two men, Kennedy and Khrushchev, could decide the fates of so many. And even today, the fact that the nuclear "football"—a set of codes ensuring that the military knows an order to fire a nuclear missile is coming from the president rather than a maverick or an imposter—travels everywhere the president goes serves as a reminder of how much power rests in one person's hands and how important it is that this individual retain composure no matter what pressure and advice he or she is receiving.

During the Cuban Missile Crisis, Kennedy found safeguards of this kind woefully lacking and insisted on a more foolproof way for the military to know it was dealing with the president. The safeguards he desired are in the mechanics of today's nuclear football, but the ultimate authority over the decision still rests with one person, the commander in chief.

Both Kennedy and Khrushchev realized the crisis was *not* a chess match just between themselves. Each leader understood that other people might ignore or misinterpret instructions from the highest officeholder and launch a nuclear weapon themselves—much as when the two Soviet generals decided to fire on "target 33." And Maultsby's straying into Soviet airspace could easily have triggered another disaster, particularly when US fighter jets armed only with nuclear-tipped missiles flew out to safeguard the lost pilot. We can't know what would have happened if they had arrived when the MiGs were still hot on Chuck's tail.

Kennedy and Khrushchev instinctively knew that the longer the crisis went on, the shorter the odds that someone at a lower level would act without consulting them. Still, neither leader was going to walk away from his duty to safeguard his country and give the other side the upper hand militarily or in terms of world dominance and influence. They had to strike a deal in which both sides seemed to win.

Helping to keep the president on an even keel was Jackie Kennedy. During the crisis she made more frequent visits to the Oval Office, accompanied by children John and Caroline, knowing that the interaction would relieve some of the pressure. In *A Thousand Days*, special assistant to the president Arthur Schlesinger Jr. touched on both the stressfulness of the crisis and the importance of Kennedy's children. "He [the president] never had a more sober sense of his responsibility. It was a strange week: the flow of decisions was continuous: there was no day and no night. In the intervals between the meetings he sought out his wife and children as if the imminence of catastrophe had turned his mind more than ever to his family and, through them, to children everywhere in the world."[4]

The risk of nuclear war was so high that Edward McDermott, director of the Office of Emergency Planning, met with Chief Justice

Earl Warren to discuss evacuating the Supreme Court justices to the bunkers at Mount Weather in Virginia. And some cabinet members had their wives and children leave Washington that weekend. Dean Rusk wryly commented that if the government leaders, including the president and secretary of state, did "board a helicopter and whirl away to some cave" and somehow survived, "the first band of shivering survivors who got a hold of them would likely hang them from the nearest tree."[5] The president, like so many others, opted not to go to Mount Weather and instead told his staff—many of whom had been sleeping at the White House for several days—to go home for the night. Pierre Salinger remembers how when he left the White House, he received a sealed envelope for his wife. He was instructed to tell her that if he and the White House staff "disappeared" the next day, it meant that a military situation required they be taken to a secure place. Salinger explained, "She was to open the envelope which would tell her where to take her children and herself to be safe."[6]

The feeling of an approaching apocalypse cast a shadow over most of the government officials who knew the details of the situation. Dino Brugioni, a senior official at the CIA's National Photographic Interpretation Center, who analyzed reconnaissance pictures from the U-2s and Crusaders, wrote, "Seeing no earthly way out of this conflict except war and complete destruction, I told my wife on a phone call that she should take our two children, get in the car, and head for my parents' home in Jefferson City, Missouri."[7]

Even the Russians at the Soviet embassy felt the wave of war coming fast and started destroying all their sensitive documents. "Black Saturday," October 27, 1962, was unlike any day in history: millions of people around the globe sensed that with each tick of the clock, the end of the world came closer.

ROBERT KENNEDY DID meet with Dobrynin and explained the president's position as urgently as possible.

In previous meetings, the Soviet ambassador had found Bobby to be a complex man with a temper who seemed to enjoy arguing.[8] But on this night Dobrynin found him restrained, nonconfrontational, and "very upset."[9]

In a written account of the meeting, which Bobby chronicled just a few days afterward, he explained that he first told the ambassador that the president was well aware that work on the missile sites was continuing.[10] He then mentioned the deadly incident involving Rudy Anderson. "We had found that our planes flying over Cuba had been fired upon and that one of our U-2s had been shot down and the pilot killed. I said these men were flying unarmed planes. I told him that this was an extremely serious turn of events. We would have to make certain decisions within the next 12 or possibly 24 hours. There was very little time left." Bobby later stated that he told Dobrynin, "We had to have a commitment by tomorrow that those bases would be removed. This was not an ultimatum but just a statement of fact. He should understand that if they did not remove the bases, we would remove them."

Bobby also addressed the missiles in Turkey, telling Dobrynin that the North Atlantic Treaty Organization had to decide the issue, but "if some time elapsed I was sure these matters could be resolved satisfactorily." He closed the meeting by saying they would need agreement from Khrushchev by the next day, or "there would be drastic consequences."

Bobby left in a solemn mood and went straight back to the White House.

President Kennedy had just finished a swim and was having a light dinner with advisor and close friend Dave Powers when Bobby returned, looking glum. As the attorney general summarized the meeting, the president looked at Powers and said, "God, Dave, the way you're eating up all that chicken and drinking up all my wine anybody would think it was your last meal." Powers retorted, "The way Bobby's talking, I thought it *was* my last meal."[11]

The two brothers then walked to the Cabinet Room for the 9 p.m. ExComm meeting. Only the individuals who were in the Oval Office earlier (reviewing what the attorney general planned to say to Dobrynin) knew of Bobby's face-to-face conversation with the ambassador. The president decided not to tell the others.

In the early part of the meeting the members discussed the difficulty of low-level reconnaissance flights because of all the ground fire from 20mm flak. Maxwell Taylor explained that armed planes preceding the photographic planes would have slim "hope of cleaning out these little air guns. . . . But we're approaching the point, I think, Mr. President, where low-level reconnaissance will be entirely impossible."

Robert McNamara then inserted his view that Sunday's U-2 missions be scrubbed and a series of low-level Crusaders go over Cuba one last time. He added, "If our planes are fired on tomorrow, we ought to fire back."

The president responded, "I think we ought to wait till tomorrow afternoon, to see whether we get any answers if [UN Secretary-General] U Thant goes down there [Havana]."

President Kennedy added that if Crusaders launched on Sunday were fired upon, and Moscow had not responded to the latest US proposal, then on Monday "we go in and take all of the SAM sites out." President Kennedy, not wanting to just fire at the antiaircraft batteries, elaborated, "I don't think we do any good to begin sort of a *half*-do-it." Instead he wanted to put out a public statement to the effect that if US reconnaissance aircraft took fire on Sunday, the United States would consider "the island of Cuba open territory, and then [would] take out all the SAM sites."

Kennedy was now clearly ready to take what he considered his next step after the blockade if his diplomatic effort failed. And he was prepared to go all in, particularly when he agreed with McNamara to call up "24 air reserve squadrons [and] roughly 300 troop-carrier transports which are required for an invasion."

After almost two weeks of deliberation, the president had decided the time for talk had run out. The Russians' response on Sunday would determine whether war began on Monday.

CHAPTER THIRTY-SEVEN

Blast Them Now!

BLACK SATURDAY'S THREE marathon ExComm meetings covered every bit of bad news except one: the high-stakes game of cat and mouse involving Russian submarines and US destroyers. No one in Washington or Moscow had any idea how close the subs, and the ships that stalked them, were to taking the world into nuclear war.

The ExComm members didn't discuss in great detail the dire threat posed by Soviet submarines. When the topic finally did arise, the president's advisors shared incorrect information.[1] Undersecretary of State George Ball asked hypothetically how the United States might respond if the Soviets announced they "were going to deploy atomic missile-carrying submarines off the coast of the United States." Secretary of Defense Robert McNamara replied that Soviet subs had already been detected off the coast, but "as far as we know, they don't carry missiles."

McNamara could not have been more wrong. Four Soviet subs, sent on a mission to Cuba before the crisis started, were now approaching the quarantine line. In addition to twenty-one conventional torpedoes, each submarine carried one nuclear torpedo—with a fifteen-kiloton explosive yield, comparable to the atomic bomb dropped on Hiroshima, Japan, in World War II—that could obliterate a US aircraft carrier.[2]

When the United States first announced the quarantine around Cuba, the Department of Defense had tasked the navy with developing a means to force a submarine to the surface without damaging it. A recently declassified memo, dated October 23, 1962, stated, "Mr. Mc-Namara would like to have some means worked out by which a Soviet submerged submarine could be given a signal to surface. It is possible that the description of the signal would be sent to the Soviet Government so that they could transmit it to the Soviet submarine." McNamara's order to develop a signal was quickly implemented, but his second point about alerting the Soviet government as to what that signal would be never reached the commanders on the submarines. The US embassy conveyed the signal to the Soviet government, but it was not acknowledged and never relayed to the subs.[3] It was a potentially disastrous failure of communication.

Navy captain R. L. Johns outlined the signal selected by the navy in a memorandum dated October 24. "US Forces coming in contact with unidentified submerged submarines will make the following signals to inform the sub that he may surface in order to identify himself: Quarantine Forces will drop four or five harmless explosive sound signals which may be accompanied by the international coded signal 'IDKCA' meaning rise to the surface."

Chief of naval operations George Anderson was only too happy to show the Soviets who controlled the waters of the Caribbean. From the start he had advocated military action, and now he got his wish, albeit in a limited form. He thought the United States should deal with the Soviets by "unsheathing the cold blue steel of power."[4] And General Curtis LeMay endorsed that notion by firmly stating, "If there is to be war, there's no better time than the present. We are prepared and 'the bear' is not." McNamara had his hands full controlling both men and had heated exchanges with Anderson.

In his approach to impending war, John F. Kennedy showed none of the boastfulness of his military advisors, and he was still measuring every reaction so that he wouldn't have to show the United States' "cold blue steel of power." The president clearly saw the potential for misunderstanding arising from the use of "harmless" but "explosive" depth charges. But no one had a better signaling means, and he allowed the instructions to stand. The quarantine applied to both ships and submarines, especially because several US military analysts warned that the subs might be carrying the nuclear warheads for the missiles being erected in Cuba. (This turned out to be incorrect. Some of the warheads were already in Cuba, and others were aboard the So-viet ship *Aleksandrovsk*, anchored in a Cuban port.)

ON OCTOBER 27, 1962, Soviet sub B-59, commanded by Captain Valentin Grigorievic Savitsky, cruised the waters near the quaran-tine line to the northeast of Cuba, shadowed by US Navy destroyers and the anti-submarine aircraft carrier *Randolph*. B-59 was a Foxtrot-classification diesel-powered submarine, not too different from the Nazi U-boats, which operated on batteries when underwater but needed to surface to run on the diesel power that would recharge the batteries. These crafts were larger than the World War II German subs and normally carried a crew of seventy-eight. Most of the B-59 crew did not even know the sub carried a nuclear-tipped torpedo, called a "special weapon."[5]

According to Russian researcher Alexander Mozgovoi, who in-terviewed men serving on that sub, including communications of-ficer Vadim Orlov, the practice depth charges, dropped by the navy ships, really rattled the crew. They exploded right next to the hull and sounded like "a sledgehammer on a metal barrel."[6] This went on for several hours. Orlov said, "The situation was quite unusual, if not to say shocking." Making matters worse, the submarine was short of freshwater, and crewmen were limited to one glass per day. In fact some of the freshwater had to be diverted to the sub's batteries—the warm water in this section of the Atlantic actually caused some of the batteries to dry out.

Captain Savitsky tried and failed to establish communications with Moscow for instructions. Unwilling to surface, fearing his sub could be captured or worse, he stayed submerged, which caused the tem-perature in the sub, with its rudimentary ventilation system, to climb each hour, ultimately reaching 122 degrees. Communications officer Orlov recalled that Captain Savitsky was "totally exhausted" and be-coming more unnerved by the minute. The crew was in no better shape, suffering from dehydration, lacking sleep, and feeling trapped.

As the afternoon of October 27 progressed, so too did the pre-dicament of Captain Savitsky. Because of the low battery charge, the sub was operating on its emergency ventilation system, and danger-ous concentrations of carbon dioxide were building up inside, causing some crewmembers to faint. US aircraft had also located the sub and were dropping the practice depth charges that most military men at the time called hand grenades. More destroyers rushed to the scene.

Communications officer Orlov later described the experience as similar to being imprisoned and pounded while inside a "metal barrel" for four hours, tormented by the pursuing ships and planes above them. One of those ships, the destroyer USS *Beale*, recorded the chase in its deck logbook, chronicling how in the late afternoon it "proceeded in company with USS Cony and the USS Murray at 25 knots to investigate an unidentified submarine."[7] The young sailors aboard the destroyers must have felt both tension and excitement. Had they known the sub carried a nuclear torpedo, however, they would have been terrified.

The destroyers arrived over the submarine in just under an hour. Exactly nineteen minutes later the destroyer "dropped five hand grenades as a challenge to submarine for identification. No response." Within a thirty-minute interval the other destroyers did the same. It must have been sheer hell for the Soviet crew in the sweltering heat with more and more blasts sounding in their ears and batteries so low the lights were dimmed to conserve power. Orlov did not think they would survive. "We thought—that's it—the end."[8]

Captain Savitsky must have felt like the Cuban antiaircraft men below the Crusaders, wondering if the next plane overflight or, in the case of the sub, the explosion might prove lethal. Some of the submariners interviewed by Alexander Mozgovoi reported that certain blasts were louder than others, making them wonder if war had broken out. Captain Savitsky likely thought along the same lines, because he became "furious" and ordered preparation of his nuclear-tipped torpedo for firing. He shouted, "Maybe the war has already started up there while we are doing summersaults here. We're going to blast them now! We will die, but we are going to sink them all!"[9]

Only two people stood between Savitsky and the order to fire the nuclear torpedo: deputy brigade commander Second Captain Vasili Arkhipov and political officer Ivan Maslennikov. The political officer agreed with the captain that war had likely started and it was their duty to fire the "special weapon." The thirty-six-year-old Arkhipov did not agree. He would not normally have been on board, but on this mission he served as chief of staff of the submarine flotilla.[10] He held the same rank as Savitsky, but Savitsky commanded B-59. An argument erupted.

It is remarkable how such a small occurrence can change human history. Had a different man than Arkhipov been on sub B-59, the confrontation at sea between the superpowers might have ended in nuclear war. Instead, Arkhipov calmed the captain down, convincing him that they did not know if war had broken out and that all three officers must agree to use the nuclear torpedo when they could not reach Moscow by radio. He reasoned that surfacing was the correct step.

Captain Savitsky reluctantly agreed, and under cover of darkness B-59 surfaced. Illumination flares dropped from aircraft immediately lit it up. The destroyers moved closer.

War had not broken out, and the sub was merely photographed rather than bombed. Many hours later, after charging the batteries, Savitsky ordered the sub to dive, and it moved away from the quarantine line. The sailors on the destroyers never knew how close they came to being vaporized by the "special weapon."

When Robert McNamara learned of these details years later in 2002, he said, "We came very close [to nuclear war], closer than we knew at the time."[11] Thomas Blanton, former director of the nongovernmental National Security Archive, said it best: "a guy called Vasili Arkhipov saved the world."

All mankind is certainly lucky Arkhipov made the decision he did. Perhaps it reflected his previous experience dealing with a crisis on a submarine. Just a year earlier he had served as deputy commander on a brand-new nuclear-propelled ballistic missile submarine, K-19.[12] The sub had a nuclear accident, and Arkhipov not only put down a potential mutiny but lent his hand to stop an overheating reactor from melting down. Eight men died almost immediately from the poisonous fumes. Arkhipov lived until 1998, but the radiation from that ordeal was cited as a factor in his death.

WE DON'T KNOW if the United States detected the movements of other Soviet submarines in different parts of the world during the crisis. One sub that the US Navy should have tracked, B-88, left its base at the Kamchatka Peninsula with orders to sail to Pearl Harbor to attack the base there if the crisis led to war.[13]

CHAPTER THIRTY-EIGHT

Invasion Imminent

THROUGHOUT THE UNITED States the mood was bleak that Saturday evening, especially after Robert McNamara issued a statement to the public explaining that reconnaissance aircraft had taken fire.[1] (He made no mention of Rudy Anderson's death.) The statement also addressed the US response: "The possibility of further attack on our aircraft and the continued buildup of the offensive weapon systems in Cuba require that we be prepared for any eventuality. . . . I have instructed the Secretary of the Air Force to order to active duty 24 troop carrier squadrons of the Air Force with their associated units."

McNamara was making clear to friend and foe that the United States was more than ready to invade Cuba. More alarmingly, though not announced, Strategic Air Command was ready to launch intercontinental missiles targeting over seventy Russian cities.[2]

Many people, including most US military leaders, endured a night so grim that they wondered if complete destruction of Earth could happen at any moment. McNamara later explained that he too felt the distinct possibility of Armageddon, writing that when he glanced outside the White House and noticed the sun sinking over the October horizon, he "wondered if I'd ever see another sunset like that."[3]

McNamara had no cause for optimism. The ongoing events of that Saturday showed that the Soviet Union was willing to test the determination and patience of both the US military and the Kennedy administration. While the firing of surface-to-air missiles (SAMs) at

Anderson's U-2 dominated much of the day's discussion, another potentially violent encounter loomed. The Russian tanker *Grozny* was still steaming toward the quarantine line, trailed by two US destroyers. The tanker should arrive at the designated five-hundred-mile quarantine line before dawn. The captains of the two destroyers had standing instructions to halt the ship in the least violent way possible. The first procedure would involve trying to ensnare the ship with a long wire cable. If that didn't work, a shot across the bow might follow, or an attempt to disable the rudder. No one knew what to expect from the Russians if one of their ships was forcibly stopped. How would they retaliate?

In Cuba the citizens of Havana prepared for war as best they could. All available nurses and doctors reported to nursing stations, medicine was moved into the basement of government buildings, and antiaircraft guns ringing the capital were manned around the clock.[4] Additional defensive trenches were dug along coastal roads near where the Americans might land. The Bay of Pigs must have seemed like a warm-up for the massive invasion that most Cubans believed was just hours away.

The Russians in Cuba also expected the worst. Colonel General Victor Yesin of the Strategic Rocket Forces, which controlled the main component of the Soviet Union's nuclear arsenal, recalls getting an order on October 27: the bombing would begin soon, and he should have plans for when and where to take cover. "We understood much trouble [was] coming," said Yesin.[5]

Fidel Castro was jubilant about the shoot-down of an American U-2.[6] Finally, the Russians were joining the Cubans in firing at the intruding aircraft, and the Americans would think twice about invading the island's airspace. Perhaps Castro fostered the myth circulating among his people that not only had a Cuban pushed the button to launch the SAMs at the spy plane but Castro had issued the order. And some reports even claimed Castro himself had fired the missiles. None of this was true, but the rumors lived on for years. (Castro even told UN Secretary-General U Thant on October 31 that Cuban antiaircraft guns had brought down Anderson's U-2.)[7]

But Nikita Khrushchev kept Castro in the dark regarding the negotiations behind the scenes. The Cuban leader was certain that war would erupt within hours and that the Cubans and Russians would fight the Americans side by side.

It was gut-check time at the White House. President John F. Kennedy and his advisors fought off fatigue while trying to remain focused on the multitude of critical situations before them. They had exhausted every option, and war was coming. Bobby Kennedy turned to a weary Bob McNamara.

> ROBERT KENNEDY—How are you doing, Bob?
> McNAMARA—Well. How about yourself?
> ROBERT KENNEDY—Alright.
> McNAMARA—You got any doubts?
> ROBERT KENNEDY—No, I think that we're doing the only thing we can do, and so on. You know.
> McNAMARA—I think the one thing, Bobby . . . we ought to seriously do before we attack them, you've got to be damn sure they [the Soviets] understand it's coming.
> ROBERT KENNEDY—Right?
> McNAMARA—In other words, you really need to escalate this.

The talk then turned to what a postinvasion Cuba and Europe might look like, presuming that anyone survived to rebuild. Bobby Kennedy said, "I'd like to take Cuba back. That would be nice." A voice cheered, "Yeah, let's take Cuba back from Castro."[8] Finally, in a moment of gallows humor shared by men with tired minds and frayed nerves, someone in the room suggested making Bobby mayor of Havana.

Before breaking after a long evening, the members of ExComm drafted a cable informing a select group of US ambassadors and fellow members of the North Atlantic Treaty Organization that the situation was deteriorating and that within a very short period the United States might have to "take whatever military action may be necessary to remove this growing threat to the Hemisphere."[9]

LATER THAT NIGHT, Bobby and Jack Kennedy had a quiet moment together, and neither was optimistic about a peaceful resolution. In fact, Bobby later wrote, "the expectation was a military confrontation by Tuesday and possibly tomorrow [Sunday]."

While some ExComm members, including Bobby Kennedy, spent what could have been one of their final nights on Earth at home with their families, others slept in their offices. President Kennedy and his close advisor Dave Powers stayed up watching one of JFK's favorite movies, *Roman Holiday*, starring Gregory Peck and Audrey Hepburn. While the president sought a few brief moments of relaxation, 11,000 marines attached to the Fifth Marine Expeditionary Force set out from San Diego, through the Panama Canal, toward Cuba. The air force called 14,000 reservists to active duty. Invasion was imminent.

CHAPTER THIRTY-NINE

The Day of the Doves

BOBBY KENNEDY STOOD inside the DC Armory on the morning of Sunday, October 28, 1962. He wasn't there on inspection, as the armory had lost its military usefulness decades before. Instead, he was enjoying a brief peaceful moment, watching a horse show with his daughters. The world might be on the brink of war, but life was continuing, at least for now. Like the other members of Ex-Comm, Bobby could do nothing but wait for the Russians to make their next move. He watched as the horses jumped and galloped and must have wondered if he would ever enjoy a moment like this again.

At approximately 10:00 a.m., RFK was called away from the event to take an urgent phone call from Dean Rusk at the State Department. As Rusk spoke, the president's brother could hardly believe what he was hearing. The Kremlin had just agreed to remove all nuclear missiles from Cuba.

In a message broadcast that morning over Radio Moscow, Premier Nikita Khrushchev spoke directly to President John F. Kennedy.

Esteemed Mr. President:

I have received your message of October 27, 1962. I express my satisfaction and thank you for the sense of proportion you have displayed and for realization of the responsibility which now devolves on you for the preservation of the peace of the world.

I regard with great understanding your concern and the concern of the United States people in connection with the fact that the weapons you describe as offensive are formidable weapons indeed. Both you and we understand what kind of weapons these are.

In order to eliminate as rapidly as possible the conflict which endangers the cause of peace, to give an assurance to all people who crave peace, and to reassure the American people, who, I am certain, also want peace, as do the people of the Soviet Union, the Soviet Government, in addition to earlier instructions on the discontinuation of further work on weapons construction sites, has given a new order to dismantle the arms which you described as offensive, and to crate and return them to the Soviet Union.[1]

Respectfully yours,
N. Khrushchev

Upon hearing the news, Bobby Kennedy drove directly to the White House. The president was getting dressed to attend Sunday morning mass at St. Stephen's Church. The First Lady had taken Caroline and John-John to Glen Ora, the family estate in the Virginia horse country, that Friday. JFK had promised to join her there on Saturday, but then the world had turned black. Now, on October 28, there was light, and with light came hope. National Security Advisor Mac Bundy, the same man who had first notified the president that the Soviets were constructing missile sites on Cuba, now alerted him that Khrushchev was standing down. Bundy approached the president's private quarters and handed the commander in chief the full text of Khrushchev's message.

"It was a very beautiful morning, and it suddenly had become many times more beautiful," Bundy later said. "And I am sure the President felt the same way from the feeling between us as we talked about it. . . . We all felt that the world had changed for the better."[2]

ExComm reconvened at 11 a.m. with a collective sense of relief, while at the Pentagon skepticism and anger reigned. The Joint Chiefs thought Khrushchev's letter was no more than another attempt to buy time until all the nuclear weapons on Cuba became operational. The Chiefs, led by General Curtis LeMay, again called on the president to order a major air strike against Cuba the following day, Monday, October 29, followed by a full invasion. The only dissenter among the

Joint Chiefs, its chairman, General Maxwell Taylor, gave the Pentagon's recommendation to Secretary of Defense Robert McNamara, while informing him that he did not agree with it. Taylor's view contrasted starkly with LeMay's.

"We lost!" LeMay shouted. "We should just go in there today and knock 'em off!"[3]

Despite LeMay's bloodthirsty blustering, Khrushchev's morning announcement was not an attempt at misdirection. The Soviets were putting their words in action. There had simply been too many close brushes with potential Armageddon: Chuck Maultsby's inadvertent incursion over Soviet airspace, Fidel Castro's firing at Crusaders and wish to strike the first nuclear blow, and Soviet generals' taking matters into their own hands with the firing of surface-to-air missiles (SAMs) at Jerry McIlmoyle and Rudy Anderson. These incidents had passed without prompting the start of World War III, but Khrushchev knew this good fortune could not last much longer. He quickly arranged for announcement of his agreement on Radio Moscow so that President Kennedy would have his answer as soon as possible.

The premier also understood that Kennedy might have a hard time keeping the reins on his generals—like Curtis LeMay—and that too had forced him to act. During a morning meeting with his advisors at his private dacha outside Moscow, the Soviet leader learned of Anatoly Dobrynin's meeting with Bobby Kennedy the night before and of RFK's warning that American generals wanted war and that the moment of reckoning had arrived. Khrushchev won agreement from his own generals and advisors to dismantle their missiles as long as the Americans promised not to invade Cuba and to eventually remove the Jupiter missiles from Turkey. Khrushchev saw the compromise as a victory for Soviet diplomacy.[4]

Fidel Castro did not agree. On learning of Khrushchev's decision, the Cuban leader went on a profanity-laced tirade. He even punched a mirror and kicked a wall. Castro was furious that the Russians had made a deal with the Americans without consulting him first. His tirade had no effect as orders to stand down went out to Soviet military commanders on land and sea.

The Russian tanker *Grozny*, which had shown no signs of slowing as it closed in on the quarantine line, stopped dead in the water. Three hundred miles away, the Soviet sub B-59 retreated with its fully charged batteries. It dove to five hundred feet and altered course by 180 degrees, while on the ocean's surface the jazz band aboard the 2,200-ton destroyer USS *Lowry* played "Yankee Doodle."

By all appearances, the crisis was over after thirteen painstaking days that had tested the wills of men on all sides of the conflict.

At the White House, Mac Bundy reflected on ExComm's shifting positions and allegiances, including his own, over the past week. Bundy said that some committee members had been hawks, and some had been doves. "Today is the day of the doves," he said.[5]

President Kennedy ordered all air reconnaissance suspended for the day; no doubt the loss of Rudy Anderson was still fresh in his mind. JFK urged his advisors to temper their public remarks so as not to embarrass or provoke Khrushchev. The president understood that work remained to be done to keep the peace. He then placed calls to his predecessors—Dwight Eisenhower, Harry Truman, and Herbert Hoover. Eisenhower praised Kennedy and told him that he was "doing exactly right on this one." Former president Harry Truman, who had never been a fan of Kennedy, concurred. "I'm just pleased to death the way these things came out. . . . That's the way to do things," he told JFK. Herbert Hoover, now eighty-eight years old, said during the phone call, "It seems to me these recent events are rather incredible. . . . That represents a good triumph for you."[6] Kennedy did not bring up his private promise to Khrushchev to remove the Jupiter missiles from Turkey.[7]

As JFK was placing his calls to the former presidents, Bobby returned from a meeting with Ambassador Dobrynin at the Justice Department. A relieved Dobrynin told RFK that the missiles on Cuba would be dismantled and withdrawn under adequate supervision and inspection. "Everything is going to work out satisfactorily," the Russian promised.[8] Dobrynin then said that Premier Khrushchev himself wanted to offer "best wishes" to Bobby and the president.

JFK knew that it was no time for a victory lap. Herbert Hoover had called his handling of the crisis "a triumph," but the president understood how quickly the situation could change course if he didn't keep a steady hand at the wheel. He also realized how a simple twist of fate could turn things back upside down. Remembering that Abraham Lincoln had been assassinated just after winning the Civil War, Kennedy joked—hauntingly in retrospect—to Bobby, "This is the night I should go to the theater." Ever protective of his older brother, RFK responded, "If you go, I want to go with you."[9]

When Bobby left for home, he recalled that his brother was sitting in the lamplight writing. JFK was expressing his condolences to Rudy Anderson's wife, Jane. Amid the hundreds of tasks tugging at the young president, he had not forgotten the U-2 pilot who didn't make it home.

The letter, typed by Kennedy's secretary the next day, read,

Dear Mrs. Anderson:

I was deeply shocked by the loss of your husband on an operational flight on Saturday, October 27th, 1962.

The courage and outstanding abilities of your husband were evident throughout his career, as witnessed by the award to him during the Korean War, of the Distinguished Flying Cross with two clusters. His tragic loss on a mission of most vital national urgency was once again the sacrifice of a brave and patriotic man in time of crisis—the source of our freedom since the founding days of our country.

On behalf of a grateful nation, I wish to convey to you and your children the sincere gratitude of all the people. I have directed the award of the Distinguished Service Medal to your husband.

Mrs. Kennedy joins me in extending to you our deepest sympathy in the loss of your husband.

Sincerely, John F. Kennedy

The president added a handwritten sentence to the letter: "Your husband's mission was of the greatest importance, but I know how deeply you must feel his loss."

The Distinguished Service Medal is the highest honor awarded in peacetime. CIA director John McCone had recommended awarding Rudy the Congressional Medal of Honor, saying the crisis was close to war and an adversary's missile had taken him down. McNamara, however, disagreed, stressing that the Medal of Honor could only be given during an actual declared war.[10]

Of course, no medal could cheer the devastated widow. She had eagerly awaited her husband's return to tell him that she was pregnant with their third child. Instead, another visit from two air force officials to her home shattered her dream. Once again, they told Jane that her husband was dead. Once again, she refused to believe them.

"You've done this before," she shouted angrily. "You should really get your facts straight before you needlessly scare people senseless."[11]

The men shook their heads.

"There is no mistake," one of them told her. "We are at the right house speaking with the correct person."

As the reality set in, Jane ran through the living room and locked herself in the bathroom. Alone, she began to weep hysterically. Marlene Powell, a neighbor at Laughlin Air Force Base and also the wife of a U-2 pilot, went to console her, and the new widow simply said, "I don't want to live without Rudy."[12]

While Jane grieved and likely wondered if her husband's remains would ever be found, the Soviets had already removed Rudy's body from the plane. A couple days later a Cuban source working with the United States reported that the body of the pilot had been taken to Gibara for embalming and was in Russian custody. "The American was described as being about 27 and was wearing a flight jacket with an emblem denoting service in Korea. Photographs of 2 children were among his effects."[13]

AFTER WRITING TO Jane Anderson that Sunday afternoon, President Kennedy left the White House and climbed aboard his helicopter to meet Jackie and the children in Virginia. When he arrived in Glen Ora, he stepped off the aircraft smiling. The president could not adequately express his relief in words, and he knew the successful outcome of the crisis owed partly to the pilots who risked it all flying over Cuba during the prior thirteen days. He did not forget those men.

Just a few days later the president visited Homestead Air Force Base to thank the U-2 pilots, Crusader pilots, and various generals gathered on the tarmac. Under the bright Florida sunshine, Kennedy strode to a single microphone—no podium, no stage, no notes—and thanked the service members for helping resolve the crisis.

Pilots Buddy Brown and Jerry McIlmoyle missed Kennedy's short speech, as they had been selected to remain inside a hangar next to a U-2 spy plane. The two pilots didn't mind—they would meet the president one-on-one and give him a personal tour of the aircraft.

Brown and McIlmoyle stood at attention as the president's limousine slowly entered the hangar and rolled to a stop. Kennedy emerged dressed in a dark suit. Buddy and Jerry gave a stiff salute, but the president wasn't having any of that formal stuff. He walked up to the men with his hand outstretched. The two pilots were taken off guard but recovered enough to shake his hand.

Kennedy must have told his staff and the generals to stay back, out of earshot, because when he asked the pilots to show him the plane, the others remained by the limousine. As the three men walked toward the cockpit of the U-2, the president turned to Jerry and asked, "What does your wife think about what you were doing?"

"She doesn't know," stammered Jerry. "It's top secret."

"Well I'm giving you permission to tell her and anyone else you want to about anything and everything you did."

Then he looked at Buddy Brown and said, "You too."

Buddy, in awe and somewhat tongue-tied, recovered and said, "Thank you, sir."

The three men reached a portable stairway leading to the U-2's cockpit. They all climbed up, and Jerry started pointing out the various instruments. Kennedy surprised Jerry yet again by asking, "Mind if I climb inside?" A seat pack and parachute had been installed just for that possibility.

"Please do." Jerry knew nothing about JFK's bad back, but the president showed no discomfort as he wedged himself into the pilot's seat.

The two pilots explained the various instruments and even pointed out on a map where Rudy Anderson was shot down. Jerry decided this was neither the time nor the place to mention his own near miss with two SAMs, and because the president did not bring it up, he assumed Kennedy was unaware of his close call.

"How do you eject?" asked Kennedy.

Jerry, now comfortable talking with the president, joked, "First thing is you make sure you have to eject!"

The three men laughed. The pilots felt like they were with a friend and briefly forgot the man sitting in the cockpit was their commander in chief.

The president peppered the two pilots with questions, and Jerry thought, "This is a military man who has been in combat. He really wants to hear what we have to say, really wants to know how the plane functions."

A full thirty minutes had passed since they had met the president, and Kennedy seemed reluctant to leave the cockpit, but they all descended the stairs to the floor of the hangar.

Just before the president walked back to the limousine, he turned to Jerry, put his arm around his shoulder, looked him in the eye, and said, "I'll never be able to thank you men enough for bringing back those pictures which allowed me to peacefully end this crisis."

Epilogue

ON NOVEMBER 5, the Cubans released the body of Rudy Anderson, still in his flight suit, to the Swiss ambassador in Cuba, and a Swiss pilot flew the remains to Florida.[1] The US Air Force conducted an autopsy and determined that missile fragments had penetrated his flight suit, triggering instant decompression, and death likely occurred within seconds. Major Anderson's body was next flown to Donaldson Air Force Base and transported to his hometown of Greenville, South Carolina, for interment on November 6.

Anderson was buried with full military honors. Jet fighter planes soared over the 1,800 mourners at Woodlawn Memorial Park, with one spot in the unit's formation left open in Rudy's honor. General Thomas Power represented the air force at the funeral. "It is because of men like Major Anderson, that this country has been able to act with determination during these fateful days," he said.[2]

Jane attended her husband's funeral escorted by an air force doctor and a nurse, who feared for the health of the unborn baby. She was inconsolable and wept openly over her husband's casket as it was lowered into the cold ground. The president and First Lady did not attend the funeral but did send a large floral arrangement. Jane Anderson quietly accepted the sentiment, but deep down she was angry. When John F. Kennedy's press secretary, Pierre Salinger, tried to set up a meeting between Jane and the president, she forcefully declined. After Rudy's death, a pregnant Jane desperately tried to get some answers and gain some insight into what had happened, but the air force stonewalled her: Rudy's military life and death were classified information. Jane blamed President Kennedy for that.

"My mother admired President Kennedy right up until my father was killed," their son James Anderson said. "All that changed after my father's death. . . . She was in the depths of despair, grieving my father's death and she was pregnant and hormonal. She took out all her frustration and anger on JFK as Commander in Chief."[3]

Rudy Anderson's family was ordered to move out of their home at Laughlin Air Force Base almost immediately. The cold treatment was customary on all military bases as the presence of a lost soldier or pilot's family was thought to lower morale. Jane and her boys moved back in with her parents in Georgia. Eight months later, Jane gave birth to a redheaded baby girl, whom she named Robyn—the daughter that she and Rudy had always dreamed of. Jane was a good mother and later became a social worker. She even remarried. But her son Tripp believes that she never got over the death of her beloved Rudy. Jane died in 1981. She was just forty-six years old. Pieces of the wreckage of Rudy Anderson's U-2 are now on display at three sites in Cuba, including the Museum of the Revolution in Havana.

STEVE HEYSER WAS invited to the White House to receive the president's thanks for taking the first crucial photos of the Soviet missile installations. But he would not meet with the president one-on-one. General Curtis LeMay accompanied him, and as they drove to the White House, he informed Steve that he had a spin on the story of who took the first photos. He said that because Anderson was dead, Rudy should be the major hero of the crisis, and the four-star general asked Major Heyser if he had a problem with that.[4] Heyser, of course, could only answer, "No, sir." Subsequently, the early air force accounts of the U-2 spy plane involvement in the crisis attributed the initial photos to both Heyser and Anderson.

When LeMay and Heyser entered the Oval Office, Kennedy sat in his comfortable rocking chair, and LeMay made sure he sat on the couch closest to the president, keeping himself between Heyser and JFK. The cigar-chomping general would control the conversation between the U-2 pilot and his commander in chief, and of course LeMay did most of the talking.[5]

CHUCK MAULTSBY BRISTLED for years over President Kennedy's off-hand remark calling him a "son of a bitch," but he continued piloting the U-2 and later earned the Distinguished Flying Cross. Chuck gave up the spy plane and returned to the skies as a fighter pilot during the Vietnam War, where he flew 216 missions, including 70 over North Vietnam.

He returned to the United States as a lieutenant colonel with a total of 233 combat missions under his belt, including those he flew in Korea. He had also earned a Silver Star, but his time in Vietnam had changed him.

"My dad had the utmost respect for the military, but his views changed during Vietnam," Chuck Maultsby II told the authors of this book. "When it came time for me to join the fight, my dad said no. He didn't want me to go to Vietnam. In fact he told me that he'd drive me to Canada himself if that's what it took to keep me out of it."[6]

Chuck Maultsby stayed in the military and eventually served as an officer for North Atlantic Treaty Organization forces in Italy. He retired in 1977 and purchased a fifteen-acre ranch in the Texas hill country with his wife, Jeanne.

"There will always be the reminders of yesteryear; when a white contrail streaks the sky," he later wrote in his memoir. "I see the silvery swept wing reflections high above me in that bright wonderful blue. . . . [But] I still look toward tomorrow. Tomorrow is the first day of something. . . . Tomorrow is and will always be toward the unknown."[7]

Colonel Chuck Maultsby died of lung cancer in 1998. He was seventy-two years old. His wife, Jeanne, survived him by almost fourteen years before she passed away at the age of seventy-eight in 2012.

IN 1963, PRESIDENT Kennedy gave the commencement address at the American University in Washington, DC. The Cuban Missile Crisis had forced him to reexamine the Cold War and his onetime foe Nikita Khrushchev. Those tense thirteen days in October 1962 had brought both leaders closer together as the world itself drew perilously close to nuclear war. Since the crisis, JFK had pushed for direct contact with his Soviet counterpart and had a special hotline installed between the White House and the Kremlin. He had a second hotline put in the basement of his home on Cape Cod so that the leaders could discuss future issues themselves without the dangers of misinterpretation.

On this day in early June, the world seemed a warmer and brighter place than it had been that previous October, during the darkest and coldest days of the Cold War. The United States and the Soviet Union were now working toward a treaty that would outlaw nuclear weapons testing, an outcome inconceivable just months before. It was indeed the dawn of a new era, something the president had promised during his inauguration in 1961. Now, two years later, he was about to give what Nikita Khrushchev called "the greatest speech by any American President since Roosevelt."[8] President Kennedy stepped to the podium, the sun of late spring splashed across his face, and spoke not only to the graduating students but to all people across the world.

> I have chosen this time and this place to discuss a topic on which ignorance too often abounds and the truth is rarely perceived. . . . [I]t is the most important topic on earth: world peace. . . . I speak of peace because of the new face of war. Total war makes no sense in an age when great powers can maintain large and relatively invulnerable nuclear forces. . . . And even in the cold war, which brings many burdens to so many nations . . . our two countries [the United States and the Soviet Union] bear the heaviest burdens. . . . So let us not be blind to our differences, but let us also draw attention to our common interests. . . . [O]ur most basic common link is that we all inhabit this small planet. We all breathe the same air. We all cherish our children's future. And we are all mortal.[9]

Authors' Note

CASEY SHERMAN

MY FATHER, DONNY Sherman, served in the United States Marines Corps in October 1962 and would have likely been part of the American invasion force of Cuba if President John F. Kennedy and Premier Nikita Khrushchev had not pulled back from the brink of war at the eleventh hour on Black Saturday. To me, war has less to do with kingdoms or states than with those we place in power. Our leaders ultimately decide who lives and who dies. We approached this book with the goal of writing an intimate story of human beings thrust into extraordinary circumstances—their hopes and their fears—across the sweeping and historic landscape of nuclear confrontation. We wanted to explore John Kennedy as a man and how the experiences of his past shaped his thinking during the most critical days of his presidency. We also wanted to focus on the human toll of war—the men who risk and sometimes lose their lives on the orders of others.

I had an idea for this book, and I knew that Mike Tougias, my co-author for *The Finest Hours*, would be the perfect partner to work with to bring this story to life. The stories told here are also very much alive in the people we had the honor of interviewing. I spent time with Robert F. Kennedy Jr. at the family compound in Hyannis Port, where we discussed his family's rich history and what it was truly like to be living as a young boy in the eye of the hurricane during the missile crisis. I cherished my time with Colonel Richard Leghorn, who was both a witness to and an architect of many of the twentieth century's most historic moments. I'm thankful for my conversation with Robert Ross, who provided me with a better understanding of what it was like to serve as a pilot during the Korean War. Most of all,

I thank Jim and Tripp Anderson and Chuck Maultsby II for sharing the stories of their fathers and their families. These men should never be forgotten.

I also want to thank our editor, Ben Adams, of PublicAffairs; our agents, Richard Pine and George Lucas, of Inkwell Management; my managers, Ellen Goldsmith-Vein and Shari Smiley, of Gotham Group; and the helpful folks at the John F. Kennedy Presidential Library and Museum. On the home front, I would like to thank my daughters, Bella and Mia, for their patience as I worked on my tenth book; their mom, Laura; my mother, Diane Dodd; my talented brother, Todd Forrest Sherman; and my uncle, Jim Sherman.

MICHAEL TOUGIAS

A BIG THANK-YOU to Jerry McIlmoyle—I simply could not have written my sections of this book without his input and encouragement. I would also like to thank Rick Heyser and Sergei Khrushchev for their insights, editor Ben Adams for his guidance and brilliant editing, copyeditor Jen Kelland and project editor Sandra Beris for their insights, and agents Richard Pine and George Lucas for believing in this project. And heartfelt gratitude to all the readers who have come to hear me speak, spread the word about my books, and offered words of encouragement. It offsets the lonely part of writing and means the world to me.

I hope that besides sharing the lesser-known story of the U-2 pilots during the Cuban Missile Crisis, this book also helps all of us understand what happened both before and during the crisis so that it never happens again.

We all owe a debt of gratitude to President John F. Kennedy for the way he conducted himself during the crisis. He listened to all opinions, deliberated on all alternatives, and constantly considered the ramifications of each potential decision. A lesser man might have succumbed to the drumbeat of war in the early days of the crisis.

Notes

CHAPTER TWO

1. "Community Remembers Missile Crisis," GreenvilleOnLine, 2012.
2. Alumni page, Clemson University.
3. Alumni page, Clemson University.
4. *The Tiger*, Clemson University, March 11, 1948.
5. Col. Charles Maultsby, *Toward the Unknown: Memoirs of an American Fighter Pilot* (CreateSpace Independent Publishing Platform, 2013), 8.
6. Maultsby, *Toward the Unknown*, 18.

CHAPTER THREE

1. William Doyle, *PT 109: An American Epic of War, Survival, and the Destiny of John F. Kennedy* (New York: William Morrow, 2015).
2. Doyle, *PT 109*, 93.
3. Doyle, *PT 109*, 109.
4. Doyle, *PT 109*, 111; "Patrick H. McMahon Dead at 84; Burned Sailor Saved by Kennedy," Associated Press, February 22, 1990; Richard Goldstein, "Gerard Zinser, Last Surviving *PT 109* Crewman, Dies at 82," *New York Times*, August 29, 2001.
5. Doyle, *PT 109*, 114.
6. Doyle, *PT 109*, 116.
7. Doyle, *PT 109*, 140.
8. Doyle, *PT 109*, 148.
9. Doyle, *PT 109*, 151.
10. Doyle, *PT 109*, 189.

CHAPTER FOUR

1. Author interview with Robert Ross, 2016.
2. Author interview with Tripp Anderson, 2016.
3. Author interview with James Anderson, 2017.
4. Author interview with Tripp Anderson, 2016.

CHAPTER FIVE

1. Col. Charles Maultsby, *Toward the Unknown: Memoirs of an American Fighter Pilot* (CreateSpace Independent Publishing Platform, 2013), 24.

2. Maultsby, *Toward the Unknown*, 42.

3. C. V. Gliness, "A Speech Worth Dying For," *Air Force Magazine*, October 1995.

4. Maultsby, *Toward the Unknown*, 81.

5. Maultsby, *Toward the Unknown*, 95.

6. Maultsby, *Toward the Unknown*, 105.

7. Maultsby, *Toward the Unknown*, 110.

8. Maultsby, *Toward the Unknown*, 111.

9. Maultsby, *Toward the Unknown*, 112.

CHAPTER SIX

1. Annie Jacobsen, *Area 51* (Boston: Back Bay Books, Little, Brown and Company, 2012), 26.

2. Author interview with Richard Leghorn, 2016.

3. Letter from Edwin Land to Allen Dulles, November 5, 1954, National Archives.

4. David Binder, "Richard M. Bissell, 84, Is Dead; Helped Plan Bay of Pigs Invasion," *New York Times*, February 8, 1994.

5. Peter Garrison, "Head Skunk," *Air & Space Magazine*, March 2010.

CHAPTER SEVEN

1. Michael Beschloss, *May-Day* (New York: Harper & Row, 1988), 105–107.

2. Organization and Delineation of Responsibilities, Project OILSTONE, United States Air Force and Central Intelligence Agency, August 2, 1955.

3. National Aviation Hall of Fame (http://www.nationalaviation.org).

CHAPTER EIGHT

1. "Is Russia Really Ahead in the Missile Race?," *US News & World Report*, May 4, 1956, 34.

2. Andrew Goodpaster's handwritten notes on July 2, 1956, meeting, WHOSS, Alpha DDEL.

3. Interview with Willy Pell, nephew of Hervey Stockman, Gizmodo.com, 2011.

4. Michael Beschloss, *The Crisis Years* (New York: Edward Burlingame Books, HarperCollins, 1991), 15.

5. John F. Kennedy, *The Letters of John F. Kennedy* (New York: Bloomsbury Press, 2013).

6. Kenneth Crispell and Carlos Gomez, *Hidden Illness in the White House* (Durham, NC: Duke University Press Books, 1988), 186.

7. Robert Dallek, "The Medical Ordeals of JFK," *Atlantic Monthly*, December 2002.

CHAPTER NINE

1. Col. Charles Maultsby, *Toward the Unknown: Memoirs of an American Fighter Pilot* (CreateSpace Independent Publishing Platform, 2013), 121.

2. Maultsby, *Toward the Unknown*, 148.

3. "Project Mercury Overview—Astronaut Selection," https://www.nasa.gov/mission_pages/mercury/missions/astronaut.html.

4. Gerald McIlmoyle and Linda Rios Bromley, *Remembering the Dragon Lady* (West Midlands, UK: Helion & Company, 2011), 131.

CHAPTER TEN

1. Col. Charles Maultsby, *Toward the Unknown: Memoirs of an American Fighter Pilot* (CreateSpace Independent Publishing Platform, 2013), 148, 176.

CHAPTER ELEVEN

1. Author interview with Tripp Anderson, 2016.

2. Gerald McIlmoyle and Linda Rios Bromley, *Remembering the Dragon Lady* (Midlands, UK: Helion & Company, 2011), 378.

3. Francis Gary Powers and Curt Gentry, *Operation Overflight: A Memoir of the U-2 Incident* (Washington, DC: Potomac Books, 2003).

4. Powers and Gentry, *Operation Overflight*, 69.

CHAPTER TWELVE

1. "143—The President's News Conference, May 11, 1960," American Presidency Project, http://www.presidency.ucsb.edu/ws/?pid=11778.

2. Sherman Kent, "The Summit Conference of 1960: An Intelligence Officer's View," CIA, https://www.cia.gov/library/center-for-the-study-of-intelligence/csi-publications/books-and-monographs/sherman-kent-and-the-board-of-national-estimates-collected-essays/8summit.html.

3. "The Second Kennedy-Nixon Presidential Debate," Commission on Presidential Debates, October 7, 1960, http://www.debates.org/index.php?page=october-7–1960-debate-transcript.

4. Author interview with Richard Leghorn, 2016.

CHAPTER THIRTEEN

1. Michael Beschloss, *The Crisis Years* (New York: Edward Burlingame Books, HarperCollins, 1991), 187.

2. Robert Dallek, "The Medical Ordeals of JFK," *Atlantic Monthly*, December 1, 2002.

3. Arthur Schlesinger Jr., *A Thousand Days* (New York: Crown Publishers, 1983), 19.

4. Sharon Whitley Larsen, "Remembering JFK and PT 109 Heroism," *San Diego Union Tribune*, November 21, 2013.

5. John F. Kennedy inaugural speech, 1961, transcript, John F. Kennedy Presidential Library and Museum.

CHAPTER FOURTEEN

1. Evan Thomas, *Robert Kennedy: His Life* (New York: Simon & Schuster, 2000), 120.

2. Edwin O. Guthman and Jerry Shulman, *Robert F. Kennedy: In His Own Words* (New York: Bantam Publishing Group, 1988), 242.

3. Thomas, *Robert Kennedy*, 121.

CHAPTER FIFTEEN

1. "Memorandum to the President—May 23, 1961," John F. Kennedy Presidential Library and Museum.

2. Michael Beschloss, *The Crisis Years* (New York: Edward Burlingame Books, HarperCollins, 1991), 186.

3. Peter Keating, "The Strange Saga of JFK and the Original Dr. Feelgood," *New York Magazine*, November 22, 2013.

4. Memorandum of conversation, Vienna, June 4, 1961, 10:15 a.m., Office of the Historian, United States of America.

5. Seymour Hersh, *The Dark Side of Camelot* (New York: Little, Brown and Company, 1997), 253.

CHAPTER SIXTEEN

1. Author interview with Charles Maultsby, 2015.

2. Author interview with James Anderson, 2017.

CHAPTER SEVENTEEN

1. Michael Beschloss, *The Crisis Years* (New York: Edward Burlingame Books, HarperCollins, 1991), 412.

2. Max Holland, "The Photo Gap That Delayed Discovery of Missiles," Center for the Study of Intelligence, CIA historical document, posted 2007.

3. Holland, "The Photo Gap That Delayed Discovery of Missiles."

4. Robert F. Kennedy oral history interview, JFK #8, February 27, 1965, John F. Kennedy Presidential Library.

5. Holland, "The Photo Gap That Delayed Discovery of Missiles."

6. JFK press conference #43, September 13, 1962, JFKLibrary.org.

7. Holland, "The Photo Gap That Delayed Discovery of Missiles."

CHAPTER EIGHTEEN

1. Michael Dobbs, "Into Thin Air," *Washington Post*, October 26, 2003.

2. Dobbs, "Into Thin Air."

CHAPTER NINETEEN

1. Author interview with Steve Heyser at Maxwell Air Force Base.

2. Michael Beschloss, *The Crisis Years* (New York: Edward Burlingame Books, HarperCollins, 1991), 4.

3. Allen Yarnell, *Postwar Epoch* (New York: Joanna Cotler Books, 1972).

4. Author interview with Heyser at Maxwell Air Force Base.

CHAPTER TWENTY

1. Dino Brugioni, *Eyeball to Eyeball* (New York: Random House, 1992).

2. Brugioni, *Eyeball to Eyeball.*

3. Robert F. Kennedy, *Thirteen Days* (New York: W. W. Norton, 1969), 53.

4. Nikita Khrushchev, *Khrushchev Remembers* (New York: Little, Brown, 1970).

5. Ted Sorensen, *Kennedy* (New York: Harper & Row, 1965).

6. Kennedy, *Thirteen Days.*

7. Ernest May and Philip D. Zelikow, *The Kennedy Tapes* (New York: W. W. Norton, 2002). All quotes from ExComm meetings are from Kennedy's tape recordings.

8. Michael Beschloss, *The Crisis Years* (New York: Edward Burlingame Books, HarperCollins, 1991), 449.

CHAPTER TWENTY-ONE

1. Buddy Brown speech, fiftieth anniversary of the Cuban Missile Crisis, George Mason University, Washington, DC, October 27, 2012.

2. Gerald McIlmoyle and Linda Rios Bromley, *Remembering the Dragon Lady* (West Midlands, UK: Helion & Company, 2011), 269.

3. Michael Beschloss, *The Crisis Years* (New York: Edward Burlingame Books, HarperCollins, 1991), 454.

4. Ernest May and Philip D. Zelikow, *The Kennedy Tapes* (New York: W. W. Norton, 2002), 169.

5. Arthur Schlesinger Jr., *A Thousand Days* (Boston: Crown Publishers, 1995), 806.

CHAPTER TWENTY-TWO

1. Author interview with Jerry McIlmoyle; PBS video documentary, John Murray and Emer Reynolds, dirs., *Cuban Missile Crisis: Three Men Go to War* (Crossing the Lines Production, 2012).

2. Robert F. Kennedy, *Thirteen Days* (New York: W. W. Norton, 1969), 31.

3. William Ecker and Kenneth Jack, *Blue Moon over Cuba* (Oxford, UK: Osprey Publishing, 2012), 75.

4. Kennedy, *Thirteen Days*, 63.

CHAPTER TWENTY-THREE

1. Robert F. Kennedy, *Thirteen Days* (New York: W. W. Norton, 1969), 44.

2. Interview with Pierre Salinger in Pat Mitchell and Jeremy Isaacs, producers, "Cuba," episode 10 of *The Cold War* (CNN, 1998).

3. Ernest May and Philip D. Zelikow, *The Kennedy Tapes* (New York: W. W. Norton, 2002), 201 (minutes taken by Bromley Smith of the ExComm meeting).

4. May and Zelikow, *The Kennedy Tapes*, 203 (notes taken from Joint Chiefs meeting).

5. Michael Beschloss, *The Crisis Years* (New York: Edward Burlingame Books, HarperCollins, 1991), 469.

6. McCone to File, "Meeting with the Vice President," 245; May and Zelikow, *The Kennedy Tapes*.

7. Priscilla Roberts, *Cuban Missile Crisis: The Essential Reference Guide* (Santa Barbara, CA: ABC-CLIO, 2012).

8. May and Zelikow, *The Kennedy Tapes*, 204.

9. Telephone recording between JFK and Dwight Eisenhower, October 22, 1962, John F. Kennedy Library and Presidential Museum.

10. May and Zelikow, *The Kennedy Tapes*.

11. May and Zelikow, *The Kennedy Tapes*, 181.

12. Beschloss, *The Crisis Years* (New York: Edward Burlingame Books, HarperCollins, 1991), 481.

13. Kennedy, *Thirteen Days*, 55.

14. Beschloss, *The Crisis Years*, 477, 478.

15. Jeremy Isaacs and Pat Mitchell, *The Cold War* (Documentary, 1998, funded by the BBC and Turner Broadcasting).

16. Gerald McIlmoyle and Linda Rios Bromley, *Remembering the Dragon Lady* (West Midlands, UK: Helion & Company, 2011), 272.

CHAPTER TWENTY-FOUR

1. Michael Beschloss, *The Crisis Years* (New York: Edward Burlingame Books, HarperCollins, 1991), 479.

CHAPTER TWENTY-FIVE

1. Ernest May and Philip D. Zelikow, *The Kennedy Tapes* (New York: W. W. Norton, 2002), 194.

2. "CBS News Special Report, October 24, 1962," video posted to YouTube by NewsActive3 on September 27, 2015, https://www.youtube.com/results?search_query=CBS+news+special+report+october+24%2C+1962.

3. Author interview with James Anderson, February 9, 2017.

4. Author interview with Chuck Maultsby Jr., September 14, 2015.

5. Clint Hill, *Mrs. Kennedy and Me* (New York: Gallery Books, 2012), 193.

6. Author interview with Robert F. Kennnedy Jr., September 1, 2017.

7. Author interview with Sergei Khrushchev, February 12, 2017.

8. William Ecker and Kenneth Jack, *Blue Moon over Cuba* (Oxford, UK: Osprey Publishing, 2012), 36.

9. Ecker and Jack, *Blue Moon over Cuba*, 95.

CHAPTER TWENTY-SIX

1. William Ecker and Kenneth Jack, *Blue Moon over Cuba* (Oxford, UK: Osprey Publishing, 2012), 95.

2. Ecker and Jack, *Blue Moon over Cuba*, 100.

3. Ian Thompson, "Vet's Mission Was to Confirm Cuban Missile Sites," *Daily Republic*, November 15, 2015.

4. Ecker and Jack, *Blue Moon over Cuba*, 104.

5. Ernest May and Philip D. Zelikow, *The Kennedy Tapes* (New York: W. W. Norton, 2002), 321.

6. Robert F. Kennedy, *Thirteen Days* (New York: W. W. Norton, 1969), 60.

7. Ecker and Jack, *Blue Moon over Cuba*, 102.

8. Ecker and Jack, *Blue Moon over Cuba*, 109.

9. "Pilot Dan Schmarr Remembered for Love of Family, Country, God," *Spokesman*, January 5, 2006.

10. History of the 4080th Wing, October 10–31, declassified 1979, 9.

11. Evan Thomas, *Robert Kennedy: His Life* (New York: Simon & Schuster, 2000) 224.

12. Michael Beschloss, *The Crisis Years* (New York: Edward Burlingame Books, HarperCollins, 1991), 489.

CHAPTER TWENTY-SEVEN

1. Robert F. Kennedy, *Thirteen Days* (New York: W. W. Norton, 1969), 53.

2. Kennedy, *Thirteen Days*, 52.

3. Ernest May and Philip D. Zelikow, *The Kennedy Tapes* (New York: W. W. Norton, 2002), 228.

4. Kennedy, *Thirteen Days*, 54.

5. Kennedy, *Thirteen Days*, 54.

6. Michael Beschloss, *The Crisis Years* (New York: Edward Burlingame Books, HarperCollins, 1991), 498.

7. May and Zelikow, *The Kennedy Tapes*, 236.

8. Charles L. Bartlett oral history #2, John F. Kennedy Presidential Library and Museum.

9. Bartlett oral history #2.

10. May and Zelikow, *The Kennedy Tapes*.

11. Beschloss, *The Crisis Years*, 502.

12. Bartlett oral history #2.

CHAPTER TWENTY-EIGHT

1. Summary record of NSC executive committee meeting no. 6, October 26, 1962, National Security Archive, George Washington University, nsarchive2 .gwu.edu/nsa/cuba_mis_cri/621026_621115%20Chronology%201.pdf.

2. Ernest May and Philip D. Zelikow, *The Kennedy Tapes* (New York: W. W. Norton, 2002), 250.

3. "Captain Coffee: Reaffirming the Invincibility of the Human Spirit," www.captaincoffee.com/about.

4. Michael Dobbs, *One Minute to Midnight* (New York: Vintage Books, 2008), 119.

5. Gerald McIlmoyle and Linda Rios Bromley, *Remembering the Dragon Lady* (West Midlands, UK: Helion & Company, 2011), 279.

6. Michael Beschloss, *The Crisis Years* (New York: Edward Burlingame Books, HarperCollins, 1991), 48.

7. Dobbs, *One Minute to Midnight*, 130.

CHAPTER TWENTY-NINE

1. Michael Beschloss, *The Crisis Years* (New York: Edward Burlingame Books, HarperCollins, 1991), 506.

2. Ernest May and Philip D. Zelikow, *The Kennedy Tapes* (New York: W. W. Norton, 2002), 263.

3. May and Zelikow, *The Kennedy Tapes*, 266.

4. Summary record of NSC ExComm meeting #6, October 26, 1962, 10:00 a.m.

5. Interview with Fidel Castro, in Pat Mitchell and Jeremy Isaacs, producers, "Cuba," episode 10 of *The Cold War* (CNN, 1998).

6. Letter from Castro to Khrushchev, October 26, 1962, NSA Archive, George Washington University.

7. Michael Dobbs, *One Minute to Midnight* (New York: Vintage Books, 2008), 52.

8. Norman Polmar and John Gresham, *Defcon-2* (New York: John Wiley & Sons, 2006), 142.

9. Tad Szulc, *Fidel: A Critical Portrait* (New York: Harper, 2000), 584.

10. William Ecker and Kenneth Jack, *Blue Moon over Cuba* (Oxford, UK: Osprey Publishing, 2012), 157.

11. Ecker and Jack, *Blue Moon over Cuba*, 201, 229.

12. Don Koser, *Strategic Air Command Casualties*, Air Force Global Strike Command, October 19, 2012.

13. Ecker and Jack, *Blue Moon over Cuba*, 179.

14. May and Zelikow, *The Kennedy Tapes*, 291.

15. Arthur Schlesinger Jr., *A Thousand Days* (Boston: Crown Publishers, 1995), 826.

16. Department of State telegram transmitting letter from Chairman Khrushchev to President Kennedy, October 26, 1962, John F. Kennedy Presidential Library and Museum.

17. Douglas Brinkley, *Dean Acheson: The Cold War Years, 1953–71* (New Haven, CT: Yale University Press, 1992), 170.

18. Robert F. Kennedy, *Thirteen Days* (New York: W. W. Norton, 1969), 69.

CHAPTER THIRTY

1. Col. Charles Maultsby, *Toward the Unknown: Memoirs of an American Fighter Pilot* (CreateSpace Independent Publishing Platform, 2013).

2. Maultsby, *Toward the Unknown*, 184.

3. Maultsby, *Toward the Unknown*, 185.

CHAPTER THIRTY-ONE

1. Michael Dobbs, *One Minute to Midnight* (New York: Vintage Books, 2008), 218.

2. Author interview with Jerry McIlmoyle, July 2015; Gerald McIlmoyle and Linda Rios Bromley, *Remembering the Dragon Lady* (West Midlands, UK: Helion & Company, 2011), 272.

3. Charles Kern in McIlmoyle and Bromley, *Remembering the Dragon Lady*, 279.

4. McIlmoyle and Bromley, *Remembering the Dragon Lady*, 272.

5. Supplement 8 to Joint Evaluation of Soviet Missile Threat in Cuba, prepared in part by National Photographic Interpretation Center (declassified 1999).

6. Author interview with Jerry McIlmoyle, January 2015.

7. Krzysztof Dabrowski, "The Loss of Major Anderson," 2012, http://www.acig.info/CMS.

8. PBS documentary, John Murray, dir., *Cuban Missile Crisis* (Crossing the Lines Production, 2012).

9. Interview with Grigory Danilevich, 2004, National Security Archive, George Washington University, www.nsarchive.gwu.edu/nsa/cuba_mis_cri/dobbs/danilevich_acct.pdf.

10. Dino Brugioni, *Eyeball to Eyeball* (New York: Random House, 1992), 476.

11. Leonid Garbuz, deputy commander of Soviet forces on Cuba, October 1962, extracted from A. I. Gribkov et al., *U kraya yadernoi bezdni* (On the Edge of the Nuclear Madness), 1998, National Security Archive, George Washington University, http://nsarchive2.gwu.edu/nsa/cuba_mis_cri/dobbs/garbuz_acct.pdf (as told by Garbuz to Gribkov).

12. Dabrowski, "The Loss of Major Anderson."

13. History of the 55th Strategic Reconnaissance Wing, declassified 1996, Forbes Air Force Base, Kansas.

14. Dobbs, *One Minute to Midnight* (excerpt in National Security Archive).

CHAPTER THIRTY-TWO

1. Gerald McIlmoyle and Linda Rios Bromley, *Remembering the Dragon Lady* (West Midlands, UK: Helion & Company, 2011) (a longer version of Maultsby's manuscript).

CHAPTER THIRTY-THREE

1. Michael Dobbs, *One Minute to Midnight* (New York: Vintage Books, 2008), 268.

2. Sheldon Stern, *The Week the World Stood Still* (Stanford, CA: Stanford University Press, 2005), 157.

3. Elie Abel, *The Missile Crisis* (New York: J. B. Lippincott, 1966), 173.

4. Edward Kennedy, *True Compass* (New York: Hachette Book Group, 2009), 189.

5. Col. Charles Maultsby, *Toward the Unknown: Memoirs of an American Fighter Pilot* (CreateSpace Independent Publishing Platform, 2013).

6. Communication from Khrushchev to Kennedy in Robert F. Kennedy, *Thirteen Days* (New York: W. W. Norton, 1969).

CHAPTER THIRTY-FOUR

1. Interview with Grigory Danilevich, 2004, National Security Archive, George Washington University, www.nsarchive.gwu.edu/nsa/cuba_mis_cri/dobbs/danilevich_acct.pdf.

2. Interview with Danilevich.

3. Leonid Garbuz, deputy commander of Soviet forces on Cuba, October 1962, extracted from A. I. Gribkov et al., *U kraya yadernoi bezdni* (On the Edge of the Nuclear Madness), 1998, National Security Archive, George Washington University, http://nsarchive2.gwu.edu/nsa/cuba_mis_cri/dobbs/garbuz_acct.pdf (as told by Garbuz to Gribkov).

4. Gribkov, *On the Edge of Nuclear Madness*.

5. Krzysztof Dabrowski, "The Loss of Major Anderson," http://www.acig.info/CMS.

6. PBS video documentary, John Murray and Emer Reynolds, dirs., *Cuban Missile Crisis: Three Men Go to War* (Crossing the Lines Production, 2012).

7. Dabrowski, "The Loss of Major Anderson."

8. Murray and Reynolds, *Cuban Missile Crisis*.

9. Norman Polmar and John Gresham, *Defcon-2* (New York: John Wiley & Sons, 2006), 150.

10. Dabrowski, "The Loss of Major Anderson."

11. Dino Brugioni, *Eyeball to Eyeball* (New York: Random House, 1992), 463.

CHAPTER THIRTY-FIVE

1. Alexander Orlov, "The U-2 Program: A Russian Officer Remembers," 1998, www.cia.gov/library/center-for-the-study-of-intellegence.

2. Author interview with Sergei Khrushchev, December 2016.

3. Sergei Khrushchev, *Khrushchev on Khrushchev* (New York: Little, Brown, 1990).

4. CIA memorandum, October 27, 1962, declassified 2002.

5. Michael Beschloss, *The Crisis Years* (New York: Edward Burlingame Books, HarperCollins, 1991), 523.

6. Beschloss, *The Crisis Years*, 523.

7. Robert F. Kennedy, *Thirteen Days* (New York: W. W. Norton, 1969).

8. Patrick Sloyan, *The Politics of Deception* (New York: St. Martin's Press, 2015); Dino Brugioni, *Eyeball to Eyeball* (New York: Random House, 1992), 464.

9. Brugioni, *Eyeball to Eyeball*, 471.

10. Kennedy, *Thirteen Days*, 105.

11. Kennedy, *Thirteen Days*, 105.

12. McGeorge Bundy, *Danger and Survival* (New York: Vintage Books, 1990), 432.

CHAPTER THIRTY-SIX

1. Col. Charles Maultsby, *Toward the Unknown: Memoirs of an American Fighter Pilot* (CreateSpace Independent Publishing Platform, 2013), 197.

2. Maultsby, *Toward the Unknown*, 199.

3. Arthur Schlesinger Jr., *A Thousand Days* (Boston: Crown Publishers, 1965), 818.

4. Schlesinger, *A Thousand Days*.

5. Alice George, *Awaiting Armageddon* (Chapel Hill: University of North Carolina Press, 2003), 52.

6. George, *Awaiting Armageddon*, 53.

7. Dino Brugioni, *Eyeball to Eyeball* (New York: Random House, 1992), 482.

8. Michael Dobbs, *One Minute to Midnight* (New York: Vintage Books, 2008), 308.

9. Maz Frankel, *High Noon in the Cold War* (New York: Ballantine Books, 2004), 151.

10. Robert Kennedy to Dean Rusk, October 30, 1962, John F. Kennedy Presidential Library and Museum; Ernest May and Philip D. Zelikow, *The Kennedy Tapes* (New York: W. W. Norton, 2002), 607.

11. Ernest May and Philip D. Zelikow, *The Kennedy Tapes* (New York: W. W. Norton, 2002), 609.

CHAPTER THIRTY-SEVEN

1. Sheldon Stern, *The Week the World Stood Still* (Stanford, CA: Stanford University Press, 2005), 165.

2. "The Submarines of October," Briefing Book 7, National Security Archive, http://nsarchive2.gwu.edu/NSAEBB/NSAEBB75/index2.htm.

3. Michael Dobbs, *One Minute to Midnight* (New York: Random House, 2008).

4. Dino Brugioni, *Eyeball to Eyeball* (New York: Random Housse, 1992), 377.

5. Submariner Viktor Mikhailov as reported in the "The Man Who Saved the World," *Daily Mail*, September 25, 2012.

6. Alexander Mozgovoi, "Recollections of Orlov, Vadim, the Cuban Samba," *Military Parade* (Moscow), 2002

7. Deck logbook of USS *Beale*, courtesy of the National Security Archives.

8. Marion Lloyd, "Soviets Close to Using A–Bomb in 1962 Crisis," *Boston Globe*, October 13, 2002 (at Havana Conference).

9. Norman Polmar and John Gresham, *Defcon-2* (New York: John Wiley & Sons, 2006), 162; see also Mozgovoi, "Recollections of Orlov, Vadim."

10. Dobbs, *One Minute to Midnight*, 302.

11. Mark Leonard and Rob Blackhurst, "I Don't Think Anybody Thought Much About Whether Agent Orange Was Against the Rules of War," *Guardian*, May 18, 2002, https://www.theguardian.com/world/2002/may/19/theobserver.

12. Polmar and Gresham, *Defcon-2*, 156.

13. "The Submarines of October: US and Soviet Navy Encounters During the Cuban Missile Crisis," National Security Archive, Electronic Briefing Book No. 15, William Burr and Thomas S. Blanton, eds., October 31, 2002.

CHAPTER THIRTY-EIGHT

1. Dino Brugioni, *Eyeball to Eyeball* (New York: Random House, 1992), 276.
2. Brugioni, *Eyeball to Eyeball*, 480.
3. Sheldon Stern, *The Week the World Stood Still* (Stanford, CA: Stanford University Press, 2005), 186.
4. Brugioni, *Eyeball to Eyeball*, 477.
5. PBS video documentary, John Murray and Emer Reynolds, dirs., *Cuban Missile Crisis: Three Men Go to War* (Crossing the Lines Production, 2012).
6. Stern, *The Week the World Stood Still*, 188.
7. Norman Polmar and John Gresham, *Defcon-2* (New York: John Wiley & Sons, 2006), 267.
8. Ernest May and Philip D. Zelikow, *The Kennedy Tapes* (New York: W. W. Norton, 2002), 400.
9. May and Zelikow, *The Kennedy Tapes*, 400.

CHAPTER THIRTY-NINE

1. Letter from Chairman Khrushchev to President Kennedy, October 28, 1962, John F. Kennedy Presidential Library and Museum.
2. Michael Beschloss, *The Crisis Years* (New York: Edward Burlingame Books, HarperCollins, 1991), 541.
3. Evan Thomas, *Robert Kennedy: His Life* (New York: Simon & Schuster, 2000), 231.
4. Michael Dobbs, *One Minute to Midnight* (New York: Vintage Books, 2008), 322.
5. Thomas, *Robert Kennedy*, 231.
6. Ernest May and Philip D. Zelikow, *The Kennedy Tapes* (New York: W. W. Norton, 2002), 408, 409.
7. Patrick Sloyan, *The Politics of Deception* (New York: St. Martin's Press, 2015), 33.
8. Robert F. Kennedy, *Thirteen Days* (New York: W. W. Norton, 1969), 84.
9. Kennedy, *Thirteen Days*, 84.
10. Dino Brugioni, *Eyeball to Eyeball* (New York: Random House, 1992), 477.
11. Interview with James Anderson, February 8, 2017.
12. Rick Hampson, "The Cuban Missile Crisis," *USA Today*, October 14, 2012.
13. Naval Message p311535z, National Security Archive, George Washington University, http://nsarchive2.gwu.edu//nsa/cuba_mis_cri/dobbs/anderson_corpse.pdf.

EPILOGUE

1. Interview with Jerry McIlmoyle, January 2016; Dino Brugioni, *Eyeball to Eyeball* (New York: Random House, 1992), 526.
2. "General Hails Pilots Who Fly over Cuba at Rites for Maj. Anderson," Associated Press, November 6, 1962.

3. Interview with Anderson, 2017.

4. Rick Hampson, "The Cuban Missile Crisis," *USA Today*, October 14, 2012.

5. Author interview with Steve Heyser's son, Richard J. Heyser.

6. Author interview with Charles Maultsby II, 2015.

7. Col. Charles Maultsby, *Toward the Unknown: Memoirs of an American Fighter Pilot* (CreateSpace Independent Publishing Platform, 2013), 251.

8. Arthur Schlesinger Jr., *A Thousand Days* (Boston: Crown Publishers, 1965), 904.

9. Commencement address at American University, June 10, 1963, transcript, John F. Kennedy Presidential Library and Museum.

Bibliography

INTERVIEWS BY AUTHORS

James Anderson, son of U-2 pilot Rudy Anderson, 2017
Tripp Anderson, son of U-2 pilot Rudy Anderson, 2016
Jacki Heyser, wife of U-2 pilot Steve Heyser, 2015
Richard J. Heyser, son of U-2 pilot Steve Heyser, 2015
Robert F. Kennedy Jr., 2016
Sergei Khrushchev, 2017
Colonel Richard Leghorn, 2016
Chuck W. Maultsby II, son of U-2 pilot Chuck Maultsby,
    2016
Jerry McIlmoyle, 2015, 2016, 2017
Robert Ross, 2016

BOOKS

Abel, Elie. *The Missile Crisis.* New York: J. B. Lippincott, 1966.
Ambrose, Stephen. *Ike's Spies.* New York: Anchor Books, 1981.
Beschloss, Michael. *The Crisis Years.* New York: Burlingame Books, 1991.
———. *May-Day.* New York: Harper & Row, 1986.
Blight, James, Bruce Allyn, and David Welch. *Cuba on the Brink.* New York: Pantheon Books, 1993.
Brugioni, Dino. *Eyeball to Eyeball.* New York: Random House, 1992.
Brzezinski, Matthew. *Red Moon Rising.* New York: Times Books, 2007.
Bundy, McGeorge. *Danger and Survival.* New York: Random House, 1988.
Chang, Lawrence, and Peter Kornbluh. *The Cuban Missile Crisis: 1962.* New York: New Press, 1992.
Coffee, Gerald. *Beyond Survival.* New York: Putnam, 1990.
Cooke, Stephanie. *In Mortal Hands.* New York: Bloomsbury, 2009.

Crispell, Kenneth, and Carlos Gomez. *Hidden Illness in the White House*. Durham, NC: Duke University Press Books, 1988.

Devine, Robert. *The Cuban Missile Crisis*. Chicago: Quadrangle Books, 1971.

Dobbs, Michael. *One Minute to Midnight*. New York: Knopf, 2008.

Doyle, William. *PT 109: An American Epic of War, Survival, and the Destiny of John F. Kennedy*. New York: William Morrow, 2015.

Ecker, William, and Kenneth Jack. *Blue Moon over Cuba*. Oxford, UK: Osprey Publishing, 2012.

Frankel, Max. *High Noon in the Cold War*. New York: Ballantine Books, 2004.

Fursenko, Aleksandr, and Timothy Naftali. *One Hell of a Gamble*. New York: W. W. Norton, 1997.

George, Alice. *Awaiting Armageddon*. Chapel Hill: University of North Carolina Press, 2003.

Goodwin, Doris Kearns. *The Fitzgeralds and the Kennedys*. New York: Simon & Schuster, 1987.

Hill, Clint. *Mrs. Kennedy and Me*. New York: Gallery Books, 2012.

Jacobsen, Annie. *Area 51: An Uncensored History of America's Top-Secret Military Base*. New York: Little, Brown, 2011.

Jones, Howard. *Bay of Pigs*. New York: Oxford University Press, 2008.

Kagan, Donald. *On the Origins of War*. New York: Anchor Books, 1995.

Kempe, Frederick. *Berlin 1961: Kennedy, Khrushchev, and the Most Dangerous Place on Earth*. New York: G. P. Putnam's Sons, 2011.

Kennedy, Edward. *True Compass*. New York: Hachette Book Group, 2009.

Kennedy, John F. *The Letters of John F. Kennedy*. New York: Bloomsbury Press, 2013.

Kennedy, Robert. *Thirteen Days*. New York: W. W. Norton, 1969.

Kenney, Charles. *John F. Kennedy: The Presidential Portfolio: History as Told Through the Collection of the John F. Kennedy Library and Museum*. New York: PublicAffairs, 2000.

Khrushchev, Nikita. *Khrushchev Remembers*. New York: Little, Brown, 1970.

Khrushchev, Sergei. *Khrushchev on Khrushchev*. New York: Little, Brown, 1990.

Lehman, Richard. *CIA Handling of the Soviet Buildup in Cuba, July–October 1962*. DCI records 80B 1676R, box 17, folder 18, November 1962 (approved for release/declassified June 25, 2013).

Maultsby, Charles. *Toward the Unknown*. Edited by Charles Maultsby II. Self-published, 2012.

May, Ernest, and Philip Zelikow. *The Kennedy Tapes*. Cambridge, MA: Harvard University Press, 1997.

McIlmoyle, Gerald, and Linda Bromley. *Remembering the Dragon Lady*. West Midlands, UK: Helion & Co., 2011.

Medina, Loreta, ed. *The Cuban Missile Crisis*. San Diego, CA: Greenhaven Press, 2002.

Mozgovoi, Alexander. *The Cuban Sambra of the Quartet Foxtrot*. Moscow: Military Parade, 2002 (National Security Archive translation).

Pocock, Chris. *Dragon Lady*. Osceola, WI: Motorbooks International, 1989.

——. *The U-2 Spyplane: Toward the Unknown*. Atglen, PA: Schiffer Military History, 2000.

Polmar, Norman, and John Gresham. *Defcon-2*. Hoboken, NJ: John Wiley, 2006.

Powers, Francis Gary, and Curt Gentry. *Operation Overflight*. New York: Holt, 1970.

Schlesinger, Arthur, Jr. *A Thousand Days*. Boston: Houghton Mifflin, 1965.

Sloyan, Patrick. *The Politics of Deception*. New York: St. Martin's Press, 2015.

Sorensen, Theodore. *Kennedy*. New York: Harper & Row, 1965.

Stern, Sheldon. *The Week the World Stood Still*. Stanford, CA: Stanford University Press, 2005.

Taraborrelli, J. Randy. *Jackie, Ethel, Joan*. New York: Warner Books, 2000.

Thomas, Evan. *Robert Kennedy: His Life*. New York: Simon & Schuster, 2000.

Triay, Victor Andres. *Bay of Pigs: An Oral History of Brigade 2506*. Gainesville: University Press of Florida, 2001.

Valois, Karl. *The Cuban Missile Crisis: A World in Peril*. Carlisle, MA: Discovery Enterprises, 1998.

Waldman, Michael. *My Fellow Americans*. Naperville, IL: Sourcebooks Media-Fusion, 2003.

Yarnell, Allen. *Postwar Epoch*. New York: Joanne Colter Books, 1972.

WEBSITES, REPORTS, ARTICLES, DOCUMENTS, AND VIDEOS

Author's/writer's name given if it appeared; date given if shown.

Attorney General Special Group Augmented on Operation Mongoose. "Feasibility, Sabotage, Overthrow, Inciting Uprising." http://s3-euw1-ap-pe -ws4-cws-documents.ri-prod.s3.amazonaws.com/9781138824287/ch7 /15._Operation_Mongoose,_1962.pdf.

Bender, Bryan. "A Pilot's Sacrifice Helped Defuse Cuban Missile Crisis." *Boston Globe*, October 27, 2012.

Brooks, Jeanne. "Piloting a Hero Home." *Greenville News*, October 13, 2002.

Burr, William, and Thomas Blanton. "The Submarines of October." Electronic Briefing Book Number 75. National Security Archive. October 31, 2002.

CIA. "Supplement 8 to Joint Evaluation of Soviet Missile Threat in Cuba." LBJ Library. October 28, 1962.

CIA memorandum, "Daily Report October 27, 1962," declassified 2002.

CIA report, "Probable Soviet MRBM in Cuba." CIADOCS #46, October 16, 1962.

"Cuban Missile Crisis: Really Touch and Go?" USAtoday.com, October 13, 2012.

Dabrowski, Krzystof. "The Loss of Major Anderson." http://archive.is/dGdj.

Deck log of USS *Beale* DD471, October 27, 1962. National Archives.

Dobbs, Michael. "Secret Heroes." *Washington Post*, October 26, 2003.

Dorr, Robert F. "U-2 Pilot Major Rudy Anderson: The Only American Killed During the Cuban Missile Crisis." DefenseMediaNetwork. October 20, 2012. https://www.defensemedianetwork.com/stories/u-2-pilot-maj -rudy-anderson-the-only-american-killed-during-the-cuban-missile-crisis.

Drent, Jan. "Confrontation in the Sargasso Sea." *Northern Mariner*, July 2003. https://www.cnrs-scrn.org/northern_mariner/vol13/tnm_13_3_1–19.pdf.

Dubivko, A. F. "In the Depths of the Sargasso Sea." Moscow: Gregory Page, 1998.

Foster, Dan. "Thirteen Days Stirs Memories of Hero, Friend." *Greenville News*, 1999 (found on Boltancestry.com).

Gonzales, Robert. Major Rudolf Anderson, Jr. Val Verde County Historical Commission. http://vvchc.net/marker/anderson.html.

Guided Missile and Astronautics Intelligence Committee and National Photographic Interpretation Center. Report prepared on October 28, 1962, at 2 a.m.

Hampson, Rick. "Cuban Missile Crisis." *USA Today*, October 14, 2012.

Harvard Kennedy School Belfer Center. "Letter from Khrushchev to Castro on October 28, 1962." National Security Archive, George Washington University. http://www.gwu.edu/~nsarchiv/nsa/cuba_mis_cri/19621028khrlet .pdf.

History of the 4080 Strategic Wing from October 10–31, 1962, declassified November 1982. Air Force Historian Archives, Maxwell Air Force Base.

History of the 55th Strategic Reconnaissance Wing, October 1962, declassified 1996. Forbes Air Force Base, Kansas.

Holland, Max. "The Photo Gap That Delayed Discovery of Missiles." CIA Library, Center for the Study of Intelligence. April 15, 2007.

Interview with Grigory Danilevich, July 3, 2004, National Security Archive, George Washington University. http://nsarchive2.gwu.edu//nsa/cuba _mis_cri/dobbs/danilevich_acct.pdf.

Interview with Major Richard S. Heyser conducted by Robert Kipp, November 27, 1962, declassified 1996. Air Force Historian Archives, Maxwell Air Force Base.

"JFK and the Crisis Crusader." Documentary video. A&E Television Networks, 2007.

Klein, Christopher. "How the Death of a U.S. Air Force Pilot Prevented a Nuclear War." History.com. October 26, 2012. http://www.history.com/news /the-cuban-missile-crisis-pilot-whose-death-may-have-saved-millions.

Koser, Don. Strategic Air Command Casualties. Air Force Global Strike Command, October 19, 2012.

Lloyd, Marion. "Soviets Close to Using A-Bomb in 1962 Crisis." *Boston Globe*, October 13, 2002 (at Havana Conference).

Looly, Joe, dir. *The Year of the Tiger*. Documentary video. 10th Mountain Films, 2016.

Mozgovoi, Alexander. "Recollections of Orlov, Vadim, the Cuban Samba." *Military Parade* (Moscow), 2002.

Murray, John, and Emer Reynolds, dirs. *Cuban Missile Crisis: Three Men Go to War.* PBS documentary. Crossing the Lines Production, 2012.

National Security Archive. U-2 report released to public 2013/06/25 (C00190094).

National Security Archive, the George Washington University collection:
- Chronology Compiled for the President's Foreign Intelligence Advisory Board (PFIAB), "Chronology of Specific Events Relating to the Military Buildup in Cuba." Undated [excerpt].
- DOD, Transcripts, SECRET, "Notes Taken from Transcripts of Meetings of the Joint Chiefs of Staff, October–November 1962: Dealing with the Cuban Missile Crisis."
- CIA Special National Intelligence Estimate, "Major Consequences of Certain U.S. Courses of Action on Cuba." October 20, 1962.

Orlov, Alexander. "The U-2 Program: A Russian Officer Remembers." CIA. 1998. www.cia.gov/library/center-for-the-study-of-intellegence.

Pedlow, Gregory. "The CIA and the U-2 Program." CIA History Staff Center for the Study of Intelligence. August 1998.

Savranskaya, Svetlana. "The Last Nuclear Weapons Left in Cuba." Briefing Book #449. National Security Archive. December 2013. https://nsarchive2.gwu.edu//NSAEBB/NSAEBB449/.

Watson, Leon. "The Man Who Saved the World." *Daily Mail,* September 26, 2012.

Zelkow, Philip, and Ernest May. *The Kennedy Tapes.* Cambridge, MA: Harvard University Press, 1997.

———. "The Presidential Recordings of John F. Kennedy." Miller Center for Public Affairs, 2001.

Index

The photo gallery is indexed as p1, p2, p3, and so on.

PST. *See* physiological support team
Psychological Support Center, 6
PT boats. *See* patrol torpedo boats
PT-109, 18–22, 27, 97–98, p3
PT-157, 18
PT-159, 17–18

Qualls, James, 149, 150, 151
quarantine. *See* naval blockade

R-14 missiles, 197
Radio Moscow, 238, 283, 285
RAF. *See* Royal Air Force
the Ranch. *See* Area 51
Rasmussen, Holt, 215
Raypenko, Alexy, 249
RB-26, 30
RB-47, 48, 121, 215, 232
Reagan, Ronald, 7
Red Scare, 97
Rendova Island, 25–28
Republic of Korea, 29
Reserve Officers' Training Corps
        (ROTC), 11
Resolute Desk, 139
Revolutionary War, 10
RF8 Crusader, 183–184
    Cuba overflights with, 185–186,
        198, 203, 213–216, 271
RF-80, 30
RF-86, 29–30, 31
RFK. *See* Kennedy, Robert
Ribicoff, Abe, 96, 153
Riley, Tad, 184, 186, 214
Ritland, Osmund, 55
Robinson, Robby, 70–71
Roman Holiday (film), 282
Roosevelt, Franklin, 108, 160,
        176
Rose, Wilburn S., "Billy," 78
Ross, Barney, 19, 24, 25, 26, 27
Ross, Robert, 30–31
Rostow, Walter, 138
ROTC. *See* Reserve Officers'
        Training Corps
Royal Air Force (RAF), 61, 75

Rusk, Dean, 109, 133, 155, 198
    end of crisis and, 283
    on evacuation plans, 269
    ExComm and, 138, 141, 142, 145,
        188, 195, 197, 217, 219
    on Khrushchev, N., bargaining
        objectives, 142
    Maultsby, Chuck, incident and,
        239
    overflights plans and, 119, 120
    on Turkey missiles, 264
Russell, Bertrand, 198
Russell, Richard, 170

SA-2 missiles, 118, 123
SAC. *See* Strategic Air Command
Sakhalin Island, 118
Salinger, Pierre, 165–166, 211, 269,
        291
SAMs. *See* surface-to-air missile
San Cristobal, 123–124, 127–130,
        132–133, 147, 185–186,
        206–207, 213, 254, p5
Santiago Bay, 194
SAR. *See* search-and-rescue
Savitsky, Valentin Grigorievic,
        275–277
Scali, John, 216–217
Schlesinger, Arthur, Jr., 96, 156,
        268
Schmarr, Daniel, 190
Schmarr, Kay, 190
search-and-rescue (SAR), 222
secrecy, 82–83, 114
Semipalatinsk test site, 84
Senate Armed Services Select
        Committee, 116
SGA. *See* Special Group Augmented
Shell Oil, 52
Shoup, David, 160, 162
Sidey, Hugh, 112
Skunk Works, 50–52
Smathers, George, 104
Smith, Bromley, 166–167
Smith, Dale, 131
Snyder, Howard, 95

CASEY SHERMAN is an award-winning journalist and the *New York Times* best-selling coauthor of *The Finest Hours* (now a major motion picture), *Boston Strong: A City's Triumph over Tragedy* (the basis for the major motion picture *Patriots Day*), *Animal, A Rose for Mary, Bad Blood, Black Irish,* and *Black Dragon.* He is also a contributing writer for *Esquire* and *Boston Magazine* and an international correspondent for FOX News. He is cofounder of Whydah Productions and lives in Massachusetts. Follow him on Twitter @caseysherman123 and on Facebook at facebook.com/casey.sherman.

Sherman has appeared on hundreds of national and international television and radio programs and is a sought-after national speaker. He is represented by APB Speakers Bureau and Gotham Group, Beverly Hills, California.

MICHAEL J. TOUGIAS is a *New York Times* best-selling author and coauthor of twenty-eight books. He is best known for his nonfiction narratives involving survival and rescue, which honor real-life, everyday people who rise to face life-threatening situations, make heroic choices, and survive against the odds. Among the best sellers he has written or cowritten are *A Storm Too Soon*, *Overboard!*, *Rescue of the Bounty*, *King Philip's War*, *Until I Have No Country*, *The Finest Hours*, *Fatal Forecast*, and *Ten Hours Until Dawn*, which the American Library Association selected as a "Best Book of the Year." His latest book, *So Close to Home*, focuses on the U-boat raids off the coast of the United States and an American family's fight for survival after their ship was sunk thirty miles off the mouth of the Mississippi River.

Tougias and Henry Holt and Co. are adapting his adventure stories into books for young adults, with *The Finest Hours*, *A Storm Too Soon*, *So Close to Home*, and *Ten Hours Until Dawn* the first to be published. Two of the young adult books have been chosen as Junior Literary Guild Selections and Scholastic Selections.

Tougias is a sought-after speaker for businesses, associations, and nonprofit groups across the country. He offers presentations on leadership and decision-making and exciting slide programs for each of his books, including *Above and Beyond*. A video of U-2 pilot Jerry McIlmoyle describing his close call with SAMs can be found on the author's website. Visit him online at www.michaeltougias.com. He lives in Florida and Massachusetts.

PublicAffairs is a publishing house founded in 1997. It is a tribute to the standards, values, and flair of three persons who have served as mentors to countless reporters, writers, editors, and book people of all kinds, including me.

I. F. STONE, proprietor of *I. F. Stone's Weekly*, combined a commitment to the First Amendment with entrepreneurial zeal and reporting skill and became one of the great independent journalists in American history. At the age of eighty, Izzy published *The Trial of Socrates*, which was a national bestseller. He wrote the book after he taught himself ancient Greek.

BENJAMIN C. BRADLEE was for nearly thirty years the charismatic editorial leader of *The Washington Post*. It was Ben who gave the *Post* the range and courage to pursue such historic issues as Watergate. He supported his reporters with a tenacity that made them fearless and it is no accident that so many became authors of influential, best-selling books.

ROBERT L. BERNSTEIN, the chief executive of Random House for more than a quarter century, guided one of the nation's premier publishing houses. Bob was personally responsible for many books of political dissent and argument that challenged tyranny around the globe. He is also the founder and longtime chair of Human Rights Watch, one of the most respected human rights organizations in the world.

. . .

For fifty years, the banner of Public Affairs Press was carried by its owner Morris B. Schnapper, who published Gandhi, Nasser, Toynbee, Truman, and about 1,500 other authors. In 1983, Schnapper was described by *The Washington Post* as "a redoubtable gadfly." His legacy will endure in the books to come.

Peter Osnos, *Founder*